Acknowledgements

Before I begin with this book, I must recognize and give thanks to a few people in my life. Without these people, there's a strong possibility this book would've never happened. It is these people that I will always think about when I think about where I come from and why I am the person that I am today. No matter what happens in my life, I will never forget these people, the things they've done for me, and what they mean to me. There have been endless people to touch my life and have an impact on me over the years. I will not be able to name all of you, but you know who you are. I am genuinely thankful for all of you and appreciate you supporting my dream by picking up this book.

To my parents, I can genuinely say that I couldn't imagine having any other pair of humans to guide me along this journey. Since the day I came into the world, you two were committed to giving me the best life possible and I can honestly never repay you for all you have done over the years. You have seen me at the times when I've been at my strongest and you've been there to pick me up through the times when I have been at my lowest. Your unconditional love through every phase and emotion we've been through along this journey is a major reason why I have found the strength to share this part of my journey with the world. In a world where parenting and guiding children has become a seemingly lost practice, you never even considered sending me into the world without instilling in me the values that even made this book a possibility. I have many goals, and goals have become a major driving force in my life. No goal for my life is bigger than my goal to make you two proud and for you to realize that your sacrifices weren't in vain. I

2

have no clue where I would be in life without you and from the bottom of my heart, I love you both more than you could ever know.

To my brothers A.J. and Preston, there is nobody else in the world I would want to share the many fights and laughs with. Our blood made us related, but all the time we spent bonding, laughing, fighting, and supporting each other made us brothers forever–regardless of our differences and disagreements. Anybody who truly knows us knows that we prepared each other for the harshness of the world (and then some) by the jokes we told and the way we treated each other sometimes. On a serious note, you two are the first friends I ever made and are a big part of the reason I have the tough skin and fortitude that I have today. I can't wait to see where the future takes us and all the great things that you two will accomplish! I love you both to the ends of the earth and I wouldn't be who I am today without you– I'll always hold the memories we've made close to my heart.

To my Granny, everybody who knows me, knows my love for you. I think some of them may be jealous, but what can we say? We have been bonded since my birth. Though I don't physically remember the first few weeks of my life with you, I have a lifetime of memories with you that solidify the special bond that we share. I hold these memories close to my heart and will forever cherish them. You played whatever role my parents needed from you throughout my life, whether it was babysitter, nurse, or "the enforcer" on those days that I let my smart mouth land me in Granny's doghouse and you were forced to remind me that the soft spot in your heart for me did not exempt me from whoopings. The older I get, the nearer and dearer I hold you to my heart, because I realize what you truly have done for me throughout my life when you didn't have to do any of it. There's my mother and then there's you as the pinnacle of women in my life, and I just want to say thank you from the bottom of my heart, for all the time, wisdom, and love you have poured into me from day one. Thank you for always believing in me and encouraging me even when I didn't believe in myself. Nobody could ever replace you and I can never repay you. I'm usually gifted with my words, but I don't think I could ever come up with the correct words to express the special place you will forever hold in my heart and how much I love you.

To Coach Maxwell, we crossed paths again at the very beginning of this crazy time in my life. When I moved back home, you welcomed me into the program with open arms and always made me feel like I belonged with you and the coaching staff. You didn't know it then, but you allowing me to get in the gym with the boys and work on my game was all I felt like I had on most days during those times of uncertainty. Though our time together has been short, the relationship we've built has had a profound impact on my life and I truly appreciate everything you've done for me. You will deservingly go down as one of the best high school coaches in Metro Atlanta high, but your legacy is so much more than what you've done for the kids from the standpoint of X's and O's. I'll never forget your willingness to get involved in my process and the energy and effort that you showed up with every day. I sincerely feel I am a better person and a better man because of my time with you and your leadership. For that, I'll always have a special place for Coach Blue in my heart no matter where I am in the world.

To the Robinsons, I've always considered this family to be my second family because the love has been there from day one. I remember moving to a new school, knowing nobody in the halls or in any of my classes. I met the twins my first day and never looked back. We spent much of my childhood together between school, practices, and spending the night at each other's houses most weekends. We got a little distant in high school, as we were all trying to find our own paths and navigate life. Then, after I moved back from Florida, it all came full circle and we picked up right where we left off. I have enjoyed all the vacations, nice nights out in the city, and all the many fun things we've done together over the years, but nothing means more to me than the bond that we all share and the love that is felt every time that we're together. I probably didn't show it very much, but I was a lost soul when you guys came back into my life and you all helped me find myself again through the many laughs and good times we have shared. I can't tell you enough how thankful I am for all the memories and the relationship that we have, simply thankful that you all were placed into my life and have been a part of me ever since. I will never forget what this family means to me and I love you all endlessly.

To my brother Trell, freshman year of college was full of ups and downs and it wasn't particularly a highlight in our lives, but our freshman year crossed our paths and I'm forever grateful for that. I appreciate you for always helping me keep my head on straight, pushing me to be my best, and inspiring me to chase my dreams at all costs. We started out as teenage boys and college teammates who didn't know what to expect from choosing each other as roommates. Now, I think it's safe to say that we got way more from that decision than either one of us could've ever imagined. We have grown into the beginning of manhood together and built a bond that will last a lifetime. Your will to win and the effort you give to your craft is inspiration to me. We talk about these things daily, but the path that you're on, success is inevitable. It's an understatement to say that I'm proud of you for all the hard work you've dedicated towards your personal development and changing your life. I know you're technically an only child, but you will always be my brother and I love you like my own blood.

To my brother Stephen, it's crazy to think that skinny kid wearing khaki pants, a button down, and loafers who sat beside me in Mrs. Hargrove's class on the first day of freshman year of high school is the same person that I call a brother now. We've come a long way since then, and I know we'll only continue to go farther. Growing up, I tried my best to be there for you, and I hope I've been half the friend that you've been to me. You were always here for me during the good, the bad, and the ugly. You know more than most people how differently my story could've turned out, and I appreciate you more than you know for being there and supporting me when times got dark and things got difficult for me. I'm not surprised by any of it, but I'm proud of you for everything you're doing, all the sacrifices you're making to build your future, and the man that you're becoming in the process. I'm excited to see all the things that the future holds for you, because you work too hard to not get to the places you want to be– I truly believe it's on its way to you in abundance in due time. Stay the course and stay solid– I know we don't see each other as much as our high school days, but I still love you like my own blood and always will.

7

Prologue

I've always known that I was put on this earth to serve others, to help those in need. For years, I struggled to answer life's greatest question of how I could have a positive impact on the lives of others. Somehow, the answer always seemed to slip by mind. I had always been a decent writer growing up and many of my English teachers told me that I had the potential to find success in a career in writing if I chose to take that path, but I was still unsure that I was capable of getting the mountain of ideas that filled my head onto the pages in a way that would resonate with others. As my experiences started to pile up and that mountain of thoughts in my head continued to grow, I realized that writing this book wasn't about me, nor was it about overcoming my lack of confidence in my abilities. It was about being the help to those who may find themselves in places in life where they feel alone and helpless.

Devoting my time and energy into something that I love to do has been a positive driving force in my life without a doubt, but I could feel in my soul that by opting to keep my thoughts and experiences to myself, I could be the very reason somebody may never hear the words of encouragement or guidance that they need to hear to get through the things they may be going through in their lives. That thought sat heavy on my mind, and I felt a responsibility to do everything in my power to make sure that I wasn't preventing someone from hearing what they needed to hear to reach their breakthrough. Those thoughts that sat heavy on my mind are what drove me to complete this project, with the goal of reaching as many hearts and minds as I possibly can.

I've been that person in need all too often in my life and I know how it feels to feel alone in those seasons of life– even when the people you love and care about the most are surrounding you. More so than anything, I want to be a voice of guidance, encouragement, and support for anyone feeling lost or hopeless in their life. I've been there more times than I can count in my own life and I aspire to help you expose these thoughts and feelings for the lies that they are and begin living in your empowering and unique truth.

This book represents many things for me. It's a milestone of achievement for me as an aspiring writer, but it's much deeper than that beneath the surface. This book is about letting go of childhood trauma that has held me in bondage for the majority of my life. This book is about challenging myself to be vulnerable and opening myself up to be a resource and a vessel towards authentic healing in a world of hurting humans. This book is about finding my purpose and fulfillment in the most dire times of my life through learning to love myself and the life that I live unconditionally and inspiring you to do the same. This book is about being my true and authentic self, no longer a slave to my fears of judgment or the opinions of others. Most of all, this book represents me reintroducing myself to the world, no longer a simple-minded, selfish, and self-sabotaging boy. This book is about me stepping into manhood as an unapologetically ambitious and hardworking man that's committed to my personal development and growth above all else, while seeking to fulfill the purpose that God has assigned me to fulfill for the Kingdom that saved me from myself and my self-destructing ways.

I want it to be known that this book was not written from a place of me looking down on you with all the answers. The process of becoming a better version of yourself is a life-long process, because there is always room for improvement within an imperfect human being. Like you, I'm a human being and am far from perfect. I make mistakes every single day of my life, and I struggle just as much as the next man to stay on the right path. In a way, I also wrote this book for me– to remind myself of everything I've been through and to hold myself to a higher standard of accountability for both how I choose to live my life and how I provide encouragement to others to live their lives.

I'm giving you principles to live by to improve your life, but I'm on this journey with you. As you start to implement these principles into your own life, I'm still working daily to master them in my own life as well. This book was written from a place of starting a journey to a better destination and trying to bring as many people on this journey with me as I possibly can. If anything, this is the book that I wish I would've come across when I was walking through my own darkness. These principles have changed my life for the better, and I would feel selfish to not give you the opportunity to be introduced to the small changes it takes in the way we think, grow, and live our lives that make a major difference in the quality of life that we experience.

If nobody else tells you this, I believe every single person reading this is capable of implementing these principles into their lives and becoming the person they aspire to be. The journey to your highest self is a journey full of peaks and valleys, unexpected twists and turns, and all kinds of distractions trying to knock you off course along the way. The journey of life is the ultimate test and it will take everything you have, but what you must overcome along the way is nothing in comparison to the destination that's to come if you stick with it. You deserve to be your highest self and to experience living at your full potential, and these twelve principles put you twelve steps closer to doing exactly that.

By picking this book up, you've already made a dream of mine come true. I can't thank you enough for your support and I'm confident that the contents of this book will give you a return on your investment. I can't wait to see all of the great things you'll do in your life and all the lives you will impact along the way! On the back cover of the book, you'll find some information on ways to contact me. I'd love to connect with you and answer any questions you may have or help in any way that I can along your journey. Once again, thank you for your support and for being a part of my journey– I'm extremely humbled and excited to share this opportunity with you. Without further ado, welcome to *12 Principles for a Better Life: Making the Most of the Gift of Life.*

Chapter One

Principle #1: Find your faith and keep it– it is your ultimate guide in life.

I'm not here to preach to you or to tell you what you should and shouldn't believe. As you will find throughout this book, I am a strong advocate for thinking for yourself and making your own decisions. My own personal beliefs don't have to align with yours and your personal beliefs don't have to align with mine– that's the beauty of individuality and freedom of opinion.

That being said, I do believe developing a relationship with a higher power and rooting your faith in that higher power is a critical step in the process of becoming all that you were created to be. I have witnessed first-hand how influential establishing your faith in something bigger than yourself can be and the doors it can open in your life. My goal is not to force anyone's hand one way or another in their spiritual choices. My goal is to simply share some insight on the benefits of rooting your faith in something beyond the natural world that we all live in and a bit of my personal testimony in my experience with growing my faith and what it has done for me in my life.

In his book *Hard Times Create Strong Men*, Stefan Aarnio discusses the importance of religion and faith in a higher power for not only men, but all human beings. He claims that without religion as a foundation, there is essentially no moral or ethical compass for society to follow. In other words, without the creation and practice of religion in the world, human actions are naturally self-serving and show no regard for moral or ethical correctness. It may sound extreme at first, but when you take the time to think about it and consider human nature– is there truth in what he's saying?

I believe there is, because human nature is savage-like in the absence of moral and ethical conditioning. Even with moral and ethical conditioning, we still struggle daily to make decisions based on what *is* right and not what *feels* right. Absent of rules and moral limitations, life's meaning is condensed to survival and reproducing offspring to continue one's bloodline and to maintain the population. Over time, society has created structure and enforced rules and regulations that are built on codes of morality and ethics. Whether you believe in a religion or not, this conscience within you to try and do right by others comes from others' belief in religion and its importance in some form or fashion. Whether you are a full-on believer in a higher power or just simply attempt to be a decent person on a daily basis, your thought processes and actions have been *strongly* influenced by the morals and ethics that are deeply rooted in religion and faith.

I want you to take a second and think about what a world with no religion at all would look like. That's right– there is no Bible, Quran, Vedas, Agamas, or any form of Holy texts in this particular world. There are no guidelines as to what is right and what is wrong in society, just a society full of people acting off of their own self-interests. Laws and justice are nonexistent. People do as they please, regardless of the effects their actions have on others. It sounds like a nightmare, right? That's because it is. Yet, this description I've provided is a strong resemblance to what the world would look like in the absence of religion and faith– roughly eight billion unruly people living purely for themselves and concerned only with the survival of their own tribes.

This is the way the world was for many years, until religion was discovered and practiced widespread enough for guidelines to be created to help us coexist peacefully and build a habitable society. The way we treat others and the lifestyles we choose to live bear importance to us now– this is greatly influenced by religion. The traditional culture of monogamous relationships and the commitment to marriage was born from religious guidance and belief. Overall, religion has provided guidance and set boundaries that have allowed the experience of life to become one that is more fruitful and purposeful for humans over the last several centuries. Though religion and its importance is diminishing in today's society, the most basic principles of how people are treated and respected are derived from morality and ethics, which are societal practices rooted deeply in religion and the role of guidance it plays in the lives of human beings.

This book is all about making the most of the life you've been gifted. In order to create a better life for yourself, you must live with more virtue and purpose. These two things are what make life most meaningful. This is why establishing a strong faith in a higher power is so helpful in your process, because religion serves as a "how to" guide for living a life of purpose and virtue. No matter which religion you choose to study or follow, all religious practice is rooted in making the proper sacrifices and following a path that propels you to a life of greater purpose and fulfillment. More importantly, all religions provide a sense of hope and peace that is beyond any hope and peace we can get from anything that's physically available to us in the natural world we live in.

Religion gives you something to live for besides yourself, while also emphasizing treating others with respect and dignity. Without any religion, you simply believe that you were put here to live your seventy-five to seventy-eight years of life expectancy and then decompose into the ground– you have no promise or incentive to make your life meaningful and impactful while you're here. As I said earlier, I respect all opinions and am very open-minded. If you're on the fence about religion and your faith, I would encourage you to evaluate the depth of life and ask yourself how difficulty and challenge serve us in our lives. Then, consider how we grow and evolve throughout life and its challenges, gaining wisdom and understanding as we mature and gain experience in life. It's worth it to ask yourself if all of this is for nothing, just for us to end up six feet below the dirt one day. Is there more to life than simply living and dying? Is everything that happens in between meaningless?

The world that we are living in today is not a world for the light-hearted. There are many heartbreaking and tragic events happening on a daily basis. From issues with police brutality, rampant increases in mass shootings over the last decade, the constant anxiety that the war on terrorism brings each of us, and all the smaller battles that we each fight in our daily lives– it can be difficult to find true hope and trust that there will be better days ahead. Yet, this is exactly what establishing your faith in a higher power does for you– it gives you the comfort of putting your faith in something bigger than yourself and allows

15

you to see past all the negativity that's surrounding you in the moment. It gives you that bit of faith in the supernatural to hold on to when the natural doesn't look so promising.

You will begin to realize that the world's problems are not all yours to bear, and you will develop impenetrable peace in knowing that your fate is not in the hands of the hate and evil that so often plagues the world we live in. By reading and gaining knowledge throughout your study of religion, you will come to find that it was already written that the world would suffer from these types of experiences, long before there was physical evidence present in the world that we live in today. Gods are all-knowing, and becoming familiar with religious teachings and readings can vastly improve your understanding of the way the world operates and give you the wisdom necessary to find peace of mind and remain hopeful in a world that so often presents us with reasons to remain hopeless.

The tragedies and sorrows that come with life are something that we all will experience at some point in our lives– faith provides a greater understanding and guide to help us through these times when we're the ones personally affected by these events. Understanding the grief that tragedy brings to ourselves and others also allows us to show more compassion when others are going through these struggles . Putting your faith in a higher power doesn't guarantee that you won't experience loss and grief throughout your life, but it does allow you to understand that there's a master plan for your life and a reason for everything that has happened and will happen in your life. Faith doesn't give you immunity from being held to the fire and tested, but it does provide you with what's needed to put the fire out and grow stronger in who you are and the purpose you've been given.

In addition to providing you with hope and peace, faith simply provides you the opportunity and challenge to be a better human being tomorrow than you were today–every single day of your life. Your spiritual journey and the journey of improving yourself go hand-in-hand. Both place a strong focus on making improvements by applying the knowledge you gain to your life and pursuing a version of yourself that is closer to the best possible version of yourself with each day that passes. By pursuing this quest in our spiritual lives, we simultaneously improve in the ways we handle many other areas of our lives as well. Spiritual teachings provide us with the wisdom to improve our lives, so through strengthening the spirit, we become more knowledgeable and understanding of life and its meaning. Improvement becomes a major focus in not just the way that we walk spiritually, but also in the way that we walk in our regular, everyday lives.

Faith is a process of growth, one where you watch yourself come into the journey with little to no knowledge on the matter and little to no faith. The more you read and learn about faith, the more likely you are to grow your "faith muscle". As with any other muscle, faith requires effort, persistence, and patience to grow. Results don't linger far behind when constant repetition meets consistency. By creating a spiritually sound environment for yourself and striving daily to live a better life, your struggles will become your testimonies over time.

17

When you commit to seeking them out, the evidence of faith and its potential benefits to your life are all around you. Placing your faith in a higher being helps you grow as a human being and instills a greater sense of purpose into your life, which ignites your spirit. Once ignited, your spirit has a strong influence on the way you go about living your life on a day-to-day basis. By placing your faith in something that is bigger than yourself and your own personal life, you open up the channels necessary for you and your gifts to be used to impact and reach those that haven't yet found faith or are struggling to maintain it– which is all of us at some point in our lives.

In a world where you are exposed to more information than one could possibly retain, deciphering what is true and what isn't true can be a tricky but immensely valuable task. Holding on to useless information only leaves less room in your mind for useful and important information. That being said, you need a reliable source for your information and guidance that you choose to hold on to. I have found faith and a spiritual relationship with God to be a safe, trustworthy source for obtaining the wisdom and guidance that I allow to fill my precious mental space.

In his book *Outwitting the Devil*, Napoleon Hill refers to this type of spiritual guidance and support as "infinite intelligence". Infinite intelligence is a fitting name for the guidance from a higher power, because infinite intelligence is exactly what a spiritual relationship provides you with. Gods are supernatural figures that are all-knowing– their knowledge and understanding don't come from the same pool of knowledge and understanding that is available here on earth. By remaining close to God in spirit and living a life devoted to Him, we're able to experience access to that knowledge and understanding that isn't found in the world amongst us through connection and the spirit.

It is through consistent communication with these supernatural beings that we are connected to supernatural guidance and correction. It's important to understand that we don't have access to this infinite intelligence, without having a strong relationship and consistent dialogue with the one who does have access to this knowledge and wisdom. Our strong faith and belief in this relationship can propel us beyond what logically makes sense, because the "impossible" only exists in the language of the natural. It is through this connection that we come into possession of *supernatural* guidance and direction, which greatly improves our chances of inheriting these supernatural bits and pieces of knowledge and wisdom that allow us to discover our unique gifts that ultimately reveal to us our true purpose in life.

Through faith and consistent communication, this intelligence is shared with us and directs us towards the things that are meant for us in this life. Allowing ourselves access to this privilege not only takes the stress off of us to figure everything out on our own, but it gives us the peace of mind that the information and guidance we are receiving is credible and coming from a source that has our best interest at heart. Sound, spiritual guidance will always lead us to make better choices, which lead to better outcomes for us. If we're constantly making better choices and getting better outcomes, this is a recipe for only one option– a better life.

There are many more benefits to incorporating faith in a higher power into our lives, but the final one that I want to discuss is that faith in a higher power assures us that we aren't alone. This is a concept many people struggle to grasp, because faith cannot be physically seen or heard. Rather, the connection comes from the spirit and is felt. This is what makes it "faith", because it is a deep belief in something that we can't physically see with the naked eye. For even those with strong faith, this idea of trusting in something that we're unable to physically see or touch can be a challenge.

There has been no physical sighting of Jesus, Allah, Buddha, or any other spiritual figure for thousands of years. To take it a step further, the sightings that are documented came from men and women who lived thousands of years ago and are documented in literatures that have been edited and revised more than any other literature has been revised throughout the history of printing and publishing. That being said, our belief and trust in these beings is essentially a blind trust at face value. Blindly trusting others is not a popular way of life in the modern world, where the majority live paranoid and fearful of the unknown and what cannot physically be seen. As a result, the majority of the modern world is living with more reverence for their fears than their faith.

I would be lying if I told you that it's always easy to sit down and find the concentration necessary to have a strong spiritual connection. It can be very difficult at times, especially when our minds and our thoughts aren't aligned with our spirit. Building a strong faith and consistent spiritual relationship is a process, but if we make a consistent effort to continuously reach out and connect, it does get easier and the connection does get stronger over time. Once the connection is developed, we will quickly find that connection to the spirit offers us a different value than the day-to-day connections that we experience throughout our lives with other people.

It's different for everyone, but the overall experience of finding faith in something bigger than yourself usually leads to relief and long-term peace. Struggles will still come and life will still run its course, but the wisdom and guidance provided by our faith gives us a foundation to stand on when the road gets rocky and things are difficult for us to understand from our own perspectives and experiences. No matter the storms we walk through in life, we can rest assured that the calm is near.

We may be shaken up and our course may be altered temporarily along the way, but we will not slip beyond what we can make a recovery from. This firm foundation makes it slightly easier to push through those hard days where we feel like throwing in the towel. Our faith allows us to see the value in the difficult times that strengthen us. It also teaches us how to weather the difficult times in life properly, so that we can receive the abundance of life and opportunity that awaits us on the other side of our struggles. Through the lens of someone with faith, there are better days coming– all we must do is be all that we can be in this very moment and keep the faith.

Some days are easier than others, but knowing that there is someone who always sees and understands us and the things that we're going through can be a great help when trying to stay on a positive track towards a better life for ourselves. The journey is ours, but it doesn't have to be traveled alone. In fact, God wants nothing more than for you to invite

Him to travel your journey with you. There's nothing that He wants more than to help you fulfill His plans and unique purpose for your life. When the going gets rough, it brings peace of mind to know that someone of greater strength and understanding than we can possibly comprehend is at our side to help us endure whatever difficulties we may face along the way.

I wouldn't include a principle as touchy as religion can be if I didn't wholeheartedly believe that choosing to put your faith in something bigger than yourself is a major key to finding purpose and becoming someone that is capable of building a better life for yourself. I went back and forth on including this principle for a while, because I know that religion is a topic of controversy and a topic that many have strong beliefs or absolute lack of belief in. The last thing I wanted was for someone to pick my book up to read it and become turned off immediately because I began with discussing religion and faith.

Then, I thought to myself: "This is *my* book, *my* story to tell. If I let the pressures of the world's opinion of me keep me from making this as authentic as possible, I'm not sticking to my own principles." Maybe somebody else would leave their faith out of the story to prevent stepping on the toes of certain audiences. It's not my intention to do so, but I'll step on the toes of earthly beings before I step on God's toes by not shining light on my relationship with Him and what it's done for me in my life. I'm not able to leave out this very important detail and part of my story. For without God's intervention and guidance in my life, I can assure you I wouldn't be here writing these words to you today.

If you already have faith, then I encourage you to dig even deeper and truly challenge yourself to grow in your faith daily. If you currently have no faith in any religion or are struggling to believe, I recommend that you simply give it a shot. Find a sermon online or maybe even call a friend that you know has knowledge of religion and discuss any questions and concerns you may have surrounding religion. Once you experience the power of a relationship as beneficial as the one with your God, I don't anticipate that you will want to go back to your life before encountering and embracing faith either. Now that I have experienced life where my faith and trust lie in something much bigger than myself, I no longer want to go back to living a life where I had little faith and felt I had so little hope– but I had to first walk through those days of little faith and hope to become the man of strong faith that I am now.

As many young adults do, I gave myself too much credit and thought I knew much more than I truthfully did coming into the real world. I didn't truthfully feel like I needed anyone outside of myself to get to where I wanted to go in my life. Despite growing up going to church a good majority of my childhood, I hardly attended church throughout my high school years and was inconsistent in my efforts to connect with my spirit and inner-self throughout my teenage years. In fact, during this time, I viewed people who went to church as some of the most judgmental and hypocritical people in the world– they were one of the last groups of people I wanted to associate with or have my name associated with. I believed in God, but I was completely turned off to the idea of giving up the things I wanted to follow Him closer.

If I'm being honest, I wouldn't say that I started the process of taking my faith more seriously until about a year and a half ago from writing this. Life had finally thrown enough at me that I was broken– spiritually, mentally, and physically. For the first time in my life, I felt stuck with nowhere to go. I had come to the realization that I knew about .000001 percent of what I originally thought I knew, and I was forced to humble myself and open my mind up to alternative ways of living to change my situation. I knew there had to be a better way and a better life out there for me than the life that I found myself stuck in.

I knew who God was my entire life, but I didn't take the time to get to know God beyond the surface of the occasional prayer and maybe coming across a few bible verses here and there. I was foolish enough to think that my own plans could triumph over God's will for my life– I thought He was someone who I made *my* requests known to and He blessed those requests and allowed me to do solely what I wanted in my life. I knew who God was, but I didn't truly know God. I knew deep down that the life I was living didn't fully honor my faith, but I knew God would forgive me– I wasn't willing to sacrifice what was "fun" and provided me the most comfort at the time.

I was interested in the good things He promised, but I was ignorant to the fact that those promises were a mute point with the way I was living at the time. I wanted the benefits and the security of a strong faith without undergoing the process of developing a strong faith and separating myself from the things and people that were keeping me from developing this strong faith. I wanted the protection of carrying the cross, without actually

24

putting in the time and effort to lift the cross above my own selfish wants and desires, dying to my flesh and surrendering my life to God.

It didn't happen overnight, but I gradually began to realize that both the world's problems and my own personal problems were bigger than me. I was never meant to feel the stress and pressure that I was feeling, leading me to feel like a complete failure. I was done carrying these powerful feelings and all the things that were hurting me. I didn't have to hold these things any longer, and as much as my pride didn't want to admit it initially, it was time to give up the charade and return home to the man who was responsible for the breath in my lungs.

I remember very vividly, I was sitting in my car outside of my house on a spring afternoon. I had just returned home from work, and as I always did, I sat and listened to music for a few minutes and caught up on the notifications I had missed while I was at work and driving back home. This particular day, I couldn't even focus on responding to the messages my family and friends had left me. I could feel that something was different about this day, that I needed to pay attention to this moment that I was about to find myself in. I didn't know what the moment looked like, but I could feel it was important and required my attention and focus.

I turned the car off and I just sat for a few minutes. I was battling serious depression at the time, a battle that was getting the best of me. I simply looked up into the clear skies and said, "God, I know you have more for my life than this." I was so defeated spiritually and mentally that I already felt dead inside. I no longer looked forward to waking up and feeling stuck in this same reality day after day. My breaking point had finally come and I had finally found the courage to seek help from who I felt at the time was my last resort.

Tears streamed down my face, as I went down the list and laid out all of my problems and frustrations that I was experiencing. I was angry at God and I didn't shy away from expressing my anger. I had been angry with Him ever since my mom's cancer diagnosis in June of 2017– the summer going into my senior year of high school. I knew I had enough on my plate going into my senior year. I knew I had an uphill battle to play well and give myself an opportunity to play at the next level, but the diagnosis sucked the endless supply of energy and life that 17-year-olds are notorious for having. I didn't understand why my mom's health was suddenly at risk and why all of our lives were being affected by something we had no control over. It had been three years since her diagnosis and I was finally releasing the anger and resentment I felt.

I wanted answers as to why I was feeling the way I was feeling, struggling with the things I was struggling with, and stuck in the miserable life that I was living. Everything I had been holding in all those years was released right there in my car, as I pounded on the steering wheel repeatedly. I was living in a world of hurt and frustration, and I had been living with all of these emotions bottled up for some time. I had tried many things to make myself feel whole again, but the truth is that I knew something was broken inside of me beyond what I could even understand at the time

Through my tears and anger, I continued to list my reasons for being frustrated and closed off over the years. I felt I had every reason to be upset about the hand I had been dealt at the point in my life, disappointment after disappointment. As I pondered all the major life changes that I had been through within the last year of my life, I pushed my head back towards the head rest of my seat and cried all the tears I had left to give.

I had reached my breaking point and something had to change, or I didn't know how much longer I could take it. I apologized for the way I had been living, all the times I had ignored what was right and chosen to do wrong instead. I wanted nothing more in life than to feel whole again, to feel like I was somebody that my parents could be proud of. I just wanted to be happy with the reflection I saw when I looked in the mirror again, to feel like myself again. I explained my feelings of rage and resentment one last time, which He already knew about. I acknowledged that much of what I was living in was brought on by my own actions, and I looked up to the sky and told Him that I was done trying to do things my way. He had finally broken me down to the point that I was ready to listen.

The sky that I had been looking at throughout this conversation was mostly clear, with only a few clouds in the sky. However, as soon as I had dried my tears off my face and prepared myself to walk into the house, clouds filled the sky and it began to drizzle. The drizzle lasted for roughly two minutes and then it stopped. The sky went right back to being mostly clear, with no rain in sight. Georgia weather is capable of almost anything. I don't put much past the impossible happening in Georgia from a weather standpoint, but this had nothing to do with Georgia's weather and I knew it immediately.

I knew right then and there that God had heard my apology and my cry out for help. It was only minutes after I had just reached out. What else could've possibly explained what I had just experienced? I couldn't physically see or hear Him, but I knew He was there and He was listening. He may have not agreed with everything I said and I was certainly in the wrong to question Him, but He heard me out and I knew he was there. On that day, my life changed.

I didn't know I was going to get out of the mess I had created or how I was going to get myself back on track in my faith. I just knew I wasn't alone, that somebody understood me and the things that I was going through at the time. Somebody could understand the feelings I was having and the battle I was fighting every single day of my life. I knew that He cared and still thought I was salvageable, even after all the mistakes I had made and disobedience I had chosen.

You see, if you only listen to what the world has to say about you and only base your actions on the trends of the world, you will be missing out on an important and an empowering piece of your life. In fact, you will be missing a major piece of your *identity*. In a way, you will be an imposter your entire life– for it is impossible to fully know yourself and your identity without knowing what your Creator has spoken over your identity and who you were called to be in your life. If you only think about how the world perceives you, you're allowing the world to determine your identity for you.

Society is a mix of both bad and good people. Not all human beings are bad and not all human beings are good– human beings are mixed into the population together to create a world of both good and bad. From the time Adam and Eve ate the apple off the tree, evil became a compliment to the good in the world. Therefore, this is a reality that will be true of human nature and society for as long as we live. There will always be a struggle of good versus evil. Some people will accept you and some people won't. That's just the way life goes.

I was able to tune out how society defined me and define myself by looking at what my *faith* said about me and the way I was created. My faith says that I'm wonderfully and fearfully made in His image. My faith says that I was hand-picked and chosen to be adopted as His son– the most righteous and perfect man to ever step foot on this earth. Over time, I came to the realization that I was exactly who I was supposed to be and that my skin and every other feature was made specifically for me. It didn't matter how anybody else felt about me, whether their opinions were good or bad– all that mattered was that my faith revealed to me how I'm seen through the eyes of the greatest man that ever lived.

Once I found God, I began to embrace my true identity. I began to embrace who God told me I am, and the opinions of others began to matter less and less to me. My identity comes from God and God alone. People will try to alter and distort this truth, but this will always be the truth– whether I choose to believe it or not, that falls on me. That realization alone has forever changed my life and the way that I live my life. Through expanding my faith and trusting in something bigger than myself, I was able to develop a stronger sense of self-worth and come to the realization that I'm worth it because God said I'm worth it. Even when I don't see worth in myself, He sees my worth and there's nothing I could ever do to change that.

Many people will judge your book based on the cover, and by doing so, they will put labels on you that cause them to miss out on all the good that lies within the pages of your story. That's the world that we live in and that's life. You can't change these people or this fact, but you can make the decision to not let their words or judgements cause you to forget the only words and judgment that truly matter.

In 1 Peter 2:15, Peter wrote, "It is God's will that your honorable lives should silence those ignorant people who make foolish accusations against you." *God's* will– that phrase speaks volumes because His will is above everything in this world. You can make the decision to continue to fill the pages of your book with goodness and purpose, having faith that the right people will look past the cover and read what truly matters– the pages that lie between the covers. By continuing on in your good work, no matter how limited the audience, you will silence the ignorance of others and write a story that brings honor to God and His will for your life.

No matter how great the story you write is, you can't force anyone to read it and you shouldn't beg anyone to read it if the cover alone is enough to turn them away. You must stay true to who you are, make sure that the pages contain your best work, and make peace with the fact that your book won't be for everybody. Even the best-selling books of all time have critics, and your life will be no different, regardless of how successful the book you write becomes.

You tune out the nonsense and harsh words by instead choosing to listen to what faith says about you. It doesn't matter which spiritual literature you choose to read or what religion you choose to follow– you're an important piece in a war against evil. Religion itself focuses on giving you the practical knowledge and wisdom that you will need to succeed in your life– sometimes you're just required to dig deeper within yourself to put it into practice and reap the benefits.

All religions teach that you were born into this world to do good things. They all teach you morality and ethics that help you treat others with respect and outline the ways to live a good and honest life. They all drill into your mind that there are trials and tribulations in life that will be overcome by your strength and your faith. They all tell you to strive to be all that you can be and that the assistance provided by your faith will take care of the rest. Most importantly, they all tell you that there is a purpose and a calling in your life– a reason to get out of bed every morning and give maximum effort to becoming your highest self.

The choice is yours. Every day, you have the choice to listen to what the world says about you or to listen to what your faith says about you. Once again, I'm not here to preach to you or pressure you into making any specific decisions in your life. My only goal is to help you become a better version of yourself and to see you reach your full potential in your life. I believe that developing a strong faith is a step that's immensely helpful and insightful in that process. I have seen first-hand what it has done for me in my life and I would feel selfish to not give you the same opportunity to find freedom and peace in your own life.

I've been there before. I've tried doing it my way, ignoring my needs for guidance and intervention. I've tried to find confidence and self-worth in sleeping with girls like it was my occupation. I've tried to find peace and clarity in my overwhelming thoughts through thick clouds of marijuana, believing that my problems and insecurities would be left right there in the ashtray with no other course of action. I've tried to find solace and distraction from my issues in the bottom of empty liquor bottles, even drinking myself to the point of being unconscious at times. I've tried to run from my problems in more ways than I can count, and I've tried to hide the pain of issues I was going through in my life in all the wrong ways.

I can honestly say no night with a girl I had no business being with has left me with the self-confidence and fulfillment that strengthening my faith has given me. While those girls were gone the next morning, the words of God remained by my side. My bed lay empty when I was in the middle of my brokenness, but the word brought fullness back into my heart and spirit. Those nights taught me how to chase instant gratification and low-hanging fruit in my life– cheap doses of dopamine that came with great risks. Reading Paul's words in the book of Galatians from the Bible taught me, "But the fruit of the Spirit is love, joy, peace, forbearance, kindness, goodness, faithfulness, gentleness and self-control. Against such things there is no law." The pursuit of a life that produces God's fruitfulness and not my own changed my life and taught me how to chase real, authentic dopamine that gives life in the midst of struggle.

I'm an advocate for marijuana because I believe it's a natural plant that was put on earth for the purpose of healing. Despite its negative reputation, marijuana helps many people every single day. No matter how much relief they bring, there comes a point where you no longer use the drugs and they begin to use you. When you're using them to cope with life and not for specific treatment, the use of any drug can quickly become a dangerous game. I can honestly say I've come down from every high I've ever experienced, even when I filled my lungs with as much smoke as I possibly could. The more I fill my mind and life with the word of God, the harder it becomes to bring myself back down to the places I've worked so hard to escape from.

I can honestly say that there isn't a liquor strong enough in the world to give me the solace and courage to face my problems that my faith has given me. My drunkenness led to repeated errors in my judgment and illness later down the road, while faith has led me to better judgment and healing. Overconsumption of alcohol put me to sleep on many nights, while consumption of the word woke me up to my greater purpose in life. The abuse of alcohol to the point of having no awareness of my surroundings put my life at risk, while getting to know the word and making the effort to apply it to my life has brought me awareness and protection.

No amount of running solved my problems– it was only learning to be still and how to put my faith outside of myself and my abilities that actually allowed me to move forward and create progress in my life. Renewing and strengthening my faith forever changed my life– I'll take it a step farther to say that it *saved* my life. I'll never claim to be

33

a saint or the perfect man of faith, as no man who is truly of faith would ever make such a claim. However, I can tell you that who I am now and who I was a year ago are two completely different people– who I am today would be unrecognizable to who I was a year ago. That version of myself would've never thought this version of me was possible, and the beautiful thing about it is that I'm nowhere near finished growing and evolving. I owe that to my encounter with faith.

I still struggle just like every other human being does, and I would be lying if I told you I don't still lose those battles sometimes. I have "Come to Jesus" meetings in my head on a regular basis to try and hold myself accountable for doing what is right. At the end of the day, I'm still human and I'm capable of the same mistakes that we all are capable of. I understand that my human flesh is sinful by nature, that faith is needed to keep me grounded and on the right track. I'm no longer swallowed up by anger and regret for the mistakes I have made in the past, nor will I be for the mistakes that I make in the future. This lack of worry comes from knowing where my help comes from and knowing that I wasn't called to live a shameful and sheepish existence. I've experienced true transformation in my thoughts, actions, and beliefs that have transformed me as a person.

Without faith and religion, life is reduced simply to living and dying. All the events that happen throughout the years in between have no major significance or meaning to us. There is a lack of guidance and direction in our lives, which will undoubtedly lead us to lives that we feel lost in. All good within humans is because of religion. Without it, we're no more civil than the animals that hunt each other for survival out in the jungle each and every day of their existence. Without it, it's every man for themselves, and we miss out on the privilege of using and combining our gifts to collaborate to create a world where we all can thrive and exist peacefully amongst one another.

We think of the top predators in the jungle to be strong and ferocious because of their ability to dominate the competition and survive. In human society, the game is much less violent and focuses much less on short-term dominance. Instead, life's race is one about building longevity and making steady improvements along the way. As a result, ferociousness and short-term dominance are empty pursuits in the game of life for human beings. That is, *restraint* and the ability to master our thoughts and urges are what truly make us strong and powerful as human beings.

This restraint and mastery does not come naturally, but it can be cultivated through the development of a strong relationship between our spirit and a higher power. Faith and religion represent all things good within us, and they are the only thing that separates humans from all other living beings. Without them, we are simply another living organism fighting for survival and advancement along the food chain. Religion and lawfulness are the root of the success of human society, the only distinguishing factors that allow us to create a society unlike any other society of living beings.

In my earlier years, I had experiences in the church that made Christianity seem like a judgmental lifestyle that would be full of ridicule. I was turned off by the idea of faith because I felt I wasn't good enough to uphold the expectations. I now understand that I'm not good enough to uphold the expectations and I never will be, but I'm still loved and

35

chosen. This walk of faith isn't about being perfect or judging others, but it's about coming to trust God with your own life and dying to self. It's about being reborn and giving your life to God so that you can walk in salvation and freedom, regardless of the times you fall short of the Glory.

I no longer see myself as a black man with a slim chance of making it in the world. I no longer worry about what people outside of God think about me and my life. I no longer question my past experiences. Instead, I see myself as knowledgeable. I see myself as a man with a calling and a purpose for my life. I see myself as a victor instead of a victim. I see myself as a man with faith and hope in a plan for a better future for myself and those I care about. I see myself as all the things my faith tells me I am, which gives me true peace of mind and the courage to wake up and chase my dreams and pursue my passions every single day of my life without the burden of trusting myself to make it all happen alone.

God sent his one and only son to endure the unthinkable on the cross, because he saw past my flaws and sins and decided that I was worth the sacrifice. Even when I don't feel worthy, God chose me to share the covenant with Him. You were also chosen to be exactly where you are in this exact moment. Despite all the flaws and imperfections we possess, we were chosen. Who am *I* to question my own worth when the greatest man to ever live doesn't even question my worth? Who are *you* to question your worth when your worth has already been proclaimed? When I found my faith, I moved closer to finding my true identity and began the process of letting go of all the negativity I had come to believe about myself.

It was done for me when I least expected it, so it can also be done for you, no matter where you are right now in your life. All I can say is God did. He filled my spirit with a desire to live with purposeful intentions. He was patient with me in my willingness to accept the challenge of choosing virtuous habits over sinful habits. It took taking the leap of faith to trust and make changes, but He traded my confusion and pain away and gave me increased wisdom and joy in return.

He had his hands on my life throughout this entire process, and He continues to have His hand on my life– I owe everything that I am to Him. Without Him, I do not exist, because my life is His. He saved me from the fiery fate that I deserve for all of my flaws and imperfections. For that simple fact alone, I make the effort to die to myself and my own selfish ambitions a little more each and every day. My ultimate hope for the man that I'm becoming is that when others see me and the way that I live my life, they see God's love in me and feel it through the way that I love them according to God's word.

Believe that there's a power that's higher than you, seek that higher power out to guide your steps along your journey, and walk in full confidence that your life is covered by a love and sacrifice so strong that even the most disruptive of events in your life will stand no chance at stopping you from reaching what was planned for your life. You'll be surprised where it'll take you in your life. You are capable of achieving whatever you put your mind to, but establishing your faith in a higher power will put you in touch with what God has in His mind for you. His plan is much greater than any plan that the human mind could possibly conceive. Your connection to infinite intelligence and wisdom will take your ability to achieve to new, supernatural levels.

His capacity of thinking and achieving is much greater than any other being on this earth. I'm a firm believer that strong faith leads to abundance and victory in your life. My life is living proof that faith leads to abundance and victory, because the strengthening of my faith has opened doors for me that I would've never imagined being opened for me a year ago– doors that I would've never discovered if I was still committed to my own foolish ways. At some points in my life, knowing that I'm still here to tell this story would be a victory in itself. I greatly encourage you to take advantage of this resource to help guide you to reach new levels in your life– it's going to cost you your old life, but you will be given an unimaginable return on your investment. Find the faith and keep it– it is the guidance that will never lead you astray on your journey to becoming all you were created to be.

Chapter Two

Principle #2: You're only as strong as your "why"- your reason(s) for doing what you do in life.

The "why" was a term I was unfamiliar with in my life prior to my sales training for a summer internship I took part in while in college. The internship entailed door-to-door sales, which is one of the most challenging methods of selling in the sales industry. Being outside on your feet and in the summer heat for up to ten hours a day– the physical demand of the job alone makes it unsuitable for many people. Even if you are able to meet the physical demands of the job, the most difficult and most vital aspect of the job is developing and maintaining *mental* toughness through the difficulty of the job.

On a given day, a sales rep can knock anywhere between 250 to 300 doors. Of those 250 to 300 doors, it's considered a good day if you encounter 50 to 60 people who have the capability of making the decision on deciding whether they want to buy the product you're selling or not. Of those 50 to 60 people that a rep encounters on a *good* day of knocking, it's considered a successful day if a rep can make four to six sales by the end of the day.

This means that on a good day, a rep is rejected on the northern end of 45-50 times within that day. Then, you must also factor in knocking empty doors or simply being ignored altogether north of about 200 times within the same day. When you put all of the time and effort that is required into your pitch and understand that compensation is slipping away with every rejection and door that is slammed in your face, it takes extreme mental strength to gather yourself and move onto the next door with confidence that one of your four to six sales for that day will be behind that door. Yet, this is exactly what a sales rep must find the mental fortitude to do if he desires to reach his sales goals for the day and for the summer.

Now that I've given you a very simplified breakdown of what it's like being a door-to-door salesman, you can better understand why the industry is so challenging to find success in. In an effort to mentally prepare me for the difficulties that lay ahead, knowing and establishing my "why" was the very first part of my training for the job. I'll never forget this moment for as long as I live, because it was one of those defining "lightbulb" moments in my life.

I was on FaceTime with my team leader for the very first training call to prepare me for the upcoming summer. I had been thinking of questions I may have to answer on the call throughout the day, and I had a few of my responses written down on some index cards that were lying on my desk. He only asked me two very simple questions throughout the entire thirty-minute call, neither of which could be answered by my note cards. The first question he asked was, "What's your reason for wanting to be successful– why do you do what you do in your life?" Immediately after, he followed up with, "What's your greatest motivation in your life?"

I looked up at the ceiling in my bedroom, as if the answers to his questions were written somewhere up there. Then, I looked back at my team leader on the phone. I took a deep breath, and I told him, "I want to be the one who changes the lives of my family for the better. I don't want my mom to be worried about the cost of her medications in the future, and I am tired of watching my dad work overnight shifts in a warehouse, followed by day shifts at Lowe's."

I thought for a few more seconds and then I answered his second question with, "My greatest motivation in my life is my family. We've been on the other side of things financially lately, which is unfamiliar territory for us. Nothing hurts me more than seeing that we're limited in the things we're able to do right now and I'm not in a position to do anything about it." I knew the job was going to be difficult, but I thought if I could just find a way to make it work for me, I would be able to make more money and help my family out.

This was a very powerful moment in my life, because at the time, I was struggling greatly with my mental health and finding purpose in my life. By asking those two simple questions and giving me a few seconds to evaluate what mattered most to me in my life and what made life's challenges worth it to me, Brandon brought back to me an important piece of me that had been missing in my life for months. He brought back the competitor in me, the kid who wanted more than anything for his family to see better days.

This experience was all about getting away from home for the summer, with hopes that I would find my footing in life again. In a few minutes, I had put my life back into perspective and reminded myself why the fight was well worth it. Again, this was at a time where I was struggling greatly in my life and my circumstances at the time had a lot to do with me agreeing to move across the country to do this internship that ultimately guaranteed me nothing. There was no doubt in my mind that I needed to get away from everyone and find myself again. I had overcome these same feelings before in my life and I was determined to find a way to do so again.

The same way that it took me a few minutes to put my life back into perspective and to remind myself of my *why*, you can also remind yourself of your why. If you've never thought about it before, I encourage you to take the time and think about the things you would do with your life if your fear of failure and the possibility of unrealistic expectations did not exist. What changes do you want to see in your life? Who do you want to impact the most with your life's work?

Take the time to evaluate what means most to you, to define *why* you picked this book up and are striving to become a better version of yourself. A strong why develops a stronger sense of self and puts you in touch with what truly means most to you in life. Once you've found this, it becomes easier to push through the obstacles and rejections in life that stand between you and your goals. The end goal has significant meaning to you, so you don't allow small bits of suffering and difficulty along the way to keep you from pursuing that goal with everything you've got.

This is why this principle is such an important piece of becoming the best version of yourself that you possibly can. Nothing can stop you when the forces that drive you are stronger than the forces that stand in your way. Constantly remind yourself of why you started your journey in the first place. If you refuse to stop moving towards the life that you want, you may be slowed down and rerouted along the way- but you will never be stopped.

It is this mindset and persistence that will separate you from the crowd and allow you to reach the goals you set for yourself in life.

Inky Johnson, one of my favorite motivational speakers and the owner of one of the most touching testimonies I've ever heard, gave me such a profound outlook on my "why" in one of his speeches. Inky says, "You must have a strong reason for *why* you do what you do, because the cycle of life will break someone with a weak reason." He goes on to state that life is bigger than each and every person on this earth, and you will eventually hit a wall of adversity in your life that is bigger than you– if you don't have a strong driving force for doing what you do. According to Inky, if you're only living for yourself or without purpose, these walls will stop your momentum and keep you stagnant. Those walls get big and challenging sometimes, so it's important that you have the drive and the motivation to climb them and keep going.

It was at this moment that I realized the power that lies within my why. I have personal goals of becoming successful for myself and my life, but every single one of those personal achievements is inspired by the prospect of putting myself in a position to change the lives of others. Leaving an impact through my compassion and willingness to serve others is my true passion in my life– personal success and achievement that has the potential to change my family's situation for generations to come is simply a by-product of pushing myself towards this greater purpose for my life.

I had experienced first-hand the truth behind Inky's words. Life is bigger than any one individual, and if you aren't in touch with why you're enduring the process, you will

43

eventually run into a wall of adversity that will force you to stop and get in touch with those thoughts very quickly. Prior to my conversation with Brandon during my sales training, I was having a hard time finding meaning in my life because my heart wasn't in what I was doing. I was going through the motions and doing what was necessary to get by, but I wasn't feeding that strong need for purpose in my life– I was playing it safe and ignoring my need for accountability.

When you make life all about yourself, you're putting yourself at a disadvantage to those who are motivated by greater forces. When you hit that wall of adversity, it's much easier to talk yourself into slowing down or even quitting when you feel as though you will be the only one affected by your actions. On the other hand, someone who is motivated to touch the lives of others and makes their goals and success about more than just themselves, understands that slowing down or quitting affects their ability to see it through that those other lives will be touched through their work. It's much more difficult to even muster the thought of giving up when you know and understand that giving up also affects the people you care about most in your life.

As humans, it is a known fact that we will take great measures and push ourselves to extreme lengths for the people that we care about. Interestingly enough, we are often more willing to suffer for these people than we are for ourselves. This willingness to suffer for the protection and advancement of those we love is one of the greatest wonders of human anthropology, but I believe it serves as standing evidence that humans are at their best when they're able to deny themselves for the sake of what's most impactful for the group.

44

Think about the man who takes a rainy jog to the car after dinner with his family while his wife and children stay dry under the pavilion and wait for him to pick them up at the curb. Rain isn't fatal and the whole family is capable of running out to the car together. However, when you love people in the way that a man loves his family, you want the very best for those people. If you can keep your spouse from having to go out into the rain and your children from running across a parking lot in the dark, that's what you do. A man doesn't think twice about doing this for people that he loves because he wants to ensure that they're always taken care of.

He isn't going to send his wife or his children into the rain while he waits under the pavilion and stays dry, because that is not his role as a husband, a father, and a man. Sure, he may get poured on for a few seconds. What's most important to this man is that his family is safe and dry. He knows the jog will only take a few seconds and he will be able to grab the car and safely pick up the most important people in his life, while keeping them dry and making their lives easier. Therefore, he is willing to take the jog in the rain to ensure that his wife and children are dry and safe– it's a small individual sacrifice that he feels is best for the entire family.

This is a very basic example of how this willingness to suffer for others is embedded within our psychology as humans, but there are examples of this all around you in life. At one point in time, we were all infants who were completely unaware of anything that was going on around us and completely vulnerable. However, somebody stepped in and fed us, clothed us, taught us how to use the bathroom properly, how to talk, how to walk, and essentially assisted with our development every step of the way until we reached the point of being self-sufficient in continuing our own development.

We call these people mom, dad, grandma, grandpa, and many other titles– but before establishing the bonds that we share with these people today, they were ultimately strangers who were willing to sacrifice more of their time, energy, and effort for another human being than they gave themselves. They had their own lives and well-beings to look after, but they still chose to prioritize another human being before themselves. Make sure you take the time to thank these people for their sacrifices and never take the bonds you share with these people for granted, for what they have done for you is one of the purest forms of love.

This willingness to sacrifice for others is a trait that is so unique in humans, but I believe that this is one of the most powerful features that we have as human beings. When the power of this is harnessed correctly and applied to virtuous and purposeful living, the power of any human is increased exponentially. It will be discussed later in greater depth, but one of the most important keys to living a better life is to live a life that serves others. When you embody your willingness to suffer for others and deny yourself in the process, you're living a life of meaning and increasing your potential to impact the lives of others in the process.

Allow the things and people that mean the most to you to drive you towards success in your life. Life is so much bigger than what you can accomplish for yourself and personal gain. Do not rob yourself of reaching your full potential and serving your purpose to leave an impact on others during your time here on earth. Most importantly, the feeling of fulfillment that you will experience in your life from sacrificing for and touching the lives of others is one of the greatest feelings that you can ever experience in your life. It is ultimately healing others that is life's best form of medicine for the soul.

Without a strong why, there's no telling where I would be or what I would be doing with my life. I would likely still be sitting around feeling sorry for myself, spending my time sulking about the few things that didn't go right in my life. Depression would most likely still have a hold on me. I wouldn't wake up and appreciate the people in my life. I may be living day to day without any specific aim or direction for my life. There are many things I could guess about the way my life would be going if I hadn't found this important piece of me, but I can assure you I wouldn't be the person I am today if I never would've found it.

Understanding my why has changed my perspective of the way I view myself and my perspective on life as a whole. It's called me to action in my life, to act on the things that feed and nourish my soul. A fire was lit within me to become successful and the best possible version of myself because I know the impact that I can have on the lives of others if I reach my highest potential. This book is only the beginning, because I'm going to give everything I have to ensure that I do my part to leave the world a better place for the future generations when I leave this earth.

Amongst all the noise and negativity in my life at the time, I was able to silence the noise and be reminded why I started my journey in the first place. Thoughts of positivity showed their faces for the first time in my life in months. I was no longer a victim to feeling completely lost and hopeless. I was reminded why I pushed myself to go above what was required of me and why I was pushing myself to try something as difficult and unfamiliar to me as door-to-door sales, in a completely unfamiliar environment– over 2,000 miles away from everything I had ever known at the time.

All of this reconnected me with who I truly am. It gave me the confidence to try new things and to develop new skills in new environments. I knew I would never live the life I desire to live and have the impact I desire to have by playing it safe and never taking the chances necessary to grow and evolve. I had to pull the trigger and take a chance, or I would never know what was on the other side of that opportunity I had been given in my life. There were risks involved with accepting the challenge but I felt like I had nothing to lose and everything to gain.

This is what truly keeps me locked in and persistent in the fight when things get difficult and I don't see a way out right away. Aspiring to live a good life and pushing yourself beyond the societal norms is no task for the weak-hearted, but I think about what this life that I've chosen has given me and the person that it's molding me in to- it's a decision I would make ten million times over, no matter how much failure it takes or how many lessons must be learned. I feel I've been through the things I've been through to become a leader and a voice, so my aspirations and lofty goals are much more to me than personal recognition and monetary gain.

Life was able to break *me* temporarily, but it was the people I love and care about who kept me in the fight until I could regain my composure. Life wasn't able to break my love and compassion for the people I vowed to provide better days for. This is who I am, and I wouldn't be a fraction of the person I am today without the support system and my appreciation for these people that runs so deeply through me. I now understand that things like my ego, laziness, and lack of self-confidence affect my ability to accomplish my goals that I have set for myself, which also affects my ability to impact and serve others. This keeps me grounded and focused on the bigger picture in life, which will not come to fruition in the presence of excessive ego, laziness, or a lack of self-confidence.

Life almost pushed me to give up on myself and my dreams, but the one person who specifically kept me going every day was my younger brother, Preston. He would tell you he doesn't know what he would do without his big brother, but the truth is I wouldn't be half the person I am today if it wasn't for Preston. I knew I was someone he looked up to and that it was my job as his older brother to be there for him at all costs. He knew that I was struggling somewhat but I could never tell him the true depths of my struggles because I didn't want him worrying about me.

I didn't feel I had much left to give, but I would think about Preston and I found a little more in the tank. I ultimately decided I wasn't going to let him see me quit. I had been determined my whole life to set a positive example for him and to be living proof to him that there were ways to beat the stereotypes and statistics that we heard so much about growing up. I wanted him to know that he was more than a number and that he could do whatever he put his mind to in his life. I refused to show him any different, so I had to find it within me to get off the ground and keep climbing.

I had fought and persevered through everything thrown my way up to this point and I had simply made it too far to stop now. Sure, I didn't always feel like putting on a fake smile and pushing through the hardest of my days, but I knew that this was bigger than just me and this drove me every single day. My brother's company and support during the darkest times of my life were a constant reminder of my why and where my greatest strength came from. There were times in my life I had mentally checked out on *myself,* but I would never even entertain the thought of giving up on Preston. I knew by giving up on myself, I was giving up on him– therefore, it was impossible for me to give up on myself. Preston is a huge reason as to why I turned my life around and why you're reading this book.

I was an athlete for the first 20 years of my life, so I know all about the benefits of building physical strength. Over the years, I have built a body that possesses decent physical strength and capabilities. However, life has shown me that true strength is not defined by how much weight I can put on the bench press or the squat rack. It comes from knowing why I do what I'm doing in my life and who I'm doing it for. It comes from understanding my purpose and pursuing my passions. It comes from understanding that my decisions affect more than just me. It comes from having the courage to continue to fight, even when it looks like the fight has already been lost.

My greatest strength in my life is knowing and understanding my *why*. I have something of great value to me to lose if I don't improve every day and put myself in the position to change lives. Any time a person has something of great value to them to lose, they also have something to live for. *This* is why I consider knowing and understanding this important piece of your life to be so critical in the process of taking your life to the next level. We all must have something meaningful to us to live for in order for us to possess the drive that this journey requires to see it through to the successful ending.

I'm going to get to where I want to be in my life because I'm going to work for it every single day. I'm going to do the work so my mom doesn't have to decide between going out to eat or paying for her medication. I'm going to do the work so my dad can load up his golf clubs into his Corvette one day. I'm going to do the work so I can be there for my brothers and their families in time of need. I'm going to win in my life, not because I'm more talented than anybody else. I'm simply going to outwork the competition through blood, sweat, and tears because I hold myself accountable for who I become in this life.

Accountability is one of the most vital concepts to understand in life, yet it's something that so many people in society struggle to understand. Your actions come with consequences. Depending on the nature of your actions, there are desirable consequences and there are undesirable consequences. Either way, you are responsible for each and every one of your actions and the consequences that come with them. Accepting this truth is accountability.

Accountability is simply something that cannot be avoided. *Somebody* must accept it at some point or another. Therefore, you have two choices– you can choose actions that leave your accountability in the hands of others, or you can keep the ball in your own court and hold yourself accountable for taking actions that propel you towards reaching the heights you desire to reach in your life. The most successful people in the world don't need to be held accountable by an outside source because they hold themselves accountable. They may use outside sources to reinforce their accountability, but the responsibility for what they make of themselves and their lives comes from within and a strong desire to be the best they can be.

Making the right decision to hold yourself accountable, paired with knowing and understanding your strong "why," can change the trajectory of your life from this current moment until your last days. When you hold yourself accountable for your goals and success, you don't need people telling you that you should work harder than the average person. You don't need people to remind you to wake up in time to make it to that important meeting for work in the morning. You don't need your employer to beg you to do your job and be a valuable member of the team. You don't need your teacher to give you countless reminders of due dates for important assignments. You don't need anybody other than yourself and your reasons for doing what you do.

You understand the repercussions of not doing what is expected of you and what must be done in order for you to reach those goals and to have the success that you desire. That alone is enough to push you to be your best. All of your responsibilities are being fulfilled because you understand that those responsibilities are standing between you and the desired end goals that you have for your life. Obstacles to success and achievement come as a part of life, but they only stay as a result of your indecision to overcome them.

Accountability itself can be its own principle in creating a better life for yourself. In this case, it can be paired with knowing and understanding your why because it is your why that you must hold yourself accountable for. Understanding the meaning of accountability is an easy concept to grasp. Living a life that embodies accountability isn't always easy, and I believe this is where so many people go wrong in their lives.

It's not always the most fun or appealing concept to focus on and implement into your life because it requires you to do what is best for you, not simply what you feel like doing in the moment or whatever comes easiest to you. This is a constant battle that you will face in life– doing what is right versus doing what is easy. The earlier that you can learn to prioritize and handle business before doing the things you want to do, the better off you will be. Accountability is simply understanding that you have the freedom to make whatever choices you desire in life, but the results of these free choices come with a price or a prize– the choice is yours. Your decisions can lead to consequences that *reward* you for your hard work, or they can lead to consequences that *cost* you for your lack of hard work.

Accountability is one facet of life that no human being will ever completely master, which makes it a life-long work in progress for every human being. I fail to meet the standards of my own accountability at times, just as we all do. By striving to become the

53

person I know I'm capable of becoming, I have grown so much through my mistakes and in holding myself accountable for my actions and the results that they lead to. As a result, I have seen improvement in every area of my life and will continue to improve as my accountability improves.

I haven't yet arrived where I'm going, but the important thing is that I've started moving towards that place and believe in the path that I'm on to get to that place. However, I also know that this path will be filled with obstacles, adversity, and growing pains along the way. It's not a linear path straight to the top. It will take me building on what I've already started, while growing in my ability to hold myself accountable for me to get there. It will take everything in the tank for me to get there. I must be strong in my "why" and remember why it all started in the first place to do the work that is required.

Have a strong definition and understanding of your why and hold yourself accountable for everything that it entails. You won't be perfect but strive for continuous progress in this area of your life. Understand that the choices you make carry weight and affect your life, so make choices that put you in a position to live the life that you desire. Push yourself each and every day to power through anything that is standing between you and your end goal for your life. The people and values that mean the most to you in life are capable of pushing you towards unprecedented greatness when you have a clear direction and understanding of where you want to go, so identify those people and those values and never allow them to stop pushing you towards your potential.

Allow these people and these values to remain near to you throughout your process and you will never be defeated by the process. Knowing and understanding your why will put you years ahead of those living aimlessly and without purpose. More importantly, it will put you exactly where you're supposed to be in your life in due time. Align your effort with your purpose and you will create a better life in every aspect for yourself.

This powerful principle has changed my life and is a major contributor to the mental strength and strong work ethic that I have today. I believe you will experience newfound strength and begin changing your life for the better through implementing this principle. The decision is truly yours, and you can either *build* yourself into the person necessary for the life you want to live or *shrink* yourself to accept the life that is given to you because of your unwillingness to grow in to the person that is necessary for the life that you want to live. There's a fine line between the two, but they lead to completely opposite results, so choose wisely.

Chapter Three

Principle #3: You will be judged regardless, so live the life that *you* want to live.

It is my personal belief that there are only two days of your life where you will not be judged by other human beings, at least not as harshly as all the days in between these two days. These two days are the day that you are born and the day that you die. People only refrain from judging those who have just entered into the world and those who have just exited out of the world. Every day in between these two days, you will be judged regardless of what you choose to do.

The day you were born, everyone was so excited for your arrival and caught up in celebrating new life being brought into the world that nobody was judging you. Your arrival was long-awaited, and they were glad that you were finally brought into the world. The day that you die, people will look back on the good times and memories they shared with you while you were alive. On both of these days, all of your imperfections are put to the side to celebrate and appreciate the *human being* that you are. It's sad that these are the only two days of life that we get this treatment or give it to others, but I believe it to be the reality of the world that we live in.

After you were born and the initial excitement of seeing you and holding you for the first time wore off, people started to analyze you closer and notice things about you that they didn't notice the first time. We've all heard the comments people make about babies. Maybe you came out with less hair than they expected, a few pounds heavier than anticipated, or a different pigmentation than you were "supposed" to be. You have now been judged for the first time in your life. From this moment forward, you will be judged for the rest of your life.

Whether you like it or not, this is simply the way life is. As human beings, we judge other human beings around us every day. If you are a decent human being, you try to make yourself aware of what you are doing and prevent it as much as possible. Despite our efforts at decency, we will still catch ourselves making judgements, because it's simply human nature. Our brains are wired to judge others around us by taking the first few things we notice about someone and putting a "label" on them.

This is because we see so many people and places in our everyday lives that we don't have time to truly process every single person, place, element, or anything in between that we may come across in our day-to-day lives. Instead, our brain tries to help us out by giving us a "summary" of others based on the first few things we notice about that person, which allows our brains to process our surroundings quicker. For this very reason, you will both be judged by others and subconsciously judge others for as long as you live.

Many of us look at judgment from others in a negative light, but all it means is that there's simply nothing you could ever do that every single person in the world would agree with. There's nothing you could ever do for not one single person to see you and put a label on you without truly getting to know and understand you. It just won't happen because that's not how human nature works. Someone, somewhere in the world will have an objection or complaint about what you choose to do. Someone else, somewhere else in the world may think what you choose to do is great. You must learn to not be bothered by this, because this is the beauty of life: It doesn't matter what others think about what you do or don't choose to do, because it's your life and you get to make your own decisions and create the life you want to create for yourself.

My father has a great saying, one that always made me laugh, but that I'm just now very recently starting to understand and embody. He said to me one day, "Son, opinions are like assholes–everyone has one and most of them stink." The first time he said it, I just looked at him in amazement. I couldn't believe that he said it, yet at the same time, it sounded exactly like something he would say. I thought it was funny, but I didn't truly understand the message behind what he was saying yet.

At the time he said this to me, I was still in high school and he knew I had a bad habit of allowing the opinions of others to get into my head. I had just told him about a conversation I had with my high school coach about my college future that night after practice and the conversation left a bad taste in my mouth to say the least. My dad could see that I was visibly upset, and he knew more than anybody else that my future as an athlete put a significant amount of pressure on me at this time in my life. My senior year had just begun, and I had yet to receive my first scholarship offer. I was so angry about the conversation I had just had that I didn't want to speak a word to anyone in the house when I came in, but he squeezed a laugh out of me and got me to explain to him what had happened. He told me that my coach didn't get the final say in my college future– only God and my effort and commitment to my dream had that type of authority.

He knew I was frustrated, stressed out by the lack of interest from college coaches, and beginning to doubt my ability to make my childhood dream of playing college basketball come true. Still, he assured me that I would get the opportunity I was looking for if I kept working and as long as *I* maintained belief in my own abilities. He had witnessed first-hand everything that had been going on throughout my process, from the time I was a small child shooting with two hands just to hit the rim, all the way to being just months away from my senior season of high school basketball. He understood my frustrations and still believed in me, even when the tunnel was getting dark and the opportunities to sign a scholarship were fading away by the day. That's who my dad always was when I was growing up and still who he is to this day– he always had my back and believed in me. Nothing I did growing up infuriated him more than allowing the opinions of others to keep my talent and ability within my shell because he knew what I was capable of doing.

Despite the heart-to-heart moment with my dad, I was still a teenager. This meant his words went in one ear, stayed for about three seconds, and flew right back out through the other ear. I continued to allow the opinions of others to dictate how I felt about myself and even how I acted in some cases, seeking acceptance and validation from my peers and sources outside of myself. I continued to let my coach's words fester in my mind, and at times, I thought about taking his word for it and hanging up my dreams of playing in college. In all honesty, I had built so much resentment for my high school coach throughout the first few weeks of my senior year that I thought about taking my chances playing AAU and making him stand on everything he had been saying to me. Luckily for me, being a hard-headed teenager also meant that I was determined at my core to prove my coach wrong and make him eat every word that he said to me that night in his office.

This went on for years, even throughout the beginning of my college years. I had reached a milestone in my life that I had been dreaming about since I was seven years old. I had silenced the words of my coach and inked my name on the bottom of a letter offering me a scholarship to play collegiate basketball, a moment he all but assured me wasn't in my future. When it was all said and done, 17 programs reached out to me by the end of my senior year. I proved my coach wrong 17 different times over the course of my final year of high school, with the icing on the cake being a coach flying from Iowa to Georgia and driving to my high school to tell him to his face that I was his priority for his upcoming freshman recruiting class. Coaches don't do these things if they don't think you can play.

I met teammates and built relationships with people from all over the country, while living out my dream of being a college basketball player. I excelled in strength training and remained competitive in practices, proving to myself that I belonged at the collegiate level despite all the times my talent had been denounced while in high school. The fear of falling short of my goal of playing college basketball that haunted my nights as a junior and senior in high school was no more– now, it was simply about making the best of the experience.

Perhaps, the fact that I took the most pride in throughout this journey was that I earned every bit of recruitment, interest, and opportunity that I got without any support outside of my family. I never had a coach send out any of my information or film to college coaches throughout my recruitment process in high school– I was told it wasn't his job to get me to the next level and that it was a waste of his time. I took those chances on myself and put myself out there to over thirty coaches and programs. I even planned and coordinated my visits on my own. I faced both every rejection and every acceptance with my family and nobody else. I learned to believe in myself and how to market myself effectively, because it was the only choice I had if I wanted to have any fighting chance of making a college coach believe in me.

Even still, I was having a hard time finding happiness and found myself concerned with how people viewed my situation from the outside. I was too concerned with the outside world and factors that weren't in my control. Instead of allowing myself to fully enjoy the opportunities I had worked so hard for and staying focused on continuing to make my own way in my journey, I caught myself wanting to compare my journey to the next man's. I saw my friends that had signed to bigger, more prestigious schools getting all the latest gear and recognition. My friends who weren't athletes looked like they were having the time of their lives at the big, party-heavy state schools.

Neither of these experiences mirrored the one I was living, and I began to question myself and the decisions I made to land me in this position. All of a sudden, I began to feel like I had underachieved and was living an experience that was less than the ones that my friends *appeared* to be living. That quickly, I lost sight of my journey and the pride I took in how hard I had worked and everything it took to get to where I was at in my life. Comparison was stealing my joy right from underneath my nose.

61

Though the blackhole of comparison distorted my reality, being where I was in my life and being given the opportunities that I had been given– it meant more to me than most kids who were in my position. I wasn't some kid who was viewed as the best player in my county, who everybody knew was going to have coaches calling after him. Basketball was an up and down emotional roller coaster for me, and my college future was never secure in my mind until I signed if I'm being completely transparent with you.

I was used to coming up short of what I set out to do on the court, trapped in a vicious cycle of disbelief in myself in my own mind. From the outside looking in, I was never supposed to be there in the first place. I beat the odds the second I signed that dotted line to agree to the terms of my scholarship. For as long as I live, I will never forget the conversation with my coach that night in his office. It placed the chip on my shoulder that I live with, even now that my playing career is over and life is about more than basketball to me now.

I understood that I couldn't be satisfied and that I would have to prove myself all over again in college, but this didn't mean that I shouldn't have been proud of myself for how far I had come. Yet, I struggled with this and quickly lost sight of the things that put me in that position in the first place– which was simply being a kid who loved the game and was willing to do whatever it took to get my name out there, including continuing to work on elevating my game and preparing myself for the next part of my journey that the majority around me had doubted I would see.

I saw others reaching their success before me, and I lost sight of the fact that my journey would be different. It had *always* been different and I was no stranger to this fact. Still, I lost sight of the person who I had become and all the improvement and growth I had experienced in this process of going against the odds and shutting up my critics. Hearing my talent repeatedly denied throughout high school, being less than appreciated by my coach, and ultimately being told that I wasn't good enough– it lit a fire in me to prove them all wrong. The hate pushed me more than anything because I couldn't stand rejection.

It took years for me to unpack and understand a brutal truth about who I was in my life up to this point. It was the hardest truth I've ever had to face about myself, and it forced me to come face-to-face with an internal struggle I knew I had been suffering from my entire life. There was nowhere for me to run anymore if I wanted to address this childhood trauma and prevent it from continuing to affect me and hinder me as I moved into adulthood.

Truth be told, I didn't want to run anymore– I was sick of living my life trying to convince *myself* that I belonged and brought value. I just wanted to feel, for once in my life, that just being myself was enough. I just wanted for once in my life, to feel like I didn't need to dumb down my actions or appearance, or enhance them, to feel like I belonged in my environment. My childhood was responsible for the root of this problem, but this problem had grown over time and was permeating itself as a significant mental burden in my life as a young adult.

I had brushed this struggle off my entire life, pushed it to the side and convinced myself that it wasn't an issue I needed to concern myself with. It was now my responsibility to first address that this discomfort around my identity was indeed a burden– one that was affecting my relationship with myself and my ability to connect and build relationships with others. Most importantly, it was time to acknowledge that my childhood experiences were responsible for the cause of this problem, but it was now, as an adult, my responsibility to heal and do my very best to not allow my childhood experiences to hinder my experiences and the quality of my relationships as I was transitioning into life as a young adult.

The trauma was simple, but one thing this life has taught me– the deepest cuts we experience often come from the ones we trust the most with the knife. As a kid, I would attend family gatherings on my mom's side of the family on occasion. My mom was the only woman in her family who had a black significant other, so we were always the only black people at these gatherings. As a kid, of course I knew that my skin was darker and I looked nothing like these people in terms of my physical features– being black never crossed my mind as being an issue until the first time I experienced being treated differently for the color of my skin, which unfortunately came at a very early age, from people who were supposed to be my family.

From an early age, I knew that there was something different about me that caused these people to simply make me feel unwelcome. I will say that there were some members from this side who did make me feel welcome and I was fortunate to meet them later in my life. My Aunt Lynne and Aunt April were really my cousins, but I called them my aunts because that's how I looked at them. My Aunt Linda, Uncle Claude, and Aunt Ellie, my mom's brothers Larry and Steve and their families- I had been disconnected and away from these people for so long that it wasn't always the most comfortable, but they did make the effort to give me a small sense of family on my mom's side around the time I was in middle school. Their families always welcomed my brothers and I with open arms and we grew close for a little while during my childhood. I appreciate them more than they know for making the effort and at least allowing me to have some positive memories of my mom's side of the family.

I didn't always see eye-to-eye with my grandma growing up, but I can never deny the fact that she loved me and invested a lot of time into me that she didn't have to. She was always there to keep me focused on my schoolwork. She drove me to my practices when my parents couldn't get off work in time. She spent many summer days at the pool with my brother and I, even though she hated sitting in the heat and getting burnt. She even used to make me sandwiches before I got off the bus, because she knew I always came in from school hungry. She wasn't perfect, I wasn't perfect– but she was always there and she was a big part of my childhood. I'll always love her and appreciate her for that.

Outside of these few people, the majority made me feel like an outcast and being around them was an uncomfortable experience for me. I didn't know what made me so unlovable and why I felt so alienated. I always wanted an explanation for closure, but I wasn't going to beg them for that explanation or for their embrace. It was a lost cause and something that I wanted to put behind me. I decided to disassociate myself from that side of the "family" at a very early age in my life, and aside from my grandparents and the few who I encountered throughout my years of middle school and high school, that decision still stands today. I don't regret the decision to remove these people from my life, because it was clear to me that these people didn't want me in their lives. However, these experiences I had as a child did lay the foundation for a nasty struggle that I fought all throughout my childhood, adolescence, and into my early years of adulthood– what was so wrong with me?

I felt like I was a good kid. I didn't find myself in trouble often, outside of a rough couple of years in middle school. Even then, it was small, disciplinary battles that I was struggling with- I wasn't breaking laws or causing any serious trouble. I stayed on top of my schoolwork and was engulfed in sports as a kid. I didn't have time for much else. I had always done my best to make other people feel welcomed and to treat people well. What about me was so wrong that these people wanted nothing to do with me?

I distanced myself from those people and tried my hardest to forget how they made me feel about myself, but it was a feeling that I couldn't shake. It bothered me to my core that those people wanted nothing to do with me. It hurt my heart that there was an entire side of my family missing from my life. It made me feel as though there was genuinely something wrong with me. There had to be *something* wrong with me for them to not even give me the decency or respect to get to know me.

I didn't know if I should've been angered by this or if I should've simply been curious– I was a kid trying to solve a problem that we still don't even fully understand as developed adults. On top of this complexity, I was trying to muster the courage to act as if there was no problem in the first place. This burning feeling of rejection put me through a roller-coaster of emotions throughout my entire childhood. I was always stuck between wanting to do what it took to be accepted and self-sabotaging to avoid putting myself in situations where there was a possibility of being rejected. I had been rejected by my own blood at an early age– the seed that this placed in my mind for a paralyzing fear of rejection can't be overstated. If they had enough reason to reject me and make me feel this way, what reasons would keep anyone else from giving me the same rejection?

Growing up, I remember sitting in history class and learning about slavery and the Civil Rights movement. I would listen to my teachers and read the chapters in the textbooks, and I always caught myself wondering how people could be so cruel and feel so entitled simply because of the color of their skin. It was sickening to learn the history leading up to these times, because it robbed multiple generations of the freedom to experience life and explore their passions. Yet, it was inspiring to me that a whole generation risked their lives so that I could live a better life than they were able to live, along with all the generations that will follow my generation. It was both heartbreaking and heartwarming to learn about the culture that I came from and the many sacrifices they made for all the people who look like me.

I would oftentimes even catch myself wondering what my life would've been like back then. Was I just white enough to be treated like a human being or was I just black enough to disqualify me from having those basic human rights and freedom? I wasn't the prototypical darker-skinned man that would've been sent to a plantation, but I certainly wasn't the prototypical white man that enslaved the darker-skinned man on the plantation either. I was learning about what one half of me did to the other half of me historically, while already being forced to try and make sense of this unjust history in my own life- almost every single year of my childhood.

For most of my classmates, whether they agreed with their side or not, there was a clear visual of what side of history they fit into. For me, on those same days that I learned about the history of how white people treated black people as a young boy, I went home to a white mom and a black dad. I would often sit down and do my homework with my white grandmother, and as soon as I finished my work, I would call my black Granny to tell her about my day and put in my request for a breakfast casserole because I was staying with her once the weekend came. That clear visual that most of my classmates had on which side of history they fit into, wasn't so clear for me.

The history of being a black man was traumatic and unjust, an awful existence of unimaginable suffering in service to men who sold and worked us to death– all while amassing massive fortunes off our back-breaking labor that allowed them to grow this industry of inhumane abuse into profitable ways of life for centuries. The history of being a white man was a tale of violence, highlighted by wealth and privilege. This wealth and privilege were often at the hands of the suffering black man. How in the world could I have both histories aligned inside my DNA?

I felt many emotions in response to this question as a kid. I always felt confused about who I was, where I fit into the world, and the types of people that I wanted to surround myself with. My parents had always taught me to never even consider color when it came to choosing friends, to treat everyone well and how I would want to be treated. I feel I did as I was taught, but it didn't mean that I couldn't still see color in myself.

I was treated differently as a kid for having darker skin and coarser hair– what if the white kids that I tried to befriend came from families who also believed in treating people that looked like me differently? What if my black classmates didn't like that my skin was lighter than theirs? The fear of rejection and overwhelming feeling of not belonging held a tight grip on me, and as I mentioned, this was something that I struggled with all throughout my childhood and subconsciously even into my early years as a young adult.

I was fortunate to meet some great people as a kid, and I grew up with the best friends I could've asked for that treated me well and made me always feel welcomed. Even still, the experiences I had as a kid never left my mind. Every holiday and special occasion that is celebrated with family was a constant reminder to me of that seed of deep fear of rejection that was planted within me. With every holiday that passed, that seed only continued to grow internally. I was terrified of feeling that feeling again. Over time, I began to prioritize being accepted over rejecting the things and people that were no good for me.

If you knew me in high school, you know that I had two hairstyles for almost the entirety of my four years in high school. I started high school at around 5'10 with an afro that had me pushing 6'4. I kept my afro, wild and nappy, until about mid-way through my sophomore year. Then, I went to the "juice cut" or the box cut. Essentially, my hair rose directly above my hairline in the form of a thin afro for a little over half a foot. I kept this hairstyle for two years straight, never cutting my hair below half a foot until February of my senior year of high school.

If you know me today without having known me in high school, you're probably thinking you've rarely seen me without curly, laid-down hair. That's because I've always favored my hair when it's wet and curly over the dry and nappy look. However, all my best friends on the basketball team had braids, dreads, and other hairstyles throughout high school. Being mixed, I already felt like I had to prove that I belonged to my teammates and was more like them than I was different. Wearing my hair in ways that showed my love and appreciation for black culture was a way that I felt like I could prove that to them, so I made it a point to leave no doubt to anybody at school, the rec, or wherever we may have found ourselves, that I was black.

The ironic thing about it is that my friends and teammates saw my hair wet and curly one day before I could pick it out at our team camp we used to go to together over the summer. They were shocked at the difference in my hair when I got out of the shower compared to how I wore it every day. I specifically remember Alex, who was one of my closest friends growing up, saying, *"That's* what I'm talking about when I say naturally curly. I wish I had those types of curls." This whole time, I had been fearful to look any more different from Alex, Jermariki, Kaceon, Devontae, Jay, Keyon, and all the rest of my friends than I already did with my lighter skin. Yet, their reactions to this difference were reactions of admiration and appreciation, not thinking of me as any less of a friend.

These were like my brothers growing up. I had known Jermariki and Devontae for as long as I can remember back to, somewhere around kindergarten and first grade. Alex and the rest came into my life around middle school. We loved and supported one another through everything and there was no reason for me to believe that my hairstyle or anything else about me would cost me the bond and brotherhood that I had built with these guys.

They never once made me feel like I didn't belong or that they didn't want me around. It was all in my head- the afro and juice cut were nothing more than a half a foot of insecurity and being uncomfortable in my own skin. That seed of fear came from past childhood experiences and the fear of seeing people I loved and accepted not reciprocate that same love and acceptance, but it wasn't my hair or any physical feature of mine that made us become friends in the first place. We love each other for who we are and what we have in common but we also respect and appreciate each other's differences- I don't know why I felt like wearing my own hairstyle would've changed anything, but I did.

We all want to be loved and accepted by others, but this desire can create a war within yourself, if it's at the expense of who you truly are. Without accepting and validating yourself, you put your acceptance and validation in the hands of others, when it belongs in your hands. Over time, I began to value this acceptance from others over accepting and validating myself, which always left me one opinion away from an identity crisis and a relapse right back into my fear of rejection. It was all internal, so it couldn't be seen, but the war in my mind was never ending.

After years of running and suffering, I finally took the time to address this problem in my life when I was forced to slow down and re-evaluate my life during a school closure and at a time when basketball was no longer there as a year-round distraction. It was one of the most uncomfortable things that I've ever had to do, but it was amongst the most necessary and long overdue. I'm thankful that I was given the opportunity through some hard times in my life, to slow down and contemplate on my life. Underneath all the hurt and the fear, I began to see someone that I could appreciate and begin to love– regardless of how outsiders felt about me.

For the first time in my life, I was able to develop self-love. This was a powerful moment in my story because I started living for myself and focusing on how I felt about myself over anyone else's opinion on me for the first time in my life. In one of the messiest and challenging times of my life, when everything felt like it was falling apart, I could simultaneously feel myself beginning to accept responsibility for letting go of the hurt that had held me back for so many years, in hopes that it wasn't too late to forgive myself and move on with my life.

I was making a conscious effort to take control of this situation that had haunted me and caused so much unhappiness in my life for years, and I had finally made the decision to refuse to continuously be controlled by fear and the lies it will tell you. Everything

72

around me may have been falling apart, but for the first time in my life, I was developing a clearer picture of who I was and who I wanted to be in my life. I began to look in the mirror and see someone I accepted unconditionally, imperfections and all. I knew the color of my skin and my ethnicity signed me up for certain troubles and struggles throughout my life, but I was also thankful to be exactly who God created me to be.

I had spent so much of my life in a state of confusion and fear, but I now realized that there was nothing to fear. Someone else's opinion of me was none of my business. I was beginning to understand that I had one life to live. It's my responsibility to become the best I can become, while making the absolute most of that life that I possibly can.

Never trade your authenticity for the sake of friendship, approval, or anything in between. If someone is meant to be in your life, they will accept you for who you are and will show interest in being in your life. If they sincerely care about your well-being and seeing you succeed, they will never make you feel like you must be somebody that you aren't to receive their friendship and support.

Your personality and all your traits are some of the most valuable things you possess as a human being because there is nobody else in the world made exactly like you. That's why we all have something to give to this world, because we're all unique and bring different perspectives, talents, and skills to the table. There is nobody who can be you better than you can be yourself.

In the world we live in today, there are so many of us suffering from fear of what people think about us. I encourage you to get rid of this fear as soon as possible, because people will judge you and that's just the way life goes. You must ask yourself, do you genuinely care more about what someone who you haven't talked to in five years says about you on Instagram more than the thoughts you think about yourself when you lay your head down at night? Nobody's opinion of you and the life you live is more important than your own– no ifs, ands, or buts about it.

People will always judge you, whether it be good or bad. Understand that it's not your business what somebody thinks about you. Not only is it not your business what someone thinks about you, but in most cases, those opinions have no direct impact on the course of your life. There are far more important things in life to spend your precious time on. Let them think what they want to think and keep yourself busy, building the life that you desire to live.

It's always the ones doing the least with their lives that have the most to say about people actively trying to do something with their lives. Your action to build a desirable life for yourself will always be far more valuable and productive than the meaningless actions others take to judge you or the mental energy you waste entertaining their ignorance. Be yourself unapologetically and squeeze everything you can out of this life you've been given.

Michael Jordan, arguably the greatest player to ever touch a basketball, mastered this principle beautifully. You would think you only hear praises and positivity about what Jordan brought to the game of basketball and the city of Chicago. After all, he went to the NBA Finals six times in his career and won every single Finals series he ever played in.

Not only did he go undefeated in the Finals, but he was also the Finals MVP in each of the six championships he played for.

You add in his ten scoring titles, nine first-team All-NBA defensive selections, five league MVPs, fourteen All-Star selections, and four Olympic gold medals with the Team USA Olympic basketball team, you get a man who had *multiple* Hall of Fame careers within a single career. One of these gold-winning Olympic teams became known as "The Dream Team", because it was arguably the most talented roster that the game has ever seen– Michael Jordan was the face of this team and the most talented player on the most talented roster that the game has ever seen. Understanding the magnitude of his success and his accomplishments, it makes you wonder what more the man could've done for himself and the game of basketball! Jordan was obviously a generational talent who reached levels of success in his fifteen-year NBA career that most people won't see in a lifetime, but guess what? Not everybody liked the way that he went about achieving this success.

You hear people say all the time that Jordan had a gambling problem, was an alcoholic, a bully, selfish, a bad teammate, and the list goes on and on. Do you think Michael Jordan cared about what other people said about Michael Jordan? You don't know much about Jordan at all if you answered yes to that question. He wasn't fazed by people's opinions in the slightest and he let it be known. He only tried to be the person that he was best at being– Michael Jordan. His only focus was on making the only person whose happiness was in his control, happy– Michael Jordan. The outside noise didn't faze him and this fact had a lot to do with his success and the fact that his name is all over the record books.

He knew who he was and refused to change for anything or anybody in the world. He worked hard and honed his skills to the point that there was no denying he was the best player on the planet, and he wanted you to know that he knew he was the best player on the planet. You didn't have to like him, but his talent was undeniable, his passion for winning was unmatched, and you were going to respect him. If you didn't, it was going to be a long and embarrassing night for you. Even if you did, it was still going to be a long and embarrassing night for you– he was head and shoulders above his competition.

As a result, he had an illustrious career that sounds like it came straight from a movie. He didn't care who believed or didn't believe in him, because he was going to turn them into a believer when the time came. He kept his head down and stayed out of the spotlight as much as one can do when they become the face of the NBA and a global icon. He understood he would be judged, criticized, and even defamed for the way he carried himself and some of the opinions that others had about him. Knowing this, he still chose to live his life the way he wanted to and won the way he wanted to win.

He cared more about how Michael Jordan felt about Michael Jordan when he laid his head on his pillow at night than he cared about how the press, commentators, and certainly fans who had never met him a single day in his life felt about him. He cared more about hanging banners in the rafters at the United Center than he cared about his teammates' feelings about how he went about pushing them to become champions. He pushed himself to become the best basketball player and the best version of Michael Jordan that he could be, regardless of how people on the outside looking in felt about how he got there.

Yes, he was one of a kind on the court and dominated in every single way possible. Even more importantly, he knew who Michael Jordan was and understood nobody else could be a better version of Michael Jordan than the man himself. He may have had unconventional ways of winning, but he also had unconventional success in the world's premiere professional basketball league. Whatever he was doing, it worked for him, and it made the city of Chicago basketball royalty for almost an entire decade, while making Jordan basketball royalty for as long as the sport lives on.

Obviously, we won't all be NBA superstars, but too many of us let the "press" and "commentators" in our lives have too much power over our thoughts and actions at times. If you really want to win and be successful, you must understand that not everybody likes people who win and people who achieve success. Some people don't like it when you find a way to win because you wake up and do the little things that it takes to win every day. They choose not to do the work that is required and stay stagnant in their own personal lives, and somehow, it's your fault that they remain in the same places while you move up the ladder.

The people who grew up around you and didn't take advantage of the same opportunities that you capitalized on especially won't always be the first to congratulate you. That's not your problem. They likely had similar chances and opportunities that were available to you and didn't take advantage of them– that's not to say that these people are bad people or lazy. It's simply to say that your success came to you because you did what was necessary for you to achieve that success, but it is not your fault that others didn't take the necessary action to achieve success in their own lives.

Always remember that being judged is a part of life but ask yourself how someone else's opinion or judgment genuinely impacts your life. The answer is usually not very much, if at all. If you find that it may have some impact, then obviously you want to put your best foot forward and make the best impression possible. Still, never trade your authenticity for someone else's acceptance. That is a trade-off that will always be too expensive for you to make. If their acceptance requires you to change who you are beyond common growth and maturation, their acceptance is not needed.

Stand strong and firm in who you are, and I'm a firm believer that you attract the opportunities and people that are meant for you in life. You may miss out on the six-figure deal for opting out of the contract extension with a company you no longer see serving your best interest. As a result of being willing to stand up for yourself and search for what will serve you, you're letting the world know by your energy, that you're ready for whatever is next for you.

It may take some time, but you will be rewarded for standing for something and having the courage to walk away from something good for something great. Good things happen when you stay true to yourself and refuse to allow your authenticity to be bought out from underneath you. Many things in life are temporary, but your authenticity is not one of those things and it should never be compromised.

We live in a world where being a follower and acting like puppets has become a popular way of life. As humans, we naturally crave the dopamine rush of being accepted and embraced by people. That being said, this principle is one of the harder ones to master sometimes and will require intentional efforts and frequent mental check-ins with yourself. If you fight your urges and the pressure of the world consistently enough to master this, you will find that you will only continue to experience more happiness and fulfillment in your life.

By freeing your thoughts from outside sources and influences, you will be able to find the things that you enjoy and that you genuinely desire to spend your time doing. You will begin to make decisions and act in your own best interest, and you will find that it is a lot easier to make yourself happy than it is to make everybody else around you happy. You are responsible for your happiness and your happiness alone. Don't weigh yourself down and take away from that happiness by trying to carry a burden that isn't yours to carry in the first place.

Your dreams and aspirations don't require counsel or approval from anyone but God. They were placed on your mind and in your heart for a reason. Discover them and pursue them. You get one life, and you owe it to yourself to accomplish and experience as much as you possibly can in the one life that you were given. For you to have any hope at reaching your full potential and making the absolute most of your life, at some point, you have to distinguish what everybody else wants for you from what *you* want for yourself.

Your friends may call you weird for not wanting to spend every night of every weekend at the bar. They may call you a nerd for wanting to read and educate yourself. They may call you unrealistic for setting such big goals for yourself. Once again, you get one life, and you owe it to yourself to do what makes you happy and fulfills you in this life.

You've allowed the opinions of others to scare you from pursuing your true passions and settling for a life that's less than you desire for long enough. Your dreams and aspirations are validated simply because they come from your mind and soul, and that's all the validation that you'll ever need. Who cares what other people think? After all, they will talk regardless.

It doesn't matter if you are poor or a billionaire. People will always have something to say. If you're poor, it might be that you need to work harder or be wiser with your money. If you're wealthy, it might be that you need to be more charitable and willing to help others who aren't as fortunate. It doesn't matter what you do or what situation you put yourself in. They will always have something to say about you. The important thing to remember is that your fear of being judged isn't stopping people from judging you– the only thing that can stop people from judging is death. Your fear of judgment is doing nothing for you outside of stopping you from being at your best and living your life freely.

This is where you ask yourself if that opinion or judgment matters to you or even reflects how *you* feel about yourself. Always be extremely selective of who you give any voice of persuasion to when it comes to your life and how you feel about yourself. Make sure those who have a voice in your decisions are credible and have your best interest at heart. You can't make everybody happy, but you can make yourself happy– and that's a big enough responsibility. Are you more interested in the approval of others or living the life that you want to live? Whatever you decide, always remember this very simple saying:

"Opinions are like assholes– everyone has one and most of them stink." - Pops

Chapter Four

Principle #4: Connect with yourself in a world that's connected to everything else.

In the world we live in today, it's nearly impossible to truly get away from the rest of the world. As a society, we have gotten so accustomed to constant connection to the rest of the world and everything going on around us that we rarely find the time to enjoy time with ourselves or even to find time to do things for ourselves. In the world of Wi-Fi and 5G internet, disconnecting from the world has become a much greater challenge for today's people than any other prior generation of human beings has ever experienced.

Technology has greatly advanced the world and some of the things that we are capable of doing as a society in today's world in comparison to even just a decade ago are truly amazing. Technology is a great privilege that we have, allowing us to stay in touch with family and friends all across the globe. It has benefited our everyday lives in many ways, making life much more convenient and efficient than in the times before ours. However, as great as technology has been for the world, it is also crippling us as a society.

The mindless scrolling and unprecedented screen times are a seemingly harmless attack on our most prized possessions as human beings– our self-image, innovation, motivation, purpose, influence over our thoughts, and overall quality of life are all being affected by technology and its massive influence on our lives. The use of technology and social media on such a large scale in today's world has given us access to more people than any other generation before us has ever had access to. This ability to connect with more people is often perceived to be a positive thing, but is it really? With the ability to connect with the amount of people that we're able to, I believe one could make the argument that we are exposed to more human interaction than we were ever *meant* to be exposed to.

The capability of connecting with others is only growing, and with it, the difficulty of distinguishing the voices of the "outside world" from our own. The noise and influence of the outside world is so loud that it's becoming extremely difficult to listen to our own voices and opinions of who we are and who we want to be in our lives. At every moment in our lives, there is a distraction competing for our time and attention. It's harder than ever before to truly mind our business and focus on what matters most to us in our lives.

The unfortunate and frightening reality of this outside noise being brought in from our exposure to the media and the outside world is it's causing us to become deaf to our own dreams and aspirations. It is quite literally killing our creativity and individuality. We are all born with our own unique paths, passions, and purposes. Yet, many people die without ever traveling their own paths, discovering their own passions, and living for their own purpose. The majority of today's society opts for a life in the shadows of other people's lives, rather than discovering themselves and illuminating their own light. Taking the path less traveled, the path that's designed for us to find our own purpose and meaning in life is not always the path that leads to social acceptance.

That path is less traveled because it is your *own* path, and having the courage to travel that path will lead you to everything you could've ever hoped for in due time. The world of "trends" has the fear of criticism at an all-time high– people are afraid to be

83

different from the masses. They are afraid to be themselves, out of a greater fear of not fitting in with the trends of society. There has never been a more advanced and opportunity-filled time to be alive as the one we're living in. Yet, here we are, wondering why so many of us are feeling lost, depressed, and unfulfilled in our lives.

Social media and exposure to media in general is very powerful in the modern world. We spend so much time on these outlets that we don't even realize the impact they have on influencing our beliefs, perspectives of the world, and the many other thought processes that make us who we are. This influx of media is slowly taking over our lives and the control we have over our own thoughts and actions. The sad truth is that the majority of us won't even look up from the phone screens and televisions long enough to realize that the largest threat to human society is right in front of our faces. We're opening the borders that protect our greatest freedom and ability as human beings, the ability to think and act for ourselves.

Through these channels, we're influenced from a young age and trained to become consumers of the media and the agendas that they push. The seed for an inability to think and process information for oneself is planted at an early age with concepts that don't carry much weight. This seed quickly grows and germinates to more important concepts as an individual ages, if the seed and media consumption go unchecked. This is happening to us and those around us every single day. The number of people affected will only rise as the media and its influence continues to grow. The media is not the only place where this conditioning of our minds is happening, but it is the fastest-growing cause and the most immediate concern.

We will get into other areas of life where this same thing is happening later on in the book, but the important concept to understand here is that the media sells what sells. That is, the media sells what piques interest and creates the "buzz". The media is a business, and like all other businesses, their end goal is to provide a service and to make a profit that pays them back for the time and effort put into providing that service. Just like every other business, they want the greatest return possible on the labor that they put into running their business and providing content.

The greatest return on this labor doesn't always take the importance of the truth into consideration, and this is why the truth is often edited or altered to create content that sells. You've lived long enough to know that there are dull moments where there isn't much going on in your life. The media knows nobody wants to read about these dull moments, and it's the media's job to light a spark in those dull moments and make them newsworthy. Sometimes, life is not very newsworthy, and that's perfectly fine. However, without news, the media industry dies, so everything becomes newsworthy.

I know the power and influence of the media from my own experiences with the media. I want to take you back to the year 2020. This was by far the most difficult year of my life, as it was for many. Between my personal life being turned upside down and the chaos going on in the world, it was this year in my life that led me to many of the lows in my life that I've discussed with you in the opening chapters. Being quarantined and stuck in the house for months, my social media intake and exposure to the media in general went up fervently. At the time, the world was entering a pandemic and America had another breakout of its own to worry about.

Riots and violence were breaking out less than thirty minutes from where I lived, in response to a series of murders committed by police officers against unarmed black men across the country. Malls and small businesses were being looted, police cars lit on fire, and it was clear that people were losing their patience with America's corrupt justice system. This anger and outrage was different from any anger I had ever witnessed in my life. It wasn't the kind of anger that showed up in a burst and then faded away. This was an insatiable anger– an explosion of emotion that had been built up and stored away for years.

After 400 years of being enslaved, segregated, mistreated, abused, and misrepresented, the anger and intolerance that resulted from this unjust treatment was erupting right before America's eyes. Equality was no longer a request from the African American community– it was a *demand* that was going to be met at all costs. The marching and rioting wasn't just about the people like George Floyd or Philando Castile, whose lives had recently ended at the hands of law enforcement's senseless abuse of power. The resistance was about addressing this continuous pattern of abusing power to degrade and disrespect our community that has *always* existed in our history– dating all the way back to the inhumane, horrific existences our ancestors were forced to live.

Our ancestors' efforts and sacrifices are a major reason that circumstances have greatly improved for us in today's world and it was now our turn to stand up for the future generations that will inherit the world from us when we're gone. It was our turn to take a stand for our unborn children, grandchildren, and the world they would live in. In order to leave this world a better place for those future generations, we simply could *not* back down and continue to tolerate being put down like dogs by those whose job is to "serve and protect" us. It was no longer acceptable to murder a defenseless, unarmed black man and there be no accountability. By law, it has never been acceptable for such a thing to take place, but history has shown otherwise. These unjust murders by police officers were eerily similar to the "lynchings" of black men that had occurred all throughout America's early history, where unarmed black men were killed without consequence. This was no longer tolerated in modern-day America and that message of intolerance was sent clearly through protests and riots that were demonstrated nationwide.

If the media wasn't talking about police brutality and the riots, next up was the debate between Donald Trump and Joe Biden for the American presidency. You had one extremely conservative candidate and one extremely liberal candidate– somebody had to lose, and that losing side was going to be forced to deal with a president that was the exact *opposite* of what they support. It's a recipe for conflict, and the growing tension nationwide only added fuel to this growing fire that was already out of control. Biden's supporters wanted nothing to do with Trump's supporters and vice versa. This election only further divided a great nation that was in the process of being ripped at the seams.

I was only twenty years old at the time of the debates, so I was extremely new to politics and even having the right to vote. I had anticipated my first time voting to be an enjoyable experience that I would be able to learn from and gain experience for future elections. I viewed it as one of those experiences that marks a new milestone in life, where you enjoy doing something that you felt like you'd never be old enough to do for about fifteen seconds and then think to yourself, "Damn, I'm getting old."

Yet, this election was very intense. Between the media coverage and events happening around the country, it felt as though this election would decide the fate of two completely different Americas for the next four years. This presidential election was about more than ordinary political campaigns and political discourse. This election was about the most powerful nation in the world being at risk of imploding on itself right before its citizens and the rest of the world's eyes. America's future was unclear, yet the moments to come were more important than ever. Therefore, there was a great pressure placed on this particular election to choose a leader.

All of this was of course secondary to the news of constant illness and death due to the global COVID-19 pandemic. All around me, I saw news of COVID cases spreading throughout the states like wildfire and death tolls rising. It became normal to see people wearing masks, constantly sanitizing in public, and waiting in lines with markers and reminders to stay at least six feet away from each other in any public setting. The CDC went live on television every single day with updates from doctors and other medical professionals on a potential vaccine or cure, updated the rising death tolls, and suggested that nobody go out in public unless it was out of absolute necessity.

On-campus college classes were canceled and I was forced to learn through lectures on Zoom and other virtual forums. It felt as though I was living in a bad dream that I couldn't wake up from for almost a year, and I didn't care what anyone said– there was nothing normal about what was becoming normalized in the world. This abundance of over-caution and negativity in the world wasn't supposed to be part of the plan for my twenties. I had heard my whole life that this was one of the most special decades of life, but it wasn't off to a great start and I feared what the next years would bring.

During this time in my life, I was looking to the media every single day to see where the next unarmed black man would be injured or killed by law enforcement– just waiting for the next viral video to be released. I dove deep into the political warfare going on in the nation, forming *strong* opinions about the parties and the candidates representing them. With all the negativity around me, you can imagine that it changed the way I viewed the world and the people in it– in a negative manner. A world that I had once thought was full of good people now seemed questionable to me to say the least.

Consuming so much negativity with little to no interaction with society made it very difficult to construct positive thoughts. The lack of interaction with my family and friends provided no outlet for these thoughts, and I began to feel trapped in my own mind. I could feel the weight of my thoughts leaving my heart broken and my spirit discouraged for what my future held. I was struggling greatly to witness with my own eyes the lack of humanity and empathy that existed in the world surrounding me.

At the time, I didn't know any better. It seemed like what everybody around me was doing, so I allowed myself to become a slave to social media and the media temporarily. I was constantly jealous of what others had going on in their lives, because I wasn't having much fun during this time period of my life. My life had been turned upside down and my future was very uncertain. I had taken a few punches in my life at this point, experienced some adversity, and made it through that adversity. This was a time in my life where it seemed as though the adversity just kept coming. No matter how strong I tried to keep my mind and spirit, I could feel myself being buried.

I had just gone from being a full-time student on a basketball scholarship to being out of school within a matter of two months after a sudden school closure. The volume of transcripts that my school had to send out for all of its transferring students was too high, so some of us were unable to get our transcripts sent off until it was past the deadline to be admitted for the spring semester. I was one of those students who missed the deadline for admissions, so now I found myself out of basketball and out of school. I wasn't happy about it, but I planned to make the best of the situation and visit a few schools and to find a coach and program that fit what I was looking for as a student and a player. Like everyone else, I had not the slightest clue that the entire world was about to be shut down.

This insecurity in my future and my circumstances at the time drove me to war within my spirit and my mind. I wanted to believe in my heart that things would work out for me. I truthfully wanted to believe that, but with everything going on, those negative voices in my head dominated my mind. I had busted my butt to get the opportunity to play college ball, and for what?

I lost focus and sabotaged my first opportunity, but I realized my mistakes and grew from them. I swallowed my pride and apologized to my coaches, showed them gratitude for giving me the opportunity to chase my dream with them, even though it didn't work out the way we had planned. I took my lessons that I learned from this first experience and became a better version of myself in my second year of college, with a new school, coaching staff, and mindset.

This time, I was much wiser and appreciative of the opportunity– I remembered the feeling of being dismissed from a team that I had spent my whole life working towards earning a spot on. I was determined to never feel that feeling again. I had endured the most difficult preseason of my life, not allowing myself to give up– even when I was exhausted and thought I had reached my limits. I bit my tongue when I was in disagreement with my coaches. I learned to push myself beyond what I thought I was capable of for the sake of my teammates. I had found an environment that challenged me and welcomed me with open arms as a transfer.

I had truthfully learned from my mistakes and was making the most of my second opportunity. Now, I had no fight or say in this opportunity being stripped from underneath me. I had no fight or say in being separated from my teammates who I had struggled with, grown with, and began to love. They became like my brothers in a short period of time.

91

Now, we were all being forced to go our own separate ways. This time, it wasn't even my own doing– it was just the hand that was dealt at the time.

I pursued the dream because I felt that it had been placed on my heart for a reason, that I could turn it around and have different experiences than I did in high school. Now, I was asking myself if all of these obstacles were God's way of telling me to keep going or if they were his way of telling me that He had other plans for me. All of a sudden, I had more free time than I ever even thought possible due to my tight schedule as a player for the previous two years. I spent the majority of this free time engulfed in the media and the negativity that it was spewing into my life.

The school closure had nothing to do with anything that I did right or wrong, yet I still felt as though I had failed miserably. I felt like I failed my parents, who sacrificed so much to see me live out my dreams and always supported me throughout my career. The very feeling I had when I called them and told them that I had mutually decided to part ways with my team my freshman year of college, the feeling that drove me to compete at a much higher level in the following year– I was immersed in it all over again.

My entire life, I always wanted to earn my older brother's respect. I felt like I genuinely made him proud when I went off to school to play ball. He used to tell everyone that I had a chance to be a special player and was excited to see me grow in a good program. I had kept him up to date with my progress throughout preseason and practice. I was excited for him to see me play in a system where my confidence and skill was growing everyday. I had given it everything I had, fought like hell to be in the position that I was

92

in– my older brother told me from a coach's perspective that it was only a matter of time before I got my opportunity. I told him I was going to stick with it, and to have to call him and tell him I was coming home empty-handed yet again– it was embarrassing.

My younger brother's support meant more to me than he could've ever possibly known. He would stand at the edge of the bleachers and be a one-man fan club at times. It didn't matter if I had two points or twenty points. He believed in me and he was going to make it clear to you that he didn't care what you thought. He hated that I had to leave home, but he used to tell me all the time that he couldn't believe his brother was a college basketball player– even when I made my mistakes and put myself in a tough situation my freshman year. He wanted to see me win, and this was something that he made very clear to me every single day that I talked to him while being away from him. Though it was out of my hands this time, I felt like I had failed him.

Most of all, I felt like I failed the kid who would lay down at night just dreaming of the opportunity to play varsity basketball, then college basketball, and eventually professional basketball. I felt like I failed my younger self, who believed he could do anything. That kid and his dreams lived within me throughout my entire process, and he was one of the reasons that I was able to endure my experiences and continuously find the courage to bet on myself and seek opportunities on the court through all the ups and downs throughout the years. He had helped me through many things in my life, but I was struggling to find him this time around.

After taking a semester off of school to focus on rehabbing a knee injury, I had ultimately made the decision to be done with ball and enroll in school as a regular student. I thought I was content with my decision, but then I came across a prep academy that was sponsored by NBA legend Tracy McGrady through a direct message on my Twitter. My time at my previous two colleges proved to me that I belonged and could compete at the collegiate level. I knew deep down that there were only a few weaknesses that were holding me back from receiving an opportunity to play in a great program, with the biggest being my mind. I began to consider how a year in prep could help me develop the skills I needed to work on, grow stronger and faster, and most importantly get me back into school and playing basketball– a sense of normalcy for me.

I talked with the coach for a few weeks, still going back and forth with myself about continuing my career or hanging up my laces. The pandemic had taken a toll on me mentally, and I felt as though this was my way out. I knew that I had to make something happen that year if I chose to play in this program, and I ultimately decided that I had unfinished business with basketball. I gave my commitment to attend Tracy McGrady's Advanced Prep Academy, roughly a month before I was scheduled to move-in and enroll. I was ecstatic for the opportunity, and once again, my family rallied behind me and sent me off to Florida for a year of prep school.

I've found peace in the situation and I have no desire to slander a coach or a program that gave me an opportunity when I needed it most, but sometimes, the truth and accountability provide cause for speaking out. I attended Advanced Prep Academy for ten days. This was ten days too long. Long story short, the coaches over-promised during the recruiting process and there was a lot to be desired when I arrived. There was a severe lack of groceries (which were included in the price of attending), clean drinking water, and most importantly, training staff to assist with injuries and recovery was nonexistent.

When you're working out three times a day and running seven miles at a time outside in the month of June in the state of Florida, you will need basic groceries, a lot of water, and treatment and recovery options to keep your body functioning at a high level. This seems like common sense but you would be surprised. Considering how quickly you dirty your clothes with a workout regime such as the one I was on at APA, it would also not be a terrible idea to include a washer and dryer machine in the team's house (which was also included during my initial recruitment). Lastly, if you tell a recruit that the program provides transportation to and from workouts, facilities, and team events, it might be a good idea to *actually* have transportation available when that recruit arrives.

I was malnourished, dehydrated, and spending my own hard-earned money at a laundromat on the one off-day that I had all week, all while using my own gas to drive to random locations all throughout central Florida. Not only was I spending my money at a laundromat, my teammates were forced to do the same– which made "laundry day" at least a three-hour process by the time everyone was able to wash, dry, and gather their clothes before piling into the Toyota Corolla and small Acura that we had access to.

I'm grateful for the opportunity that APA gave me to continue my basketball career in a difficult time in my life and I believe they had great intentions to develop me into a better man and basketball player, but you give the keys to the show to a clown and the result is sure to be a circus– and a circus it was. Needless to say, I spoke my mind on the misinformation that was spread to me during the recruiting process when I was informed that I was "required" to cut the grass and do chores around the team's house after a week of using my own gas to go back and forth to the facilities and buying my own food (on top of helping my teammates out who had no money for food).

I just thought it was funny that my coach and the athletic director cited these chores as part of our end of the contract. I figured they must've only printed out the parts of the contract that highlighted what we were required to do as players, so I quickly reminded them of the *other* part of the contract that they must've neglected to read before sending out to their players. How are you going to claim to run a prep school that makes better men, yet as the "leader", you aren't even a man of your own word?

Keep in mind, prep school is usually for kids who are in their first year removed from high school. Every single one of my teammates were fresh out of high school, with no college experience whatsoever. I vividly remember Coach saying to us, "Get used to this, because it will be similar in college." On top of forgetting how to read the other side of the contract he had just cited, I guess he also forgot that there was someone who had been in two college programs in the room as well.

It made me angry that he was taking advantage of my teammates' youth and inexperience. I was quick to tell my teammates that this was *nothing* like college. In college, you have a meal plan that allows you to eat multiple times a day, water is provided

96

at every workout and team event, transportation is provided by the school, and there are trainers on site to assist you with any tweaks or injuries that you may experience while training.

I looked at them, pouring sweat from the hot sun. I told them they were their own men who could make their own decisions, but I would be *damned* if I even snipped an inch of grass from that yard. After all the lying he did to get me there, I shouldn't have been surprised that Coach was offended by me sharing the truth with my teammates and encouraging them to hold him accountable in front of his face.

He was embarrassed that one of his players was defying his authority in front of the team and it was written all over his face. He wanted to tell me to run seven miles with no water so bad– I could see it in his eyes. Now, I was raised better than to tell a grown man to kiss my ass, but on this day, Coach DeLoach figured he had a situation on his hands and decided to invite the lead director, Leo, over to the team's house for some reinforcement– so I told *two* grown men to kiss my ass.

There were a few words exchanged, no grass was cut by my labor, not a single one of my fingers were lifted to do the "mandatory" chores I had been assigned, and this resulted in me packing my things to the tune of Coach DeLoach screaming, "Hurry up and get out of my house!" He didn't have to tell me twice. For the third time, I was headed back home– only this time, I had no regrets. That program was the biggest joke of a program I've experienced, and T-Mac should've been offended to have his name attached to such a sorry organization. I've lost my love for arguing since, but I wouldn't have handled the situation any differently today than I did two years ago. As with my other schools and teammates, I met brothers for life at APA and I will always have their backs. That is all I'm going to say about my time at APA.

Pops, I hope you're paying attention, because this is for you– "Mandatory my ass!" This is an inside joke between my family and I, but essentially, Pops set the example for how to handle outlandish "mandatory" demands from people who you in fact owe nothing to when he was pushed too hard by a front desk associate to attend a "mandatory" breakfast meeting with a sales rep to discuss upgrading to a larger condo at the resort my parents were members at. Based on the quote, you can guess how that worked out for the poor associate at the front desk. I'll admit– this is out of my Pops' typical character, but I guess seven hours in the car can get the best of anyone from time to time. We've had to ask for the complimentary cookies that used to be given to us at the beginning of check-in every year since this incident.

Having already transferred once to a university that closed my first semester there and dealing with a knee that was less than fully healthy, I could see my window of opportunity slamming shut right before my eyes. I wasn't the type to complain and I certainly knew that life wasn't always fair, but I truly felt that I didn't deserve the hand life was giving me at the time. Some of it was my fault and some of it was just life, but that didn't make the pill any easier to swallow at the time. I got my laughs from the incident at APA with my family when I arrived back home. Deep down, I was heartbroken because I knew I had likely just exhausted my last chance to play basketball competitively.

Two years prior, I felt on top of the world as I brought my dream of playing college basketball to life. Now, it felt like I had thrown it all away in a two-year timespan with a combination of poor decisions and unfortunate breaks. As a 23-year-old today, I know a few poor decisions and unfortunate breaks are all it takes to derail *anything* in your life. However, you put all of this on a 20-year-old kid who had little experience with the reality of life– you can imagine it was a difficult time in my life. I was facing the music of my choices yet again and it wasn't a sound that was beginning to haunt me.

As most people who don't separate factual information from the media do, that 20-year-old kid lost himself in the world– he stopped thinking for himself and protecting himself from outside influence. The kid who once made a dream board of playing college basketball and worked at it every single day had been overtaken by negativity. Without realizing it, he was choosing to hold onto this anger and negativity rather than taking positive steps back towards becoming the person that helped him achieve his dreams in the first place. Life was throwing haymakers, and for the first time in my life, I didn't know if I had it in me to stay in the fight.

I became infuriated by all police officers, for the actions of a few bad police officers. I listened to the media and believed I couldn't associate with people who didn't have the same political views as me. I blamed my situation on coaches and circumstances, instead of taking a long, hard look in the mirror at myself. I was a ticking time bomb, ready to explode at any moment. I became angry at the world, spending days on end just continuing to scroll and make myself miserable. I became so consumed by everything going on and everybody else around him, I failed to realize that I was neglecting the person who needed me the most during this time in my life– myself.

The moment I decided to stop waking up and filling my mind with the negative influence of the world, I started to look at my situation and look for positive steps forward. While the issues at hand in the world were important, there was nothing that I could directly say or do to have influence over the outcomes of those situations in the way that I had influence over the outcome of my own problems going on in my personal life. My priorities shifted, because I realized that I had lost touch with who I was and I didn't want to continue living my life this way.

I realized that the only way to help my situation was to help myself, which involved spending less time plugged into the world and its problems and more time on finding solutions to my problems and finding myself again. I had my moment of weakness and feeling sorry for myself. I had shed all the tears I could shed, out of a combination of anger, frustration, and the feeling of not knowing what was next for me. I came to the realization that problems followed me everywhere I went for a reason– I was the problem and I needed to change my mindset. I couldn't change the past, but I was determined to put my best foot forward and create a better future.

Notice, I said "problems" when speaking about the world and "solutions" when speaking about my personal life. The world will always have problems, complaints, and everything in between. Yet, the world offers limited plans of action towards solutions to these multitudes of problems. This is because it's easier to point out the problems and call others to action than it is to look in the mirror and ask ourselves what we can do to inspire or be the change ourselves. Everybody wants to see change in the world, but only a few take the initiative and put in the effort to do their part in being the change in the world.

Listening to the media teaches you nothing but how to consume negativity. What you put into your mind and spirit has a great influence on what you put back out into the world. The media informs you of the negative problems of the world, but it fails to educate you on ways to find solutions and reverse the negative trends– it doesn't want you to learn how to solve problems, because without problems, the media cannot live.

The media is filled with negativity by design, not coincidence. The media doesn't exist without negativity, because it's the fear and caution that the media engrains into the minds of so many people that keeps it relevant. Like any other predator, the media feeds on the fear of others. It tailors its coverage to feed those fears, keeping people reliant on the media to keep them informed and living in fear.

People who focus on positivity, don't consume themselves with the media and fear. These people understand that negativity is already in abundance. Therefore, these people focus on creating and filling the world with more positive outlets. These people fight fear with faith and they fight problems with viable solutions. If you want to be at your best and live a purposeful life, you must learn to find solutions in a world full of problems and people who are unmotivated to solve them.

I'm not telling you to never use social media again or that it's all bad. I'm suggesting that you be mindful of the content that you consume from social media. Use social media for what it was made for, leisure and entertainment. Don't allow the media to turn you into a sheep, someone who forfeits the right to think and act on their own accord. Don't allow the fear it promotes to deplete you of your courage and faith. Make sure that you're using social media, not being used by social media.

Always remember that the media's end goal is viewership and relevance. They oftentimes don't yield their most viewership by giving the full truth. The media is a business and we all know that business has a way of fogging the code of ethics and morality. Learn to disconnect from the world and focus on the changes you can make within yourself to be a better version of yourself, and you end up helping make the world a better place in the process.

So many of us are going through life living to please others or even wishing we were in someone else's shoes. Do you *truly* believe you were given the privilege of life to wish you had someone else's? I'm not the one who gave you the privilege of life, but I can say I'm fairly confident that you were given your own life to follow your own path and discover your own truths. Get connected to who you are and what's meant for you– nobody can take this away from you!

Write your own story and follow your own path. The plan for your life was custom-built for you. Why would you trade it in for a replica of someone else's plan? There is no one else in the world who can walk the path that was meant for you better than you can walk that path. It took years for me to understand and embrace this, but I'm challenging you to waste no more time in your life questioning your worth and being fearful to separate yourself from the masses to pursue the path that is for you.

In my own personal experiences, the hardest part of staying the course of your path isn't even navigating the obstacles along the way. It's simply tuning out the outside noise and having the courage and confidence to pursue the path that doesn't look like everyone else's. If you're able to do this, you will be built to survive the path because it was meant for you. You may trip and you may stumble, but everything needed to conquer the difficulties of your path is within you if you dig deep enough and stick to your principles.

Do yourself a favor and ignore what everyone else is doing and focus on your own path and paving your own way. In today's world, this can be difficult to do but it pays enormous dividends in the long run. Your own life is always the best place to put your greatest investment, because you will never regret taking a chance to better yourself. You owe it to yourself to discover who you truly are, your path, and to fulfill your purpose in this life.

What do *you* think connecting with yourself means? The answer is it could mean many different things and the answer is different for everybody. However, there are some universal practices that we can all implement to find that connection with ourselves. The topics discussed are not the only ways, and I encourage you to learn about yourself and find your own ways to connect with yourself as well. I want everyone who reads this to be able to find value in the content, so for that purpose, we will focus on universal methods that have been known to help humans on a large scale.

One of the most important things to remember when seeking a connection with yourself on a deeper level is that you must first spend time with yourself. For some of us, alone time isn't even in our vocabulary. Many of us struggle with being alone for many different reasons, but it is critical to learn to appreciate and make the most of your alone time to identify your purpose and the correct path for yourself. Our minds tell us that we fear being alone, because our minds crave the comfort of having other people around. We receive dopamine from being around and interacting with other human beings, which is a beautiful part of life and our experiences as interdependent human beings.

Being alone doesn't provide us with the dopamine and comfort that our minds so desperately crave, so the majority of us naturally tend to avoid being alone as much as possible. However, dopamine isn't always needed to understand yourself and to help yourself out of your struggles. As I'm sure we're all aware of by now, life is not meant to be composed of all positive experiences and rushes of dopamine. Sometimes, sitting in those lows and reflecting on the negative situations and circumstances that you want to reverse in your life is exactly what you need to sprawl yourself into action with a plan for overcoming those lows.

While being alone can be difficult at times, I can tell you from experience that trying to go through life without knowing who you are is even more difficult. This is a life that you're making yourself susceptible to by not embracing the beauty of who you are and taking the time to grow in your own understanding and appreciation of yourself. I would describe it as more of a transitional process because you have to reprogram your mind to get it to transition away from its natural patterns and comfort zones that are preventing you from experiencing the freedom to explore yourself as an individual and form a stronger sense of identity.

Like any transition, it takes time, there are growing pains, setbacks, and failure, and you will be uncomfortable in the initial stages. Change is simple, but it isn't easy. Changing lifelong habits is even more difficult. However, once you make the transition and begin to see the benefits, you'll never want to turn back to neglecting yourself ever again.

Whether it be taking time in private to pray, meditating and calming your mind, or going to the gym and having a good workout, there is true peace in being away from the rest of the world and being one with your mind, body, and spirit. The silence can be deafening sometimes. You're able to truly connect with yourself and think clearly, with no outside influence or judgment. There is nowhere to hide from the things in your life that are holding you back and the problems you're struggling with. It can be a very uncomfortable feeling being faced with the thoughts you've been avoiding for so long, but it is never in our comfort that we grow.

I must ask you though, how much comfort does it truly bring you to distract yourself from your flaws and your problems– to put off finding the *real* solutions? You can stall all you want, but a problem remains a problem until it is met with a solution. Living a better life isn't about hiding your problems– it's about facing them and overcoming them once and for all. This is far from the easiest thing to do in life, but you're here because you want to see improvement in your life. If you haven't picked up on it yet, nothing worth having in life will come easy.

Journaling is also a very effective method to connect with yourself on a deeper level. You don't have to be the author of a New York Time's best seller to simply write your thoughts and ideas down on paper. When you first start, it will likely feel ridiculous and like you are talking to yourself– you may be encouraged to close the journal and move on to the next method. If you'll hang in there and stay consistent though, you will realize that writing things out onto paper often brings clarity and better understanding when you can physically see the writing.

When you write them down, these thoughts start to cross your mind more and more. Eventually, your brain begins to process these thoughts and subconsciously centers your thoughts and your being around deriving meaning from your thoughts and bringing these thoughts to reality. Getting your thoughts out of your head and on to paper gives your thoughts and ideas life– they suddenly become works in progress rather than just occupying space in your mind that is already overpopulated with thoughts.

When you are alone and thinking of a few things you want to write about in your journal, these ideas are where your mind is at the moment. Regardless of what you find yourself doing in life, these thoughts that you have during this time are important and they're trying to convey something to you. If you knew you would be successful in these ventures and didn't have the fear of failure or a false reality in your mind, these thoughts are what you would pursue. If you had no fear of being rejected or embarrassed, these thoughts are what you would pursue.

The journal is only for you, so there is no need to try and impress your parents, your friends, or anybody else in the world. This is why you are able to connect with yourself and your passions. After a while, your brain recognizes these as being important desires of yours. Even when you're sleeping, your brain is subconsciously hard at work processing and thinking about ways to make your thoughts become reality. Of course, you still must put in the work and the time necessary, but your subconscious thoughts can play a major role in pointing you towards the right opportunities. Simply putting your thoughts and ideas on paper isn't enough in itself and it doesn't guarantee success, but it does put your mind and body in better alignment to pursue the true passions and desires of your spirit.

Writing your thoughts down is also a great way to keep the mind clear. Thousands and thousands of thoughts cross your brain each day. There isn't room for all these thoughts to live in your mind and for you to maintain your productivity, or much less, even think about attempting to increase your productivity. Thoughts can be extremely heavy at times and the dangerous thing about them is nobody knows that you're having them unless you tell someone or express them in some shape or form.

If you are the type of person that likes to deal with their own problems, writing your problems down and acknowledging your true feelings towards these problems is a great way to begin the process of finding solutions to these problems without feeling like you're putting your problems on someone else. The human brain often reacts to things seen in writing differently than it does to thoughts that go unexpressed. Even though you're the one who is writing about your own problems, it is likely that seeing the problems in writing will help you see both the problem and possible solutions more clearly.

By simply writing them down, the problems or whatever is bothering you has been released from your mind. They may still live in the mind for a while but putting them on paper allows for an outlet of some sort, meaning they are no longer solely in the mind. Your mind is already carrying a heavy load, doing its best to process the millions of signals being sent to it every single day. Be kind to your mind and lighten the load whenever possible. There is real personal discovery, growth, and healing in consistent journaling and becoming more aware of what means most to you in your life.

Your body can only go as far as your mind will allow it to go. The importance of mental health and clearing the mind is uber important to exponentially improving your life. Many people across the world, myself included, have made a habit of writing in a notebook and transferring these thoughts from their minds to paper. Once again, this doesn't guarantee you will be completely free from your mental struggles and battles. However, failing to connect with yourself and take care of your mental health does guarantee continued mental battles and limited hope for different results in the future.

It's a small, simple habit that can sometimes feel pointless in the beginning stages. It can also be uncomfortable at times, especially for those of us who struggle with expressing our emotions. You may not get the release you were hoping for the first few times and that's perfectly fine. If you stay consistent and pay attention to what your mind releases during these times, it will grow your self-awareness and put you in touch with an authentic understanding of yourself and guide you to a much healthier, clearer headspace.

I no longer allow the media to have the negative influence over my mind and my life that I used to. I'm no longer the young, angry brown boy who was terrified to be stopped by the police. I'm no longer someone who has a crippling disbelief in himself. There are many things in life that I used to believe I was, but I never truly was. All it took for me to expose these poisonous lies in my life was to get to know myself well enough to find my own definition of who I am and who I'm not.

It didn't happen overnight and it wasn't through some snap of the fingers like a magic trick. Through constant affirmation, education, and the investment of time into getting to know and understand myself, I'm learning how to control the biggest threat to my potential– myself. Before it became my reality to be free from these things, these thoughts were simply put to paper in a journal. Before I made peace with the past, I had to sit in my room in silence and contemplate the mistakes I had made that led me to the situations I was in. It was a series of highs and lows but I committed myself to growing through what I was going through by allowing myself to feel all the painful emotions and extracting meaning and lessons from them that led to a stronger connection with myself and a clearer mind to dictate my future with.

Another great way to connect with yourself is to get into the habit of exercising. It doesn't matter how much or how little you start out doing– all that matters is that you get started somewhere. Exercise and small doses of pain and discomfort allow you to reach deep within and connect with yourself in a unique way. If you truly get into the habit and allow yourself the deep connection that exercise can bring, you will discover that there's so much more to prioritizing exercise and a healthier lifestyle than the physical benefits.

The process of exercising is symbolic of life, in the sense that it requires a certain amount of pain and sacrifice to reach the goals that you have for yourself. It requires discipline and consistency to reach lasting success and transformation in your physical health, much like it requires discipline and consistency to transform any other area of your life for the better. I believe this is one of the main reasons so many people find therapy and healing in exercise and personal fitness– it's a time to invest in yourself and to implement these disciplines and consistency into your daily routine. It's a short period of time in your day where you agree to sacrifice your comfort, push through some pain, and work towards the goals that you have for yourself.

The workouts can be grueling and there will be times where you can think of a thousand other things you'd rather be doing, but the hardest part is actually getting up off your butt, changing into your exercise clothes, and willing yourself to the gym, the basement, or wherever it is that you choose to workout at.

The experience is different for everybody, but the fitness community is a positive community. There are a few exceptions, but for the most part, you are surrounded by people who simply aim to be healthier and better than they were yesterday. It's very rare that you will speak to someone in the gym or on the track, and they don't give you a

110

friendly smile and wave, or maybe even a few words of encouragement if you look like you could use them.

This is a principle that we will discuss later in the book, because it's a life-changing lifestyle habit that I believe is very powerful and has the capacity to invite massive transformation and improvement to anyone's life. That being said, I won't unload everything here. All I need you to take from here is that making time to exercise and get your body moving is a great way to do something positive for yourself, while decompressing from the rest of the world. It's a way to give some of that much needed time, attention, and love that you crave to yourself.

The last way to connect with yourself that I'm going to cover is simply taking the first thirty minutes that you get out of bed for yourself. Leave your phone on the charger and take time to plan your day, undistracted. Plan out your success. For me, I like to write two small goals I want to achieve within the day before I get started with my day. Be intentional about what you do throughout the day to become a better person and to better yourself.

Your goals can be as simple as making it to the gym and getting a good workout in. Maybe you want to drink one less cup of coffee today. These goals and successes are yours; nobody else can define their meaning or significance to you. What you will begin to notice is that these goals are on your mind throughout the day, whether you stick to them successfully or not. This is what you want from this process, putting success on your mind early in the morning to shift the flow of your thoughts towards that success and holding yourself accountable for reaching whatever goals you have set for yourself.

You want to write your desired success out onto paper to bring it to the forefront of your mind, which gives you an increased awareness of the things you must do to obtain this success. Small wins are still wins, which are positive changes that have the capacity to have a positive impact on the rest of your life. You aren't going to turn your entire life around in one day, but if you focus on winning each individual day, life will stand no chance at keeping you where you currently are. If you want to win the day, it is critical that you win the *morning* and properly prepare yourself to be successful throughout the day.

After you have written your goals (it can be more or less than two), I want you to visualize yourself achieving those small goals. Make the vision a reality by bringing the moment to your mind. I want you to truly connect with this visual and feel the feeling of conquering the task at hand. The feeling of victory is a powerful feeling, one that we all desire to feel in life.

If you truly connect with your visual and desire to feel that feeling that you've created within your mind, it's going to be a lot more difficult for anything to stop you from bringing that great feeling you visualized to fruition. Many of us don't reach our goals in life or our full potential because we have doubts and fear. Kill these doubts and fears by taking a moment to visualize what it would feel like if you stuck to the plan and everything went right instead of counting on everything to go wrong.

If you don't believe you will be successful and get to new places in your life, how can you expect anybody else to believe that you will be successful and level up? When you believe in yourself and understand that you can do anything you put your mind to, you gain control over your thoughts and are able to take command over your doubts and fears. This is equivalent to turning the difficulty down on a video game, where you are competing with players who are forced to remain on the higher difficulty setting. You're figuring out how to slow down the game of life and employ strategy, will, and belief in yourself.

As a result, you have more control over the outcome of the game than the competition does. You're less likely to remain on the same level because you have removed the weight of self-doubt and lack of confidence from your back. This is what taking that extra time in the mornings for yourself will do for you over time. Life is hard, but we tend to make it much more difficult than it has to be with our lack of preparation and poor use of our resources.

As most people do in the world, the first thing I did when I woke up for most of my life was check my phone. I would usually start with checking my text messages and within five minutes of my alarm going off, I was nose-deep into my Twitter feed. What I failed to realize is that I was giving the world power over my thoughts and my mind subconsciously– allowing the negativity and thoughts of the outside world to shape my attitude and state of mind for the day before I even gave myself a chance to step into the day on my own terms.

I didn't plan out my success for the day, much less visualize it and attempt to feel it. Therefore, I lacked the extra belief in myself to go out into the world and take what was mine. Rather, I hoped my desire within my mind was enough to take me to the places I wanted to go. I dreamed big and did many of the surface level things right, but I was missing the little things that truly separate the elite from the average in life. I *hoped* for my desired results instead of working hard and *believing* in myself and the work that I put in to take me to where I wanted to be in my life. In my mind, my fate was not in my own hands.

As a result of missing these little things, I lived my life in constant doubt and fear of failure. Instead of picturing myself getting the A+ on the big exam in class and how good it would feel, I worried about getting the F and how I would explain it to my parents. Instead of picturing myself asking the beautiful girl out on a date and the great feeling I would have if she accepted my offer, I pictured being rejected and talked myself out of approaching the girl. Instead of trusting the work I was putting in and visualizing the dotted line of the scholarship I would sign and feeling the joy of celebrating with all the people closest to me, I always had a deep fear of not being good enough to ever bring that moment to fruition. I was a slave to my fear and my self-doubt. I was a prisoner of my own mind, and if you've ever experienced this in your life– you know the mind is the highest security prison that exists.

As simple as it sounds, devoting the first thirty minutes of my day to planning small successes and visualizing myself being successful has had a profound effect on my life. In fact, I would say it's a major reason I decided to face my fear of failure and write this book in the first place. Writing a book was always something I wanted to do, but I had little faith in myself to accomplish this feat not too long ago. Winning my mornings and shifting to a faith-driven mindset from a fear-driven mindset gave me the confidence to pursue this long-time goal of mine that has now come to pass.

That responsibility that I told you I felt to those who needed these words, came upon me in the morning. I knew that there was a possibility no one in the world would ever lay eyes on this book but I decided to visualize myself working hard and creating something meaningful and impactful anyways. Once I began connecting with myself in the morning and not the Internet, it became very clear to me that the creation of this book was something that had genuinely been placed on my heart and I eventually came to trust that I had the talent and means necessary to pursue this dream of mine.

I wasn't going to continue this miserable pattern of self-sabotage and projecting fears onto myself by visualizing a failed book and lack of support. Just as love is the only thing that can drive out hate– positivity, confidence, and faith are the only things that can drive negativity and fear out of your life. Taking the first thirty minutes or so of my mornings to plan out and visualize my success gave me that positivity, confidence, and faith over time to overcome my fear of finishing this project and sharing my story with the world.

Give yourself a chance to wake up and get those thoughts that drive you crazy onto paper. They may seem unrealistic to you right now, but you will be surprised how your mind will work in your favor to drive you to success– if you feed it the right thoughts and visuals. No matter how far away the goal may seem, close your eyes and visualize the moment that you reach that goal and feel the feelings of that moment. Empower yourself through building confidence and thinking positive thoughts. By doing this, your self-doubt and negative thoughts about yourself have no choice but to flee in defeat eventually. You control your own thoughts and success. You are the master of your own fate. You're in the driver's seat of your life and the roads of fear and self-doubt are toll roads that you simply can't afford to go down any longer on your journey.

As I mentioned earlier, these are just a few ways to connect with yourself that have helped me along my journey. I find new ways as time goes on and I learn more about myself- you will also find new ways. This is what's so great about seeking improvement within yourself– there's so much information available to you, *if* you just take the time to seek it out. Improvement is inevitable if you put in the time and effort it takes to improve, which you will find is usually a very small portion of each day that compounds on small portions of the days that follow. Slow down and regain control of your life and your thoughts, for it's much better to move at a slower pace in the right direction than at the speed of light in the wrong direction– or to remain still in your paralyzing doubts and fears.

I picture the outside world as a fast-paced machine that was installed without reading the instructions. The machine is operating so fast that it may take a while to notice, but you will eventually notice that there is a malfunction in the machine and seek repairs and improvements that will produce the final product you desire. It may take multiple adjustments and tools, but you will learn how to take away parts and add parts to this machine to get an output that is more suitable for you and your needs.

It's easy to get lost in this world with the immense pressure and overexposure that the media tends to put on us, but my advice is to remain focused on yourself and redirect that pressure to be accepted and validated by others into pressure to become a better version of yourself that *you* accept and value. At the end of the day, you're the only one who can live for you and define you. Why not put in the time and effort to become the very best version of yourself that you can be? Why not do the necessary work to build yourself into a person that you love and appreciate?

Social media is a great way to stay connected with family and friends and a place to enjoy your downtime. Unless you are an influencer of some type where your livelihood is dependent on social media, I would recommend not letting it be anything more or less than a place to stay in touch with loved ones and healthy forms of entertainment. It was never meant to determine or define how you feel about yourself or who you are as a person. We have given it that power over us and it's time to take that power back.

The majority of what you see on social media is a "front" or fake– it captures a moment of a much more complex story or situation that you know nothing about. Stop comparing yourself and your life to what you see on the Internet and commit to putting the necessary work into yourself in real life. If you do these things, your life will inevitably improve and you will have a lot more to show for it than a few pictures on your Instagram with comments and likes from people you aren't even in close contact with anymore or have never even met in person.

It's a crazy thought at first, but you will survive being disconnected from the world. You very likely will *thrive* being disconnected from the world. You have been conditioned and fallen into the habit of overexposing yourself to the media and the outside world, but no generation of humans before you needed it to survive and neither do you. Essentially, social media is a drug that brings comfort and distorts reality– when not managed properly, it's just as destructive to the brain as any other drug.

I want you to think about what social media has *truly* done for you in your life, in terms of adding *value* to your life. You've been able to stay in touch with people you care about and had some good laughs, right? For some of you, maybe you found a career and an opportunity in social media. Most of us have not found that in social media. That's great for those that have, and I am by no means trying to downplay their careers or ways of life. I'm simply saying that social media has added very little value or worth to many of us who use it.

Now, I want you to think about some negatives that social media has brought into your life. The answer is different for all of us, but some of the more common ones consist of anxiety, constant feelings of comparison, and feeling behind in life. These are all heavy feelings to deal with and they are all capable of causing even more complex, threatening problems for us down the road.

The important thing to remember is that social media does not always reflect one's reality– it's a "snapshot" of their best moments and the highlights of their lives. If you put your head down and stop letting petty, irrelevant things strip you of your value for yourself, you will build a life that is full of your best moments and highlights. These moments will continue to grow, and eventually they will no longer be "snapshots", but your everyday reality. The quality of life that you create for yourself is the real cause worth being focused on, not how many likes or views you get on a social media post.

For some of you, the difference between continuing to work your lives away for a small piece of the pie and becoming the head of an empire could be your inability to put down the phone and focus on the real life you have in front of your face. Disconnecting from the world and connecting with yourself on a deeper level is the only way to truly find yourself and your passions, get out of the habit of living for the acceptance of others. and to stop settling for less than you're capable of in your life. It's the only way to discover what makes you tick and to identify which causes are worth your efforts and sacrifice, and equally as important, which causes aren't worth your efforts and sacrifices. It's the only way to truly give yourself a chance to live a life of fulfillment and virtue, because your purpose and virtue lies within you– not the world or social media.

At the end of the day, the responsibility of fulfilling your purpose and building a life that makes you happy is on you and only you. There are many people who will be willing to help along the way, if you simply get to work and show them that you are serious about getting to the places you say you want to go in life! If you don't take anything else from this principle, make sure you get this: **Make sure you're as happy in real life as you appear to be on your social media.** Heck, make sure you're even happier in your real life than you appear to be on your social media. If you can do this, social media and the outside world won't be a problem that you deal with and that's my goal for everyone reading this. Don't be afraid to unplug from the world at times–you just might mess around and discover who you really are and your true potential in a world full of lost souls and wasted potential!

Chapter Five

Principle #5: The only competition is who you were yesterday– the poison of comparison will contaminate your path.

This is a principle that I wish I would have learned and understood much earlier in my life. I struggled greatly with comparison as a teenager, and even now as I'm into my early twenties, it's a principle that I'm pushing myself to master more and more each day. Even knowing the harmful effects of engaging in comparison and having the knowledge and experience that I now have, comparison is still a destructive habit that I struggle with from time to time in my life.

As I said in the introduction before I started the book, I'm not writing this book from a mountain top looking down at everyone else struggling. I'm right there on that mountain with you, fighting to stay positive every day and climb my own mountain. I'm still in my process, just like you and everyone else around you. I wouldn't have it any other way because this process is what makes this journey so difficult, yet so fulfilling. I wouldn't rather share these difficulties and growing pains with any other bunch of people.

Avoiding comparison is one of those habits you must become very intentional about, and you must ultimately decide that your own personal life and your own personal goals are too important to be wasting precious time and mental energy worrying about what's going on in the lives of other people and things that won't help you reach your own goals. You must become intentional about this avoidance, because subconsciously, you've been categorized and compared to others your entire life. As harmful as it can be to our mental and emotional well-being, comparison has been around us, is around us, and will be around us for the rest of our lives.

The world that we live in today will put you in a living hell if the only measure you have of yourself is based on how you're doing compared to someone else. As we discussed earlier, the people living on the planet right now have more access and exposure to the lives of other humans than any other era of human beings ever has before. With all the media and platforms we have for sharing information, it takes no time at all to tap into the parts of someone else's life and accomplishments that they have shared with the world. From what they're willing to share with the world, often the best bits and pieces of their lives, we tend to make a diagnosis of how life is going for these people.

This is going to be hard for many of you to believe because we've been conditioned most of our lives to try and "keep up" with our peers and allowed society to paint this picture of what success should look like in our lives– but it doesn't matter what anybody else in this world is doing. As long as it is not a direct threat to your well-being or success, what others are doing has absolutely no effect on you and your life. I've discovered that minding your own business and focusing on yourself will protect you from wasted mental energy and unnecessary pain in many cases. Real power doesn't come from keeping up with peers and succumbing to the pressures of the world. Real power comes from remaining still, continually growing, and creating your own definition of success and chasing it every single day in your life.

Fulfilling your purpose in this world is something that nobody else can do for you. Whatever your purpose in this world is, that purpose was, and is, a gift to you in your life. There is not one single person in this world outside of the one whose eyes are reading these words at this exact moment that can fulfill *your* purpose in the world– much less someone that can fulfill that purpose better than you can.

To be clear, I don't mean there is nobody that can do your day job better than you. Your day job likely isn't your purpose. Your purpose is whatever lights that fire and drive inside you. It's that thing that doesn't even feel like work to you because it's what you love to do. There's a deep sense within you that this work was meant for you. That's because it was.

It's the voice in your head that screams to keep trying even when the last fall was scary and did a lot of damage. It's the thing that bothers you so much that you lose sleep over it, whether it be from putting in long hours and sacrificing sleep to see it through or it is resting so heavy on your mind that sleeping simply becomes difficult. It's that thing that's so much bigger than you that it scares the absolute hell out of you to think about it, both the feelings of finding the courage to accept the challenge and the fear of falling short. It's that one thing that you will spend most of your life piecing together and chasing. Your purpose is your reason for being here and your duty to both the world that we live in and the world that your offspring and the future generations will inherit from you.

If you are religious, then your purpose and your faith work as one together as the most important thing in your life– your purpose is deeply tied into your religious beliefs and what has been spoken to you. If you are not religious, your purpose is the most important thing in your life and the most determinant of both how you will spend your time here on earth and how you will measure your success throughout the course of your life. Either way, the purpose for your life is extremely powerful and plays a major role in the direction of your life. As with any other important tasks you are faced with in life, starting as soon as possible and remaining consistent are key to giving yourself a chance at success in this endeavor.

If nobody else can do the job for you and there is nobody that can do the job better, then it's safe to say that the job is already yours. Better yet, the job was *assigned* to you. You must simply commit to enduring the path that has been created for you to finish the job. Your endurance on this path will determine if you reach the end of the journey and complete this job that has been assigned to you. It's simple to understand, but it's far from easy to accomplish.

Worrying about what someone else's job is and what they're doing on their own separate paths won't help you along your own path or help you complete the job you've been assigned. This is a very simple concept to understand. By worrying about what lies ahead of someone else on a separate path, no action is taken towards overcoming what lies ahead on the path in front of you. Your inaction towards traveling your own path has only kept you stagnant in places you were capable of moving forward, while decreasing the time you have left to reach the end of the path. We as a society have made this a much more difficult concept, due to our overexposure and overindulgence in the Internet and other

124

forms of media that give so much access and insight into the paths around us that have nothing to do with our own.

Understanding this concept will exponentially improve the happiness, fulfillment, clarity, and overall quality of your life. The most important thing that we fail to understand about comparison is that there is absolutely no victory in it– it's an endless game in our minds that subconsciously shifts our priorities and mental energy from the things we can control in our life to things that we can't control.

Comparison takes life from the empowering thoughts that we possess and gives life to the limiting, negative thoughts that we possess. Comparison is a thief of both your joy and your appreciation for your own life. Comparison is a distraction from all the positive things in your life that are working for your good. Most of all, it's an act that lacks action, which makes it a complete waste of two of your most valuable gifts in this life– your time and energy.

This principle is one of the most important boundaries you can implement into your life if you are struggling with constantly feeling less than others, anxiety about your future, or simply feeling lost in your life. I'm a firm believer that we all have our own times to peak in life and that you can never go wrong by waking up and giving it your all every single day. At the end of the day, your goal is to fulfill your purpose and live a life that makes you happy but getting there is a process.

We find ourselves in such a rush to get to that point in life, where we feel like we have it figured out and have made it. The truth is, we never have it all figured out in life.

Life is a never-ending game of evolution and growth and those who never stop evolving and growing tend to win at this game of life. When it's all said and done, we will look back on the journey and realize that it was the actions we took in the times that we didn't have it all figured out that will give us true fulfillment and appreciation for the lives that we create for ourselves.

Those times where it feels like you won't reach success or you feel like giving up on yourself, only make you stronger and create a sense of resiliency in you to get the job done. You need yourself more than you need anybody else in this world, whether you're happily married with kids or struggling through college and single. To be the best spouse, parent, or individual that you can be, you need to be there for yourself daily. You can't expect to be there for someone else if you have yet to learn to be there for yourself. So many of us never find this concept of self-care and learning to love ourselves before we involve ourselves with the lives of others. As a result, we find ourselves trying to learn how to take care of ourselves while also juggling with managing our other obligations to others.

This is why it's so important to avoid the trap of comparison and take small steps towards a better version of yourself everyday. By focusing on yourself and appreciating the life that you have, you will empower yourself to make drastic improvements over time and you will enjoy the process of becoming a better version of yourself. It may feel difficult at the moment to let go of comparison and the idea of "catching up" to everyone around you, but you must remember that you're running your own race and there's a finish line designed just for you and your needs in your life. Just because you aren't where everyone else is, doesn't mean you aren't exactly where you're supposed to be at this moment in your life.

Hank Aaron didn't become one of the all-time leaders in home runs by comparing himself to Babe Ruth and the other great sluggers before him. He earned his spot on that leaderboard by focusing on his craft and improving every single day. He didn't come into the league feared by opposing pitchers and his beginning numbers were no indication of the massive career that lay ahead of him. He came to love the *process* of forging his own way and it wasn't long before the entire league knew who Hank Aaron was.

He didn't doubt himself or get caught up in the success of others– he applied that energy to his own game and gained confidence in himself through the repetition that he put in. He focused on becoming the best Hank Aaron that he could be. He focused on maximizing his talent and gifts to cultivate the skills and strength that could be used to contribute to his team's success. His talent eventually became undeniable and the work that he had put into becoming a better player had paid off in huge dividends. Through running his own race, he became one of the most respected players in the history of the game.

By focusing on himself and staying out of the trap of comparison, he made a name for himself and paved his own way into the record books of baseball. These broken records eventually led Hank to the MLB Hall of Fame. His decorated career and massive success did not come from comparing himself to anybody else, or living in the shadow of the greats that came before him. Rather, his success was a by-product of enduring his own path and shining the light on his own legacy that he had created. It's important to note that *what*

Hank was able to accomplish was inspiring, simply amazing. However, it was in *how* he went about doing it that teaches us the importance of running our own race in life.

It took hours and hours of unseen work outside of team practices and the bright lights of the stadium for him to become the version of Hank Aaron that's in the Major League Baseball Hall of Fame. You would be amazed at what you could accomplish by being consistent and believing in yourself too! There's many of you in the world with the potential to have your own Hank Aaron-like story, but the question is will you ever stop comparing yourself and just focus on putting in the work to be better than you were the day before?

Babe Ruth was great. Hank Aaron was great. Both can be true at the same time because greatness isn't defined by one single parallel or any distinguishing factor. The success of others doesn't mean there is no room for you to become successful as well. Become inspired to find your own success, and work hard at it every single day until someone is looking up to you for their own inspiration to be successful on their own terms one day.

Never fear success, but rather be inspired and *learn* from those who are successful. Don't just sit on the sideline– learn and take purposeful actions and you will soon realize that it was never your ability that was keeping you on the sideline. It was your inability to kill fear and self-doubt the whole time that stopped you from even trying to get in the game that you are fully capable of playing at a high level with the right attitude and mindset.

I want you to take a moment and imagine how much further and how much happier you could be in your own life, if you gave all the time you have spent comparing and analyzing the lives of others to things that directly impact your own life in a positive fashion. Most of you probably just reevaluated your lives slightly, didn't you? I know I did a significant amount of reevaluating when I asked myself this very same question. When you think about all the time you've spent focused on other people's lives, it becomes apparent that all that time would have benefited you much more if it had been invested into a cause that actually mattered and benefited you.

Don't beat yourself up over this because this is human nature. It's a pattern that takes a significant amount of practice, discipline, and self-awareness to break. Taking this moment to contemplate the time you have wasted was not to "guilt trip" or get down on yourself, but simply to bring awareness to an issue that has a relatively simple solution and the potential to bring an endless amount of benefit to your life. Solving life's greatest problems and challenges starts with finding the simple solutions to the simple problems first and this is a simple solution to a simple problem that many of us experience in our lives.

One thing about time is that once it's gone, it's gone forever. You can't get the time that you have wasted back, but you can change your habits and behaviors and make the most of the time you still have. You can commit yourself to only giving your time and energy to things that will advance your life, whether it be spiritually, mentally, or physically. When you stop holding yourself to other people's standards, you make room to be able to define your own standards. When you develop your own standards and define what success looks like for you in your life, you find the clarity to appreciate your own progress and growth towards that success.

It can be difficult to shake the natural urge to compare yourself to others, but once you start to see the progress you make in your life by doing so, the measuring stick no longer looks the same to you. You will become focused on eliminating the things that have held you back for so long and seek more of what helps you move forward in your life. It's when you stop chasing to have the same life as everybody else and simply begin building your own life that you will see your life begin to change right before your eyes. Your focus will realign you with the things you can control and you will find much more satisfaction in the process.

Don't get caught up in where you are right now in your life. Focus on where you want to be a month from now, six months from now, a year from now, and so forth. I recommend writing down a few things you'd like to see change– once again, seeing it on paper makes it seem real and attainable before it becomes reality. Resist the urge to believe you can hold onto this list within your brain that already has thousands and thousands of thoughts locked inside it. Bring the change to life by spelling it out for yourself.

Once you have written these few things down, look at this list every morning when you wake up and do your absolute best to *only* engage in actions that will push you towards these goals you have set for yourself. Find a way to tune out what the world is saying and doing. Just go to war with yourself every single day for the duration of that goal that you have set for yourself, whether it be a month or five years. Use each day as a day to get closer to your goals and to work at becoming the best version of yourself.

Over time, you will find that your life has become simplified and that you have become significantly less invested in what the people around you are doing or how they may feel about the things that you're doing. This is what you want, because there is no point in investing into things and people that do not return the investment back to you. It's time to stop watering dead plants in your life by giving them your time, attention, and focus. It's time to stop giving other people's thoughts and actions, which are things you can't control, power over you.

After a while of being on this journey, you will become focused solely on the goals you have set and your progress. The only comparison that will matter is where you currently are in comparison to where you were when you started. This is the only comparison that counts for anything in life. Measuring backwards helps you slow down and appreciate your progress along the way, and it creates a situation in which victory is not only possible, but very attainable.

Life is already hard enough as it is. There's absolutely no need to make it any more difficult than it already is, so focus your mind on the things that you can control and trust that the energy you put out will come back to you in abundance when the time is right. Seeing yourself make the effort to win daily and take control over the very things that have held power over you in the past can create momentum that lasts a lifetime and leads you to the success that you've only been able to dream about up to this point. The consistent effort and resistance to the pressures and noise of the outside world is how you reach the peace of mind and confidence that frees you from the struggles of the poison that comparison brings into your life.

Now, this process isn't going to be a walk in the park. Everybody would have the life they desire and be living on their own terms if it were an easy thing to do. This process will require you to be brutally honest with yourself, to acknowledge and admit that there are areas that need improvement in your life– weaknesses in who you *currently* are. It will require you to address insecurities and other areas of your life that trigger comparison. The ability to honestly evaluate ourselves and identify weakness within ourselves is essential to continuous growth in our lives.

We tend to avoid these conversations with ourselves out of fear of appearing weak or embarrassing ourselves, but there is no greater strength than knowing your own weaknesses and attacking them at the root. All strong people were once weak at some point in their lives before they became strong. Consider it a blessing if you're struggling in your life currently. Struggle is what builds the strength that's going to take you to new levels. Without the presence of struggle, there can be no strength.

Before you can strengthen a weakness, you must first recognize it as a weakness. After all, this is what makes focusing on improving yourself so rewarding– there's always room to improve because you will never be perfect. No matter how strong you become and how much improvement you make, there is always weakness somewhere. Understand that you are human and deeply flawed and learn to embrace this fact, but also understand that this doesn't mean that you have to continue to be controlled by fear, addiction, anxiety, or any other problem that has been holding you back from becoming your highest self. Hard work and discipline seems miserable to most, but those that endure it understand its importance to living better lives. Having the discipline to focus on your own improvement regardless of what's going on in the world around you is essential to becoming your highest self and to fighting off the danger of comparison.

To give you a real-world example of how comparison can rob you of your happiness and prevent you from appreciating your own story, I want to share a bit of my own story and how comparison has gotten the best of me in my past. I'll be the first person to tell you that I didn't come anywhere close to my ceiling as a basketball player, and it wasn't an issue of talent that was the cause for this. A major contributor to my shortcomings was constant comparison and worrying about what everybody else around me had going on. Even worse, I had a paralyzing fear of what others thought of me.

Almost everything that I just talked about in this principle, I struggled with greatly throughout high school and into my early years of college. That's how I know avoiding these things is best for you. I have lived in the personal hell that comes from trying to co-exist with these unhealthy habits and it's not a fun life! I speak on all of these principles from experience and from the heart, because I want to educate you through my personal experiences so that you can avoid making the same mistakes that I've made in my life.

I loved the game of basketball for as long as I can remember. I told my parents at an early age that my dream was to play basketball at the collegiate level. I wasn't caught up in divisions or levels at that point. I was simply a kid who wanted an opportunity at the next level. The older I got, I grew taller, ran faster, jumped higher, was able to lift more weight, and understood the game more and more. I could see myself improving in every aspect of the game as the years went on. Yet, I was unable to showcase my abilities and talent when it mattered most and the opportunities finally came.

It was the most frustrating, disheartening few years of my life at the time. I watched films of my favorite players, watched films of myself playing and tried to catch my mistakes. I even looked for the weaknesses in my game that my coaches didn't point out to me because I wanted to be a better player than I was. I spent hours and hours in the gym on a daily basis. It seemed like I was doing more than most kids my age at the time, but I had nothing to show for it when the lights shined brightest. I had all this ability and was dying to be noticed for it, but I couldn't ever put it all together in game situations– where all the hard work is supposed to pay off.

I didn't realize it back then, but after having a few years to reflect and grow my knowledge, I now have a better understanding of why I struggled so greatly to play freely and showcase my abilities. My inability to reach my potential had nothing to do with the defenders that were in front of me or the X's and O's of the game. The simple fact of the matter is that I was defeated before I even stepped on the floor. My fear of failure, worry of what others thought of me, and constantly worrying about how I compared to others stripped me of my confidence and consistently limited my production on the court.

Anyone who knows basketball will tell you that the best defenders know their opponents' strengths, weaknesses, and their tendencies. My mind knew all three better than anyone else on the floor and it was the best defender I ever played against. Though the shots I took were few, I shot roughly 47% from the field throughout my high school career. I made almost half of the shots I attempted. There are many things in life that lie but the numbers are not one of them. It was never the other team stopping me. It was always my mind stopping me.

It had my number every single night and made me work hard for every positive contribution I made to the game. This is what great defenders do. They make doing even the simplest things much more difficult. They provide resistance to things you know you're capable of doing. They fluster you and take you away from your comfort zones. They force you into doing the things that you are least skilled at and the least comfortable with.

Even though I did a lot of things right to physically become the player I wanted to become, my major weaknesses were internal and mental. Doubting myself and this extreme fear of failure took away from my abilities and made the game I grew up loving to play feel like a mentally exhausting game of chess. I was frustrated that the time and effort I was putting into the game wasn't paying off. I was frustrated that the skill set I had worked to develop was largely unseen by the world. I was sick of this invisible voice tormenting me, holding me back, and making something I once enjoyed so draining to me.

More than anything in my life at the time, I wanted to be able to play basketball with a clear mind and without fear of failure. I tried many things and I put up a fight for much longer than most would've in my situation. No matter how hard I fought, it seemed that there were other plans for my life. This took its toll over the years and even though I was given the opportunity to play college basketball, I never gained complete control over my mind and continued to struggle with comparing myself to others and doubting my abilities throughout my college career.

I know there was potential for a much better outcome and overall career for me. There were moments where I would be able to silence the noise temporarily and do the things that I knew I was capable of doing. There were moments I would ignore the pressure and make the correct play. There were many moments, even in college, where my athleticism took over and I simply was just too big and skilled for the defense to stop me from putting the ball in the rim. These moments created some of my best memories on the court, but they were just so rare in comparison to the moments that my mind got the best of me. It was soon back to the constant whispers and voices in my head that kept me from playing freely.

As a result, I ultimately decided to step away from the game after a few seasons in college and an attempt at prep school. I was proud of myself for achieving a life-long dream of mine and sticking with it as long as I did, but I knew I had reached a point where I needed to prioritize my mental health. Every man has a breaking point and I pushed myself hard to do everything I could to stay strong and not give up on my dreams prematurely. Deep inside me, I knew I had reached this point and knew that it was time to close this chapter in my life.

I had my share of experiences throughout my childhood and other factors in my story that may have contributed to my struggles, but I ultimately don't blame anyone but myself and my inability to let go of comparison for my mental struggles. Physically, I was in the best shape of my life at the time that I made the decision to step away from basketball. It was never an issue of physical ability, talent, or athleticism. I had a chronic weakness that posed a great threat to my future even after basketball. Mentally, I was beyond weak. I wanted to solve this problem, so I wouldn't experience the same problems in my new life away from the basketball court and all the things I had been through with the game.

I had allowed the outside noise to become the inside noise within my mind and it was a battle that I no longer had the energy to fight. Comparison and spending excess amounts of time worrying about things that were out of my control robbed me of having my best possible experience with something I devoted much of my childhood and teenage years to. I *allowed* comparison to take these things from me, without even realizing it. Comparison is a thief that comes and takes whatever you allow it from underneath you, so it's very important that you have the necessary boundaries and protect your peace of mind from this disruptive thief.

I didn't tell you this information to bore you with flashbacks from my life or to win your sympathy for my struggles. I'm not proud to say the game I loved became a mental struggle for me and it's still not the easiest topic for me to discuss, even to this day. However, I have come to understand why my journey resulted in the way it did at some points in my life through self-reflection and gaining wisdom that I didn't have at the times I was first dealing with this battle. I have learned to forgive myself for what I didn't understand during these times, but I also understand that there is power in my experiences and that they can be used to make a difference in the lives of others who may be going through similar battles in their lives.

There are still days that I wish I could go back and do things differently. Even three years later, I sometimes catch myself wondering what opportunities I may have been able to afford myself and my family if I would've just been able to focus on my craft and enjoy the present at all times. However, the most important thing to me is that I use my story and my experiences to be a voice of guidance and support to lead others away from this destructive path.

Just like I'm advising you to avoid comparison and to appreciate your own process, I'm still learning how to do the same thing and learning how to forgive myself for the times that I was unable to avoid comparison and appreciate my process earlier on in my life. It's a daily focus, but it's a focus that I owe to myself to make sure that I never find myself in that negative headspace that I've worked so hard to crawl out of again. Avoiding the tendency to compare our processes lives to others' is something that we all deserve freedom from, but it doesn't just happen for us. It first requires us to learn to accept and appreciate our own processes, to fall in love with our own unique paths.

I have a firm belief that every experience provides us with something for future use and application. This experience has made me appreciate my growth into becoming my own authentic person and no longer being a slave to my mind and the opinions of others. If I can help anybody else gain this knowledge at an earlier age and help them avoid having a similar experience, this book will go down as a success to me.

For me, the reward isn't found in how many copies I sell or the compensation I receive. I know from experience the road that comparison takes you down mentally and I don't want to see any of you on that road. Believe in yourself and focus your time and energy on improving yourself. By focusing your time and energy on yourself and things that directly benefit you, you will only continue to improve as an individual and improve the life that you live.

Your path looks different from others by design because it *is* different from others. Learn to embrace it, appreciate it, and to avoid comparing it to the paths that others are traveling. My life and my mindset changed when I took my focus away from other people and the things outside of my control. I began to realize that I was in control of my own thoughts and my focus, and I made every effort to only give these two important life forces to what mattered most. I've said it before and I'll say it again– it was done for me, so I know it can be done for you.

Whether you struggle with comparison or not, I advise you to fill your life with as much positivity as possible, in as many areas of your life as possible. If you look hard enough and open up your mind and heart, you can find positivity in almost any situation. There is enough negativity surrounding you already. The goal is to subtract from the negativity in the world, not add to it. Find who you are and embrace it to the fullest, because nobody else can be that person but you.

Don't lose yourself and downplay your own accomplishments and achievements because it's not as "prestigious" as what someone else around you accomplished or what you originally envisioned for your life. They're operating on a different time and path than you are, and you couldn't have possibly predicted everything that has happened in your life leading up to this very moment. You don't know when they started or what kind of help they may have had, or anything in between. It doesn't matter how they got there or that they got there first. Believe in yourself and that through the work that you're putting in, you'll reach your own goals and milestones at the right time in your life.

Life is a beautiful gift and there's enough resources for more than one person to win and more than one way to win. Run your own race and avoid the ugly cycle of worrying about where others are in their own separate races. It's a disservice to yourself and the work you have put into your own journey and life. Be eager to reach your own finish line, but don't forget to enjoy the journey and everything that leads up to finishing the race.

Learn to find happiness and appreciation for what you do have in your life and where you're at in your journey, and this is where promotion and opportunities to reach new levels show themselves in your life. When your energy reflects gratitude and appreciation for the present, the world can sense by your energy that you're ready for promotion and opportunity. The universe knows more about us than we give it credit for and all possibilities in your life begin to open for you as the universe senses your energy and appreciation for the things and opportunities that you already have.

I like to think about this using the example of your parents when you were out at a restaurant and you finally felt like you could handle an adult meal. In most cases, the adult meal first crossed your mind because you saw one of your friends or cousins order off the adult menu and now you want to follow suit and keep up. Some parents may take your word for it, but most will say something along the lines of, "Show us you can handle all of your kid's meal first, and then we can see about you getting more food if you're still hungry."

It's not that they don't want you to have enough food or that they're trying to embarrass you. They simply want you to show that you can appreciate and not waste what they've already given you before they feel comfortable investing more money into feeding you and putting more on your plate. They want you to understand that you don't have to waste your energy trying to keep up with what your friends or the other kids at the table are doing. As long as you're focused on your plate and you get full, that's all that matters. More will appear on your plate when more is needed to fill you up.

Life works the same way. You must show appreciation and prove that you can handle your current blessings and where you currently are in life before life gives you more blessings and responsibilities. This isn't because life doesn't want to bless you, but because it wants to ensure that you're ready for your blessings when they do come.

Life won't give you a promotion if you're struggling to complete the tasks required by your job now. Life won't give you a raise if you have already shown that you can't responsibly manage and show appreciation for the money you currently make. You can't lie to life and put on a poker face like you may be able to do with other people because it senses the energy that you give off. It's all timing– just because you don't have it yet or aren't where you want to be yet, doesn't mean you can't appreciate the things you do have and the places you are along the way. Life's timing will protect you from mishandling your blessings and opportunities through teaching you patience and gratitude.

As strong and mighty as Superman is, he can do nothing in the presence of kryptonite. All of his powers become weaknesses and he is no longer able to function and fulfill his purpose to the world as Superman when exposed to kryptonite. I believe comparison works the same way in our lives as kryptonite does in Superman's life. It is vital that we avoid this poison in life. In a world that is already hard to win in, do yourself a favor and choose empowerment and positivity in your life whenever possible. Just because others appear to be doing better right now, it doesn't mean that you aren't doing what you're supposed to be doing or the best that you can do.

Always remember, we all have our own times to peak in life and it's the journey up the mountain that you will look back on and find the most fulfillment in once you have conquered the mountain. There is nobody made exactly like you in this entire world and that is your greatest power and responsibility in your life– be you and stay true to who you are and what your purpose is in this world. The world needs you at your best every single day to live with a purpose and to impact those you were called to impact! Learn to love and appreciate *your* life and enjoy it to the absolute fullest– you will miss out on the beauty of your own life by constantly comparing it to the life of others.

Chapter Six

Principle #6: It takes both rain and sunshine to produce a strong harvest.

When a farmer plants his seeds for the upcoming season, he understands that there will be many factors that go into having a successful harvest come the end of the season. The most important of these factors is the proper balance of exposure to sunlight and rain that the crops must receive. The farmer must consider many things in his preparation for a successful harvest but nothing is more important than ensuring that they receive the sunlight and water needed to grow.

If the crops get too much sun and not enough water, they will be full of energy and nutrients above ground but their roots will not have grown strong enough to support the crops' energetic and lively state. The crops will remain full of energy and nutrients above the soil for a while but eventually the entire crop will die off due to the weak roots at the foundation. Without having a strong foundation and strong roots, the life of a crop can only be sustained in the short term.

On the other hand, if the crops get too much rain and not enough sun, they will be lacking the necessary energy and nutrients to continue to grow and produce, despite having roots strong enough to support that growth should the crops find the needed energy and nutrients. Just as important as it is to strengthen the roots to sustain a harvest, it's equally as important to fill the harvest with the energy and nutrients needed for the harvest to sprout above the ground as well. A strong foundation and strong roots mean nothing without also having the proper energy and nutrients to produce growth.

The farmer understands this and makes his best effort to provide this proper balance to protect and grow his harvest. After all, his life is directly affected by how he chooses to manage his crops and how strong his harvest is come the end of the season. He knows a successful harvest is needed to live the life that he desires for himself and his family, so finding this balance of rain and sunlight is a practice that he devotes his life to.

I'm not sure if you caught onto the analogy, but we're all "farmers" in life. Rain and sunshine are facts of life. They have shown up in all the days of the past and they will continue to show up in all the days of the future. They are very different from each other but they each provide things that are needed for our survival and growth. They are *essential* to life and growth– without these two things, there is no growth and there is no survival. The key to continuous life and growth is the proper balance of the two and understanding their functions in your life. This function is strengthening you to survive in your environment and keeping you at the balance that is needed to sufficiently support your growth and life.

The "rain" is the difficult times in your life. Rain is often perceived to bring darkness, gloom, and sometimes even depression to us as human beings. For some, it brings calmness and relieves stress. Regardless of how you perceive rain, it is inevitable and something you must get used to dealing with in your life. You must go through situations and times that test you, because they develop you into a stronger version of

145

yourself, teach you valuable lessons about life, and force you out of your comfort zones that are hindering your growth. Without the seasonal rain and tests, you will never be able to fully appreciate the energy-giving sunshine that comes as a result of enduring the rain and withstanding the challenges that come with life. Without the proper amount of rain and struggle, your roots will lack the strength to support all the growth that you are capable of achieving.

Navigating the difficult times in life allows you to appreciate all the great times that are coming in your life. Abundance and peace are on the way but life must first ensure that you are grounded and prepared for all the goodness that is coming your way. Abundance and peace do you no good if you mishandle it. For your own protection and for you to be able to extract the most out of your seasons of abundance, life has waiting periods and times where you are first put through times of trial and tribulation before reaching your breakthrough.

Though it may feel like a punishment at times, these difficult times are the exact opposite. They're designed and placed into your life to strengthen you and prepare you for your upcoming seasons of abundance and breakthrough. If you only knew the blessings that are coming your way if you remain in good spirits and stay consistent in doing the right things in your life, you wouldn't even sweat the tests and difficulties that life throws your way.

The "sunshine" is the other half of the spectrum. You finally receive the peace and abundance. You got the good news that you made the Dean's list for the semester. You saved up enough money to get the new car you've been dreaming about. Anything that is positive and brings happiness to you is part of the sunshine in your life. It has stopped raining and you are reaping the rewards for withstanding the rain that came before the sunshine.

The good times and recovery that never seemed possible when it was raining for days on end have come and the rain feels like it was worth every single drop now. The rain makes sense now. You had to go through the things you went through to get to where you are, to develop an even greater appreciation for yourself and your strength. You now understand that the rain served a purpose in your life and wasn't just a senseless punishment. You now see that some of the things that you were holding onto out of fear of finding nothing better, may have been holding you back from finding exactly what you were looking for.

It's important to remember that becoming a better version of yourself and creating a better life for yourself is the journey of a lifetime and there is no way to get an "ETA" for when you will arrive at your desired destination. As with any other journey, there's ups and downs throughout the course of pursuing the destination of your highest self. It takes both rain and sunshine to keep you strong, to rid you of the things and people that are no longer serving you, and for you to progress and grow along the way.

Growth is "desired" by all, but growth is only experienced by those who do the necessary work and put in the necessary time. Most people acknowledge the beauty and excitement of growth, but most don't have the patience or discipline to commit to being uncomfortable long enough to see long-lasting growth in their own personal lives. This is why you see so many people around you settling for lives that they aren't fully satisfied with and stuck in versions of themselves that they desperately want to outgrow. They have the desire for growth and change in their minds, but they have found comfort and are unwilling to takes the risks that are necessary to bring change into their lives. That comfort keeps them from making an effort to do the things that they truly desire to do in this life.

Imagine the only place you're allowed to drive your car is down the street to the local grocery store. The weather conditions stay the exact same and you pick up the same exact groceries, week after week. You know you're capable of making it to the store, getting all your groceries, and returning home safely. You know what the outcome of every trip is because nothing ever changes in the routine. The weather, the route, and the destination are the exact same every single trip. You've always wondered where the other roads and highways will take you, but you're fearful to discover those answers for yourself because this trip to the local grocery store is all you've ever known and it's comfortable and familiar.

This life sounds like it would be boring and predictable, doesn't it? You'd rather take the risk of getting lost going somewhere you're unfamiliar with than confine yourself to that same route to the same grocery store, right? I can't speak for anyone other than myself, but I'm hoping that the vast majority of you would rather take the risks to explore than to be stuck in the same cycle your entire lives.

There is much more to see and experience in life than the same trip, in the same weather, to the same mundane destination. Yet so many of us are settling for that familiar grocery store and those same groceries over and over again. We're fearful of opening ourselves up to the world and experiencing new emotions, environments, mindsets, risks, and everything else that this beautiful world has to offer outside of what we have become comfortable with and ultimately settled for.

Though we don't legitimately limit ourselves to the same local grocery store, this is the exact ideology that you buy into when you neglect to pursue growth and choose to instead suffocate yourself in the comfort of your life. You keep the same level of skill, knowledge, and discipline all throughout your life. You get older with each year that passes, but you grow very little as a person over time. As a result, you continuously get the same results. There is little to no expectation for change over the course of your life because you've been shopping at the same grocery store your entire life.

You wonder why the "groceries" are the exact same as they were last week, and the week before that. The simple answer is that it's a conflict of interests– you haven't made the effort to change your grocery list, so the groceries will continue to be the same until you do so. You haven't changed anything about yourself or the things you do on a daily basis– why should anything change? It's fine for you to feel uncomfortable walking down the aisles of the new grocery stores you're unfamiliar with, but you can't expect to ever know what those aisles have to offer if you never take the plunge and courageously go explore them for yourself.

Changes in your circumstances come from doing the small things daily that help you achieve your goals and fulfill your purpose. Changes in your circumstances come from becoming open to experiencing feelings of discomfort and unfamiliarity for the sake of your growth and to simply enjoy the adventurous side that life has to offer. Before you expect the results to change, you must first make changes in what you do to achieve those results.

In other words, you can't have growth and success without standing in the rain and experiencing some discomfort throughout the process. The road can get very bumpy and it'll push you to your limits at times. You will certainly question yourself and your strength along the way, but you will find a way to redefine and reinforce that strength as a result of having stood in the rain.

Enduring the rain and the difficulties is what makes the journey meaningful. When you finally get to the end, you can look back at all you endured to get there— all the times you could've quit, taken the easier route back to that same old grocery store, or parked the car and saved yourself from suffering the brutal conditions of the journey. Without difficulty, there's nothing that makes the pursuit of the journey meaningful to us.

A common misconception about suffering is that it's only felt by some of the world, when it's truly felt by everybody in the world. Suffering is inevitable in life, no matter who you are or what you choose to do. It requires suffering and sacrifice to become successful and build the life that you desire. Likewise, choosing to accept a life that is not desirable to you also brings suffering every day. The life that you desire becomes the sacrifice due to your choices and lack of action towards that life that you desire. Will you suffer *through* difficulties along the way to your destiny or will you suffer *regret* from the comfort you buried yourself in to end up with the undesirable life that you're living?

There's beauty in suffering, beauty in struggle. Your strength is not defined by how you respond in a state of comfort and knowing– how you respond when you're struggling and faced with the unknown defines your true character and strength. Life, regardless of who you are, produces suffering. Those who find the riches in life beyond monetary gain and material status find meaning in the suffering.

When a farmer's harvest is under a thunderstorm, the farmer knows that the crops that survive the storm will be stronger and a better product as a result of surviving the conditions that they were forced to grow in. They have experienced the stress and the pressure of the constant rain, yet they found a way to hold on and become strengthened by the temporary storms. Eventually, the sunshine must peak back out and refill them with whatever it is the storm may have left them depleted of.

The same is true for us as humans. You will be stronger because of the things that you endure, even when they look like they will only bring damage to you in the current moment. You will be a better final product because you decided to choose growth and to outlast the conditions surrounding you, even when the conditions surrounding you felt suffocating at times. Just as the farmer will find in his crops that survived the storms to be valuable and resilient, you will find more value and worth in yourself for having experienced difficulty on your path to success and fulfillment.

You understand that the storm was for your greater good and that you are a better, stronger version of yourself for having endured the temporary pain and suffering that was required to reach that understanding. The rain came, but as it has throughout its entire history, it also went away. On the other side of the rain and the challenges of life, there is a version of you that is resilient, battle-tested, and prepared for whatever may come next.

The brightest, most refreshing sunshine usually comes after it has been raining for an extended period of time. The skies have been pouring what seems to be nothing but rain for consecutive days, maybe even weeks on end. You're wondering how much longer it will continue to rain, wondering how much more you can take. Then, suddenly, the clouds clear up and the sun peeks its head for the first time in weeks.

You've been seeking sunshine through all the rain you endured and that sunshine that's now beaming from the sky is the fruit of your labor, sacrifice, and your commitment to growing and developing yourself in the presence of the undesirable rain. We all strive for sunshine in our lives, but it's important to note that the sunshine that gives us the most satisfaction is often on the other side of the storms we don't want to subject ourselves to. Without the rain, the sunshine in your life can never be properly appreciated and celebrated.

Don't wish for a life without rain because that would be wishing for a life with no meaning. Rather, ask for the strength and courage to find calm in the chaos of the process of learning to endure the rain. The most treacherous of storms often build the strongest harvests because those harvests are better prepared for whatever conditions life may throw them into next. The harvests that weren't put under immense stress and pressure during their process of growth will not have the same strength as the harvests that were pushed to their limits during their process, because those harvests have never been forced to grow through the conditions that those that were challenged were forced to grow through.

When you feel like life is just constantly beating you up and you can't catch a break, you're almost there. I know it's tempting and your brain is screaming at you to throw in the towel and just give up. I'm begging you to do the exact opposite and remain steadfast in your consistency despite the discomfort and the pain. It's at our breaking points that we are delivered from the stress, the heartbreak, the grief, and the many other negative thoughts and emotions that have been attacking us for so long in our lives.

It's when the rain is starting to feel too heavy that we feel the storm lighten up and we are finally able to see the sunshine peeking through the clouds as they clear up. Life will often test you to see how much rain you're willing to endure for the life that you desire. This life that you desire requires you to become a version of yourself that has been through the rain and stretched beyond your current capacity, so life produces the rain that will stretch your limits beyond the ones you currently have. If there is something that you *genuinely* desire in your life, I need you to understand that the rain is inevitable but there isn't enough rain in the world to keep you from obtaining that which you truly desire in your life.

Just as you can't control the weather outside, you can't always control the weather in your life. You can only control how you respond to the weather, but you will find in time

153

that the ability to control your response is a greater power than the ability to control the weather itself. Your response to adversity and uncomfortable situations is where you will find your true power and strength in your life. The same circumstances that can cause you to lose your way, set you back, or even give up on yourself, can also push you to become more disciplined and help you grow through the pain and suffering. It's a choice you must make for yourself, to sink or to swim.

You can make the decision to stay on the ground whenever life throws its punches, or you can make the decision to take the punches and get back up and continue fighting. Both the decision to waive the white flag of surrender and the decision to take the punches and stay in the fight, come with pain and sacrifice. One is the pain of regret and living a life of mediocrity. The other is pain that subsides and builds you into a stronger fighter, edging you closer to the triumph that follows the pain that we fight through.

It's only a matter of time before someone taking life's punches to the chin gets the opportunity to throw a few punches back at the opposition. Be the fighter that gets knocked down and gets back up. I know laying there on the floor, avoiding the punches feels like it will bring relief to you in the moment. That temporary relief is nothing in comparison to the strength you will build from continuing to fight. Half the battle is simply staying in the fight and actually making the opposition beat you. There are only so many punches that they can throw and all it takes to change the momentum of the fight is one chance to return the punches.

Your life matters. Serving your purpose to the world and impacting others matters. Don't let the rain rob you of your courage to do what matters to you in your life. The rain can be treacherous but it's temporary, and there is a lot to be learned from the rain in life. There is a lot of growth to be discovered in the rain. In fact, there is no growth at all without rain. Luckily for us, the sunshine always follows the rain and provides the necessary relief that makes going through the rain all worth it in the end.

Your legacy is forever and worth every step it will take to get there. Embrace your experiences and allow them to empower you. Not every experience is a pleasant one, but every experience is an opportunity for you to master your reactions to your experiences. Every experience serves a greater purpose in the bigger picture of your life. In learning to focus on what you can control, the power is no longer in the experience's hands and is solely in the hands of how much power you choose to give the experience over you.

You're taking power from situations and circumstances that were likely out of your control in the first place and giving that power back to yourself and the things you can control. This is how you embrace the rain and find ways to get stronger in the midst of struggle and adversity. The rain is inevitable, but with the right mindset and approach, these seasonal rains will provide you with the growth, understanding, and strength necessary to become the person you desire to be and an individual who is fit to live the life that you desire to live.

Life is many things, but above all, life is a mental game. If you can keep your composure and develop a strong mind, you will find that nothing in your life happens *to* you. Everything that happens in your life happens *for* you. My perspective of life changed forever when I shifted to this mindset. Everything that happens in your life happens for a reason and serves a purpose, whether you can see it right now or not. If you can find the strength to hold onto what the experience is teaching you and not self-destruct in the emotions and feelings that come with the experiences, you'll find yourself able to thrive and grow in any weather conditions that you find yourself in. Learn to appreciate both the darkness and the light that you will encounter along your journey and it will make you infinitely more satisfied with who you're becoming as you march towards the final product.

If you had endless access to the sunshine and the absence of stress and pressure in your life, there would be no purpose for you getting out of bed every morning and working to become a better individual. The rain regulates the sunshine to keep you grounded, adaptive to changes in life, and firm in your purpose. The rain brings undesirable experiences to your life at times but there is something of equal desire to be gained from every experience in your life. Train yourself to find the positives in negative situations. Train yourself to find the lesson in the season of suffering. It is in these times that true growth and transformation takes place within our lives, and it is in these times that we prepare ourselves to step back into the sunshine a new, improved version of ourselves.

Perception is everything. If you can shape the way that you think about situations in life, you can also shape the way in which you respond to situations in life. The more controlled and rational your headspace is when responding to adversity or times of difficulty, the easier it is for you to start the transition from the rain back into the sunshine. The quicker you find and retain the lesson or the gain in the situation, the less time you will spend wrapped up in the loss of the situation. By having a clear head and looking for what the experience is trying to teach you or how it will develop you for the future, you begin the process of bringing the light into the darkness.

All of us, as human beings, have failed an infinite number of times in our lives. What separates the successful from the unsuccessful is the ability to earn from every failure and come back stronger. The successful don't allow themselves to stay in their defeat too long or to take the bad weather in their lives personally. To become a better version of yourself and to increase your happiness in your life, you must learn to find a way regardless of the weather. Take a deep breath, gather your thoughts, and get back into the fight. If your better future and the best version of yourself aren't worth fighting for, what in life *is* worth fighting for?

When you're driving and get caught in a heavy rain that seemingly came from the middle of nowhere and you can no longer see the road clearly through the windshield, do you panic, lose all control, and crash your car? If that is your response to bad weather when you're driving, I urgently advise you to familiarize yourself with Uber or Lyft and return your license to the nearest DMV immediately without further question. The answer is no. You don't do either of those things. You remain calm, turn your wipers and hazard lights on, and slowly make your way to the side of the road.

You may need to stay still for a moment and get yourself together, ready to ease back into the rain in a calmer, more calculated state of mind. You may need to look at the GPS and familiarize yourself with the route, so you aren't distracted looking at the GPS when you're focusing on the road ahead through the strong rains. Either way, you don't panic and you don't give control of the situation to the temporary storm. No matter how scary the storm may be, there's so much more that's worth discovering and experiencing on the other side of that storm. Sometimes we're forced to slow down and re-evaluate our course, but panicking and opening ourselves up to unnecessary danger is never the answer.

You should approach your life the same way. Vehicles are equipped with hazard flashers, windshield wipers, defrost functions, and several other tools that assist you when you get caught in the middle of a situation that calls for you to slow down and proceed with caution. You may not realize it, but you also are equipped with several tools that will assist you in the middle of these times in your life where life is telling you to slow down and carefully consider your next moves. Everything you will ever need to be successful and find your way in life lies within you.

That's why these principles are so important. That's why doing the difficult things that build you stronger and prepare you are so important. Get to know yourself and identify your tools and the skills within you that help you withstand the rain and make a conscious effort to sharpen these mechanisms every chance you get.

Before I started my journey and gained a better understanding of the way life works, I amplified every bit of rain in my life and gave it much more control over my life than was necessary. Every inconvenience or bump in the road felt like a worst-case scenario event in my life. This mindset caused me to be miserable and held me back from finding lasting happiness at many stages in my life, even when I was in situations that I had always dreamed of being in and that I worked my butt off to get put into.

I finally got tired of living that life and made the decision to change my mindset. Understanding the roles of rain and sunshine in life played a major part in establishing the understanding and peace that I find in my times of struggle now. In addition to helping me through my times of struggle, I make it my personal mission to grow in every experience. It no longer has anything to do with what I'm going through and how it makes me feel. Instead, it now has everything to do with what I'm going to learn from what I'm going through and how I'll feel when I get to the other side of the suffering.

I have gained strength and understanding beyond what I ever would've thought possible. I've experienced growth in myself and learned to remain calm in situations that used to ruin me. I now classify very few events as "storms" in my life, but I think back to the farmer and his harvests when I do find myself in these seasons of waiting and enduring.

I'm learning to define my own experiences and how to extract the lessons and the benefits. The pain and suffering are temporary but the lessons and benefits are forever. For someone who has struggled mentally and with responding to adversity most of my life, this shift in my mindset and witnessing myself grow into a more mature and patient human being in my personal life has been one of the most rewarding parts of my process. It is my wish for anyone else who may be struggling with the storms in their lives at the moment to reach the same reward.

I was watching *Blacklist* one night in my room, which is one of my favorite TV shows that I've ever watched in my entire life. One of the main characters in the show is Raymond Reddington, who is one of the most dangerous criminals in the entire world that has turned himself in to the FBI to be an informant against other criminals. I love Reddington's character in the show because he always finds a way to make ends meet and to keep going. He finds himself in near-death and other extreme situations quite often, but he is the best at what he does and he remains calm and survives every situation that threatens him. Not only does he survive, but he puts fear in the hearts of his rivals.

In this episode that I was watching, Reddington was opening about some of the events in his life that led him down the path of becoming the most dangerous criminal in the world and the events that led to him agreeing to turn himself in to the FBI. Trauma, pain, and tragedy turned Reddington cold. At the end of his rant, Reddington says, "It's the children whom the world almost breaks who grow up to save it." I thought this quote was so powerful and profound because it *is* the ones who have been tested the most and endured the most that become the strongest and most capable in the world.

This quote made me reflect on the difficult times in my life, and I realized that I am who I am because of the rain that I've endured. I have the vision that I have and the passion that I have for others because I've been stuck in those same shoes of hopelessness and depression before. The world did in fact almost break me. I remember those nights

160

sitting in my car all alone. I never wished to hurt myself or to end my own life, but there were plenty of nights I wished to no longer feel anything or to have to go through the exhaustion that came with living life at the time. I remember it all. It's through remembering these exact feelings and emotions that I reflect on how I have become the person that I am today and wholeheartedly accepted the responsibility I have to be a voice of reason and compassion for those who are suffering in silence.

Saving the world can have many different interpretations. It's impossible for the world to be saved by one person, but I believe one person finding the strength and courage to use their experiences to better themselves and those around them starts the momentum that can grow and save the world over time. My original desire was to feel alive again, to feel like I had a reason to get out of bed in the morning. At my lowest, that was genuinely all I wanted in life. Over time, this was no longer enough for me. I know that I have had the experiences I've had and gone through everything I've gone through to help others through their own struggles and battles in their lives.

As I was continuing to encourage myself and make improvements, I knew it was my responsibility to encourage others and help them improve themselves also. Those feelings of brokenness and frustration with my life will stick with me for as long as I live. They serve as a constant reminder of a place that I never want to return to again in my life. More importantly, those feelings also remind me that there are many people *still* going through these experiences and feelings and that's something that carries a significant amount of weight in my heart. My hope is for nobody to feel like that about themselves or their lives, and while it is impossible for this to be the case, I know that I can focus on leaving a positive impact every chance that I get the opportunity to do so.

I believe that we all have the capacity to be broken by the world that we live in, but we also have an equivalent capacity to restore ourselves and grow into stronger, healed, and healthier human beings in the face of this brokenness. Feeling broken and lost today is not a guarantee that you will feel broken and lost tomorrow. These are feelings and emotions that are completely normal to feel throughout the course of life. This is the beauty of the journey. This is what is going to make reaching your destination for your life so fulfilling to you. You endured the path and stuck with it, all the way to your desired destination. To take yourself to a place of higher value and desire, you're going to have to take difficult roads that you don't want to take from time to time.

I know how much my dreams and desires mean to me personally. I know how much they push me every single day of my life. Dreams and desires are beautiful things to have and they become tangible when they're met with a plan of action and a strong work ethic to bring them to fruition. Dreams are some of the most valuable things we have in life and they must be protected and invested into at all costs.

Healing in the world begins with taking our passions and dreams back, living inspired and with a purpose in a world where the masses are just breathing and occupying space. Though I can't save the world, I'm committed to saving myself and bringing as many people with me as I possibly can along the way. Though it doesn't look the way I imagined it, I'm grateful for every bit of the process that has led me to being where I am in my life at this very moment.

You'll eventually see the bad weather in your life in a different light- if you take the time to slow down and open your mind to new perspectives. If you'll mute the noise of the problem for a moment, you'll find a way in the process of dealing with the problem that's going to propel you forward in some way in your life. You don't always have control over your problems in life, but you do have control of your perspective of your problems and most importantly, your *responses* to those problems.

Life is a privilege and it's a beautiful experience, no matter what you're going through right now– the world has a way of making us forget that sometimes. Every breath that you take, you're a breath closer to death. There will come a day where you draw your last breath and all you will be left with is memories and what you made of your gift of life. It sounds extreme and unpleasant to put your life into that perspective but that's how quickly life goes. That's why it's vital that you make it a priority to live everyday like it's your last, because one day it will be, and it will be too late to make the most of something that's already came and went.

You owe it to yourself to make the most of every single breath, to experience life on your own terms and conditions. You owe it to yourself to *live*– some of these experiences come with pain, struggle, heartbreak, suffering, loss, and even death in some cases. This is what makes the breath in your lungs so precious and valuable because you get the opportunity to experience life to the fullest. Even when you find yourself broken and struggling, there is an equivalent place of wholeness and peace through your experiences and the lessons that they teach you.

Have courage and optimism through your rainy seasons in life and understand that all rain must eventually come to an end. Even when it's raining, every raindrop is a new blessing and opportunity for growth. As humans, we tend to give meaning to our experiences based on how they make us feel. Not every experience will leave a good taste in your mouth. Without the bitter taste of struggle, the sweet taste of success and victory would be meaningless. See past the pain and your feelings– open your eyes to the lessons and the growth. You make peace with your emotions over time, but the lessons you learn and your growth as a person stick with you forever and allow you to walk through the rest of your life more healed and prepared for what's to come.

Life is too precious to be wasted being angry at the things we can't change. Life is too precious to limit yourself to the same local grocery store and the same groceries. It is better to get caught in the rain from time to time than to go your whole life sheltered from the rain and never truly experiencing the gift of life. You're built to do the difficult things and to take the chances necessary to have the life you desire. You're built to withstand the rain and grow stronger through your failures and shortcomings. You're built to let go of the things and people that were required to break and fall apart along the way. You've already suffered, so you might as well get something out of your suffering.

Take every experience and choose growth and peace, no matter the difficulty. Coming from experience, you will love and appreciate the people in your life and your life itself more than you could've ever imagined. These experiences make you who you are and your fight to become better in the face of the ugliest of storms will inspire more people than you could ever imagine. No matter how many times you may fall or find yourself traveling off course, I want you to know that the way you continue to fight in the midst of your struggles is admirable, a true sign of the strong character that is being built within you. I believe in you to do these things and exponentially improve your life throughout the process. The simple question that remains– do you believe in yourself to endure the necessary seasons that come with creating a strong harvest?

Chapter Seven

Principle #7: A better life requires better habits– habits are everything.

Research supports that it takes roughly 21 days of putting the body into a specific action before that action becomes a habit, which is essentially an action that has been repeated so many times that the body begins to perform the action subconsciously. That is, the action becomes muscle memory– the body no longer requires any thought to engage in the action. However, just as this research applies for building good habits, it also applies to bad habits as well. Therefore, it's important to always watch what you're doing on a daily basis because these habits develop and reinforce themselves quickly and with great strength.

21 is an optimistic number if you ask me. You can start the process of building a good habit for yourself right now, at this very moment. If you remain consistent, this good habit will become a natural action for your body after roughly three weeks. That means it takes less than a month to see results of improvement in yourself through your daily actions and decisions. Given how long we have been careless with our actions and making the wrong decisions in life, it's almost an anomaly that our bodies are able to adapt and begin the course of correcting these bad habits and decisions in such a short period of time.

Habits are very small intricacies in our lives. From the surface, they tend to seem insignificant and to be just a small part of our everyday life. While they are essentially just a small part of our everyday lives, these habits have significant influence in shaping the lifestyles that we live and the people that we become in life. These small habits build on one another and *compound*. It is through this process of compounding that our habits become the single most important determinant of how successful (or unsuccessful) we become in our lives.

If you want to experience victory in your life, you must first develop winning habits. You must become consistent in doing the little things that set you up for success every single day. This is what separates those who live life to the fullest and those who merely exist in this life– consistency in the small, mundane areas of everyday life. Many people can stick to a routine or new lifestyle for a day or two, but who can stay consistent for weeks, months, and years– especially on the days when they don't feel like it? To become successful and of greater value, you must engage in consistent actions that render success and add value to you as a person. A successful life isn't given, nor does it come by chance or "luck". A successful life is built by building winning habits and making the commitment to sticking to those habits.

One thing you must constantly remind yourself of is the fact that as long as there is breath in your lungs, it's never too late to make the decision to start living a better life than the one you are currently living. No matter how much time you feel you have wasted in your life, you have been afforded more time and have every opportunity to be more intentional with what you choose to spend this time doing. No matter how much opportunity you feel you have watched pass you by, all it takes is capitalizing off the right one when it presents itself. No matter how "out of it" you may feel, you're very much still in it because there is breath in your lungs that you can use to become wiser, better, and purposeful.

This is the crazy fact about life that we often neglect– *one* positive decision could change the trajectory of your life forever. It's unlikely that one single decision will change your life alone, but that one decision could very likely put your foot in the right door, your talents in front of the right faces, and direct you towards alignment with the people and surroundings that *will* go on to change your life forever. It's the small actions that we choose every day that make up the sum of the quality of life we create for ourselves.

I believe an important realization that we neglect to make concerning our daily habits is that they reveal to us how we see ourselves and how we value ourselves. The things that you train your body to do on a daily basis speaks volumes of how you perceive yourself. Sometimes, correcting bad habits is simply a matter of developing a better self-image and stronger concept of self-love. Before you can create a better life for yourself, you must first learn to see yourself as capable and deserving of creating the life that you desire for yourself. You must also love yourself enough to choose habits that push you towards a better version of yourself that will bring these desires to reality. If you don't first see yourself as capable and deserving of a better life, it is highly unlikely that you will develop the love for yourself that is necessary for you to push towards the uncomfortable, disciplined, and transformational process that you will be required to undergo to bring that better life that you dream about to reality.

When I think back to the times where I was most unhappy in my life, I was living like I had nothing to live for and had lots of bad habits. I was essentially at a place in my life where I didn't want to feel anything anymore. Therefore, I developed habits that allowed me to become numb to the reality of my life. These habits were never a solution by any means. Not once did they help me find myself or make me feel any better in the long term. All these poor habits did was temporarily distract me from the growing problems in my life.

At the time, I didn't love myself enough to recognize the destructive nature of abusing substances to feel numb for a moment rather than seeking out healthier alternatives and long-term solutions. In my mind, feeling nothing and being distracted from my problems was better than the reality of having to feel and process the feelings and emotions I was going through at this time in my life. The illusion I painted for myself by avoiding my problems was much more pleasant than my reality at the time, so I held on tightly to that illusion and hid from the real work that needed to be done for as long as I possibly could.

I allowed myself to go down this dark path because of a poor self-image and a severe lack of love for myself. I saw myself as incapable of finding the strength, so I *was* lacking the strength to dig deeper and do the meaningful work that would guide me towards a more purposeful and fulfilling life. I became so comfortable with my habits of abusing sex, drugs, and alcohol to numb myself that I had no interest in pushing towards the authentic dopamine that would help me out of the hole I was stuck in. I had no interest in the uncomfortable and disciplined habits that were the true solution to the test I was being given. As a result, I was failing this test miserably.

Eventually, I became more disgusted with the life I was living than I was fearful of feeling the thoughts and emotions that I had been avoiding for so long. I was extremely lost and my spiritual life needed a lot of work. Mentally, it was a struggle every single day to control my thoughts and find peace. Physically, I woke up every single morning to the reality of being back in my hometown and trying to figure out who I was without a basketball in my hand for the first time in my life. Nothing in my life was going the way I wanted it to go, but I knew there had to be more to life than getting drunk, smoking weed, and chasing validation from females all the time.

I knew that I didn't want to feel this way forever and that the habits I had chosen were not going to help me become the person I aspired to be or to build the life that I desired to live. I knew that the habits I had chosen did not reflect who I wanted to become, nor who I truly was. I was acting out because life had knocked me flat on my back and I wasn't sure how to respond. I wasn't sure how the changes would come about, but I knew I had to make a change, or I was going to end up living a life that I wasn't pleased with.

I had finally come to my senses and made the decision that I owed it to myself to turn my life around and take control of my life. I was still upset with myself and didn't see myself in the most positive light initially, but I made the decision that I was ready to invest the time and energy required for me to truly heal and to learn to love myself correctly. I was only 21 years-old and my life was just beginning. Just because I had fallen into the habit of making poor choices over the last year and a half of my life didn't mean I had to continue to make poor decisions for the rest of my life.

I had finally developed a genuine hunger for a better life and I knew that meant separating myself from the habits that were destroying me. I had finally made the decision to pursue a life that was free from depression and emptiness, even after the bartender stopped pouring shots and the music stopped playing. I was a long way down the wrong path, but I knew that path led to nowhere I was interested in going. Something had to change, and that "something" was actually *someone. I* had to change.

This breaking point is different for everybody, but this is the point you must reach to develop a legitimate hunger to better yourself and the life that you live. You must reach this point where you're no longer content with doing the same things and living with the same results, or you'll continue to do the same things and accept the results you've been getting. You must come to the realization that the output will continue to be the same if nothing changes in the input. This realization forces you to consider alternative courses of action and direction in your life.

You must examine your current daily habits and look at what version of yourself and what type of lifestyle they've produced for you and will continue to lead you towards. It's difficult to look at yourself in the mirror in this way, to acknowledge faults and shortcomings in your preparation for success. Though difficult, this is critical to identifying where improvements can be made and will be one of the best investments of your time and energy for your future self. Being able to look in the mirror and be brutally honest with yourself will change your life for the better.

You must open your eyes and acknowledge the habits in your life that consistently bring negative results and consequences to your life. You must acknowledge the habits that are keeping you in a cycle of falling short and losing in your life. Lastly but certainly most important, you must ultimately get tired of settling for less than you are capable of and continuously putting yourself in positions that keep you from obtaining the things you desire in your life and from going the places you want to go.

The constant taste of defeat in your life must sting enough to push you to take decisive action that will lead to better-tasting success in your future. Everyone experiences the pain of losses at some point or another in their life, but not everybody grows from their losses and makes the changes necessary for them to learn to win. Everybody who is winning in life was at one point in time losing in life- but they stuck to the work, found ways to improve, and made the necessary changes. Thus, they found a way to make it happen.

Once you have taken inventory of your habits and identified those that constantly lead you down the wrong paths and into undesirable situations, it's time to get to work on yourself and replace these habits with habits that lead you down better paths and into better situations. A habit becomes a habit because you have repeated the action multiple times in your life, to the point that your body begins to identify the action as part of your nature.

Your body even offers resistance when you first decide to stop engaging in the habit because it has been trained to perform the habit.

Change is one of the simplest concepts to understand in life from the logical understanding that you must do something different if you desire a different outcome. However, the human in us (our human nature) makes the process of change one that is much more complex than understanding the surface level logic behind change and its importance in guiding us towards better lives for ourselves. These complex ideologies come from various sources in our lives, and they make creating change one of the most uncomfortable and undesirable functions for humans.

There are many elements of our human nature that cause us to choose habits that aren't the most beneficial to us in our lives. The human brain's desire for comfort and homeostasis not only allows but *encourages* us to remain in the same actions and habits, even if those habits aren't leading us towards success or a life that we desire. Human emotion can oftentimes cause us to develop strong feelings that allow us to become attached to certain things and people to the point that we're unable to use logic and sound reasoning in our decision making. As we discussed in the first principle, by nature, humans are self-serving creatures whose habits solely support our own survival and well-being. When unconditioned by society, our human nature is no different than any other living species.

It's no secret that we are extremely flawed as human beings. In fact, developing strong, good habits requires us to go against all our natural instincts. The bottom line is that any habit that pulls you further away from who you want to be and where you want to be in life needs to go. By releasing these habits, you create room for the positive habits that will allow you to push towards becoming the person you want to become and living the life that you desire to live. Creating a better life for yourself starts with creating a better *you*. What you choose to do in your everyday life matters significantly, because these acts will ultimately lay the foundation for the finished product of who you become in your life.

The key to becoming your desired finished product by the end of your life is to find a way to tip the scales of life in your favor through the implementation of positive daily habits. You may be under the impression that you must immediately drop all your bad habits and turn your life around within a short period of time but that is an unrealistic expectation and not the case at all. The *end* goal is to rid yourself of your bad habits, but there is a process that must take place between the start and the end. It's important to understand that this is a gradual process, and you cannot suddenly quit all of the bad habits you have trained your body to do for weeks, months, and years of your life with the snap of your fingers.

The Compound Effect, a great book written by Darren Hardy, changed my life and my perspective on habits forever. I could write another book on the ways this book has impacted me alone but there was one quote in particular that stuck with me. When discussing the importance of habits, Hardy alludes to a quote from the great success mentor and life coach, Mr. Jim Rohn. He writes, "Success is not something you pursue. What you pursue will elude you; it can be like trying to chase butterflies. Success is something you attract by the person you become." This quote made such an impact on my life because I had never considered the perspective of tying success in my life to becoming a better *person*- I always thought of success as independent of who I was and completely dependent on what I achieved in my life. This piece of wisdom put into perspective how important my daily habits are to becoming successful in my life.

As we've already discussed, your daily habits play a major role in defining who you become in your life and the life that you live. Therefore, a major part of becoming the person you want to become and living the life that you want to live revolves around aligning your daily habits with the things you value and desire to attract most in your life. When you align your habits and actions with your values and desires, you begin to attract the things, people, and opportunities that you desire. You don't have to go aimlessly chasing them and make a fool of yourself in the process.

Reading this book by Darren Hardy was life-changing because it put me on the offensive side of life for the first time in my life. After playing defense for so long and just reacting (poorly) to what was happening in my life up to this point, this book got me thinking about what I could do to help myself out of the unfulfilling life I was living. It taught me that I could become whoever I wanted to become and attract whatever I desired in my life through my daily habits. It drilled home to me the importance of daily habits and how much the seemingly small things in life count for, which is much more than we like to give them credit for. It reminded me that I am the only one responsible for my life and making the choices necessary to live the life that I want to live.

In the same way that Hardy inspired me to go on the offensive in my life and to be proactive in shaping myself into the person I aspire to become and designing the life that I desire to live, I want to challenge you to go on the offensive and bring the fight to your life through your daily habits. Identify what you value and desire the most in your life and then make a conscious effort to build your daily decisions and habits around attracting those things and people of high value and desire to you into your life. The process is much easier said than done and will require you to sacrifice those comforts that are holding you back from the life that you desire, but becoming someone who is able to effectively use their mind to make sound decisions that attract the things they desire most is what maturation and personal development is all about.

Once again, the process of changing your habits is a gradual process. The last thing you want to do is attempt to quit all your bad habits all at once. This is a recipe for failure early in the process, which is the exact opposite of what you need in the beginning stages of changing your habits. Rather than setting yourself up for failure that will discourage you, set yourself up for success that will encourage you. You can do this by starting small with one or two simple habits that you want to include in your daily routine going forward.

These habits could be as simple as making your bed before you leave the house in the morning and leaving the house ten minutes earlier than usual to give yourself some cushion and avoid unnecessary stress to start your day. The start can be as simple as that– the important thing is *getting started* and committing yourself to adding these very simple actions to your daily routine. The size of the actions truly does not matter because they're simply laying the blueprint for the massive reconstruction to come in your life. All that matters is that you stay consistent in doing them. Through creating these simple habits, you will come to realize that though they are simple, they're effective and beneficial to you right away.

Making your bed in the morning starts your day off on the right foot. If you don't do anything else right for the rest of the day, you'll know that you started your day off right by making your bed. Don't get me wrong. Making your bed doesn't guarantee that every day will be great and all of your problems will go away, but it does put you into a great habit that allows you to be successful at the start of the day. No matter how big or small the task, you can never go wrong with making the effort to start your day off on the right foot.

Making your bed every morning also contributes to maintaining a clean living space, which allows you to feel less cluttered and more organized. A clean living space has been scientifically proven to decrease feelings of stress and anxiousness. We often tell ourselves that we're too busy to keep our living space as clean as we'd like or don't have the means to hire someone to do it for us at the moment. Making your bed before you leave the house isn't going to miraculously declutter the rest of your living space and organize all the shelves that line your walls, but it will shift your mindset towards appreciating your living space and doing the small, daily things that are necessary to make gradual improvements holistically in your living space.

This is a very easy way to start your day with a small win, which when combined with other small wins throughout the day, builds momentum to create the massive wins in your life. The massive wins often get the most recognition and appreciation, but it's the multitude of daily, small wins that do the heavy lifting to make the major wins possible. These major wins are just the tip of the iceberg, what becomes noticeable to both us and the outside world. Beneath the surface, way deep into the frigid waters that lie below the surface, is the foundation of the tip of that iceberg– the numerous small wins and daily actions that nobody saw or applauded that led to the breakthrough that everybody sees and applauds.

Similar to making your bed in the morning, it takes hardly any effort to leave your house ten minutes earlier than you normally would. It's such a small detail in your day that it seems like it's insignificant. That is, until you notice how much less stressed you are during your commute to work or other important places. Traffic and minor inconveniences no longer add stress to your mornings. Your habit of speeding to work that puts you at risk of a speeding ticket or an accident no longer seems necessary. Eventually, you get in the habit of leaving ten minutes earlier to go *everywhere*, because you begin to appreciate the calmness of not feeling rushed. This is another very easy way to start your day with a small win that has the potential to give life to the much larger wins that you will make room for in your life along the way.

One small habit is all it takes to start your days off in a positive direction. Very little time or effort is involved in adding these habits into your day. As crazy as it seems, this is how the changes that will move mountains in your life begin. You likely will choose different habits to start with than the examples that I gave but the principle remains the same.

The start of becoming a better version of yourself often takes no longer than fifteen minutes of your day. These fifteen minutes will likely become the wisest investment of fifteen minutes you ever make. You can and will radically change yourself and your life by showing up for yourself in the smallest ways to begin each day. Never underestimate the power of taking small steps towards progress in your life because the truth is all progress starts small.

After you have successfully implemented your initial habit or two into your daily routine, push yourself to add in one or two more over the next few weeks. Once again, they don't have to be your worst habits or the ones you struggle with the most. Continue the path of simple and low-demanding changes. Get into the habit of creating better habits before you try and attack the habits that have been attacking your potential for the majority of your life. Early on in this process, gaining the psychological advantage over your mind and proving to yourself that you can create additional success for yourself through small commitments is the main objective.

You will find that through committing to just a few small, barely noticeable changes in your life, you have already created small improvements and success in your life. These changes aren't major, so the success may not seem major at first either. Like all progress, all success must start somewhere too. There is no such thing as success that is too small because success is a compounding element– major success comes as a result of many small successes stacking on top of one another.

However, going back to the example of starting habits I gave, making your bed in the morning could encourage you to also tidy up your office space. You've noticed the benefits of not having clutter around your living space at home and you now want to bring those same benefits to your workplace, and guess what? Your other daily habit also has resulted in you getting to work a few minutes earlier each day, which provides you some extra time to begin this process of tidying up your office space and creating an environment that allows you to feel your best, while also performing your best work.

Your good habits are now working together to accelerate your output and your productivity. This productivity is not only limited to your home or job, but it becomes an area of focus no matter where you are. This is the greatest power of committing to making small changes in your daily habits because implementing those small actions will create the time and opportunity to begin other small actions in your daily routine that will also accelerate your output and increase your productivity.

This is exactly what happens when you just begin *somewhere.* You notice the positive results of these changes and you naturally start to look for other areas that you can improve and experience these same benefits in all areas of your life. Before you know it, you're a much more productive and efficient human being- and living a much higher quality of life as a result. You're only a decision and a few habits away from the life that you dream of but it's the patience to continue to nourish those habits in between the transformation from small success to major success that will take you there.

The "snowball effect" is normally given a negative connotation because we use it to discuss how negative occurrences can create the momentum for more negative occurrences to pile on top of those we're already dealing with and create an entire downhill mess in our lives. Is it possible that the same effect could be used to describe positive occurrences in life? Could we apply the snowball effect to packing the snow back on and rebuilding our snowballs into stronger, more durable snowballs that don't fall apart so easily this time? I would argue that this is a strong possibility and the perfect example of this is the process of continuing to pile on healthy habits.

Why don't we create an uphill surge with all the positive momentum we have created in our lives for once? What is true of negative occurrences in our lives can also be true of positive occurrences in our lives, *if* we are willing to shift our mindset and understand that everything in life works in a balance. There can be no negative without positive to maintain balance and vice versa. The same way that negativity can build up in your life and spiral you into a low point in your life, positivity can build up in your life and propel you to places you could've never even imagined. There's always going to be negative around the positive and positive around the negative, but what's going to really separate you in your life is becoming someone who is willing to go for it and put their faith in the positive.

When you experience those negative build ups and see yourself headed for a low in life, understand that there is an equal opportunity for a build-up of positivity and breakthrough, right beyond your fears and limiting beliefs. You'll be amazed at how the universe works to maintain balance in your life once you understand balance and seek it out. It does a person no good to be naive to the fact of the potential for negative results in life, but one must also understand that there is the same potential for positive results and breakthrough in their life. Perspective is everything and you can't expect to build a life with a strong foundation with weak faith and a weak mindset.

Newton's first law is a staple in physics and it will also be a staple in your development as a human being. Whether the law works in your favor or against you is up to you and the habits that you choose for your life, but it will play a role in your development one way or another. The law simply states that "an object that is in motion will remain in motion, unless its speed and direction are affected by an outside source".

Your self-sabotaging ways and your poor habits that lead you down the path towards a life that leaves you unfulfilled and continuously falling short of reaching your potential is that object in motion. Gone are the days where that object remains in constant motion against your goals and ambitions. That object in motion may feel like it's moving 100 miles per hour in your direction right now. You may feel lost and hopeless, terrified to step in its way. It may feel like it's taking everything out of you and beating you into submission.

I've been in this exact place in my life more times than I can tell you. I'm here to tell you that you aren't alone in this battle against the internal pain and shame it's bringing you to be stuck in habits that are below your standards for yourself. I'm also here to tell you that no matter how defeated and hopeless you may feel, *you* are the only one with the power to turn the tide and win this battle. *You* must become the "outside source" to disrupt this constant motion of mediocrity and unfulfillment in your life that is keeping you in bondage. Your *habits* must become the force to put control over the outcome of your back in your possession.

There are endless choices of ways to spend your time in today's world. Amongst these choices, there's no shortage of ways to focus on your personal development, but I believe there are three areas of your life that you must focus on daily to improve your quality of life: spiritual wellness, mental wellness, and physical wellness. These are the areas of your life that your habits must compliment the *most* if you desire to grow as a human being and seek better results in your life. While these are not the only areas of life that contribute to growth and better results, these three areas of focus are instrumental in shaping the life you live and the person you become in your process.

Spiritual wellness is the most important focus of your health as a human being because it is at the head of everything else in your life. Without a healthy spirit that satisfies your needs, it's impossible to satisfy any of your other needs and to find fulfillment in any other area of your life. There are many different interpretations of spiritual wellness, but I prefer to keep it simple and focus on just two very important concepts– the spirit and the soul.

You're probably wondering what's the difference between the two, as they are often mistaken for one another. However, they're very different and serve completely different purposes, despite their similarities. I didn't research these or include any exact definitions because I have my own perspective on these two concepts that I believe help to distinguish one from the other.

Your soul is what makes you human. It allows you to exchange energy with other human beings, which allows you to complete functions such as creating memories with other human beings and feeling emotion. In essence, your soul is what connects you to the rest of the world. You feel energy from others and you give off energy that is felt by others. This connection and exchange of energy occurs on a deeper level beyond what meets the eye, so it can't be physically seen but can be felt. This connection is what you experience when you feel connected or attracted to another human being beyond "the physical" -there is a connection beyond what can be physically seen.

Your spirit is your deepest level of connection to a higher power. To simplify this concept, I would describe your spirit as your deepest connection to all things good and virtuous within you. This connection is deeply tied into the core moral and ethical values that you possess, along with your thought processes and your perspective of your life and its meaning. Your greater purpose that you have been reminded of throughout this book is found within your spirit, where it will hopefully be discovered by you and brought into fruition through a flame within your soul and relentless commitment to yourself to avoid the path of least resistance. Whether you believe in a higher power or consider yourself to have no religious affiliation at all, your spirit is the realm that you must become aware of to know and understand what drives you to live a life of purpose and meaning.

That being said, your spirit and your soul have the biggest impact on who you are as a person. If you lack awareness and fail to implement habits into your life to strengthen your connection and understanding of these two very important parts of yourself, you will be lacking in many other areas of your life as well. The reason that these are such an important part of who you are and learning how to bring your desires into your life is because *everything* else in your life is shaped by these two things.

The spirit and the soul lead your thoughts, decisions, and actions as a human being. If you're following a weak, uncertain leader, how can you have confidence that you will end up where you're supposed to be? The simple answer is that you can't have definite confidence that you will end up where you're supposed to be by following a leader who is undeveloped, uncertain, and has yet to prove they can reach the places they claim they can help you reach. These two things are very important. Feed them the right things and get to know them well, because they need to be sharp and strong to *lead* you in everything that you will do in your new and improved life.

Developing habits to strengthen your spirit could be as simple as starting your mornings with a ten-minute devotion to spend time getting to understand your faith on a deeper level. Developing habits to strengthen your soul could be as simple as pushing yourself to speak to strangers more, allowing yourself to both release and experience new forms of positive energy in your soul and feel more connected to your sense of humanity. These are two very simple examples that show just how simple it is to invest in strengthening these critical components.

The bottom line is you're not serious about improving yourself and creating a better life for yourself if you can't devote fifteen minutes of your day to become more in touch with your spirit and your soul. Stop disrespecting your potential and value your life. It only takes a few changes to create the momentum that can change the rest of your life. If you continue to neglect the basics and fundamentals of small changes, how can you ever expect to reach the mastery that is required to create the bigger changes you desire in your life?

The next core area of focus that your habits should support is your mental wellness. Allowing unhealthy thoughts to go unchecked for too long eventually leads to an unhealthy mind, so it's important to always be aware of your thoughts and the state of your mental space. You must take responsibility for feeding your mind positive and constructive information, while protecting it from harmful, unnecessary information. If you feed the mind whole, unprocessed information, the mind grows strong and healthy. If you allow the mind to become consumed by junk and processed information, the mind grows ill and lethargic.

Your mind and your thoughts are shaped by your spirit and your soul. Then, your body follows your mind. Similar to your spirit and soul, if you have a weak and unhealthy mind, your body will follow through with weak and unhealthy actions that hinder you from

186

growing into your highest self and living life at your full potential. Your body's physical performance can only be as strong as your mind allows it to be. Get your mind right, along with your spirit and your soul, and your physical body will follow through with a strong performance to eventually provide you with the favorable outcomes you seek in your life.

I will continue to emphasize the power of small changes in your daily habits throughout this chapter. You don't have to go from being overly stressed, anxiety-ridden, and a chronic overthinker to a calm and collected monk overnight. In fact, you will never be completely "calm" if you're pursuing a life that's meaningful to you. Small doses of stress and anxiety are essentially healthy indicators that you're pursuing something that stimulates you and has meaning to you. These feelings mean that your success means something to you, that you are alive and well in your pursuit to fulfill your purpose in your life.

These feelings simply indicate that you're pursuing *life*, rather than just wasting your breaths. As often as we forget this truth, it's supposed to be difficult at times. It's scary, stressful, exhausting, and downright nerve-wracking to begin the process of building something without the guarantee that the finished product will be one that is sufficient. These are normal emotions to experience in the process but it's important that we make sense of these emotions and allow them to push us *forward* into our purpose and not backwards into a corner of fear and inaction.

Once again, building the habits that will allow you to win in this life is a matter of making small sacrifices that compound on top of one another to create massive change in your life. Winning in life doesn't always have to look like becoming the wealthiest person on your street or buying your dream car for yourself. Without a doubt, those are positive milestones and major wins if those are the goals that you set for yourself. However, it's important to understand that there were many small, tedious wins that built on top of each other to eventually create the possibility for those milestone wins. Just because you aren't at the end of the road yet, it doesn't negate all the good that you've done and will continue to do on the way to your bigger successes.

There's nothing wrong with having breakthrough goals and aiming for milestones of high achievement, but you must first learn to seek the small wins that are available for the taking in your everyday life. Seeking these small wins out, doing the work that's necessary to obtain them, and remaining consistent is what will *begin* the process of changing your life for the better. Society has us under this notion that you can wake up and change your life any day that you choose, and this is true to an extent– but that one day is just the beginning of a much deeper process. You must learn how to win small before you can realistically expect to win big.

The final core area of focus that your habits should support is your physical wellness. While there is more to life than the way you look, you can't put a price on having good health and being able to show up for yourself and the people counting on you day in and day out. You're working hard to become a better version of yourself and create a better life for yourself and you must keep yourself healthy and feeling fresh to be able to enjoy the fruits of your hard labor.

If you are experiencing numerous health issues that resulted from your decisions in your habits, then you won't be able to reap the benefits of all your hard work to the fullest. In essence, all of this would be for nothing. The bottom line is you must physically be here and feel the best you possibly can for you to end up at the best possible destination in this beautiful journey called life. The goal isn't to improve your life, just to lose it prematurely to poor health– the goal is to be here, feeling healthy, and with the means to continue to make positive contributions to society for as long as you possibly can.

There is no denying the fact that it can be difficult and expensive to maintain good physical health at times. It's often more expensive to buy the right foods and more time consuming to prepare them in more natural, organic ways than simply dropping them in a boiling fryer full of grease that will do the trick in just a few minutes. Without a doubt, it takes discipline and requires an investment of your time, energy, money, and commitment to live and feel your best.

We make investments every single day of our lives, investments that we have decided are worth the risks and sacrifices. I must ask you which of these investments are worth your time, energy, money, and commitment if the quality of your life is not worth at *least* the same investment? The answer is none of them are because you are worth the investment today and you will be worth the investment for as long as you live.

Get active and move. Take the time to learn how to cook more whole foods and healthy meals rather than living off the easy and "cheap" processed foods that flood the shelves. You may save yourself a little cash in your wallet by buying these foods but they place a heavy tax on your nutrition and overall wellness. Gradually reduce your sugar intake, as too much of it will cause inflammation, weight gain, and could increase your risk of diabetes, among other health issues. Cut back on your alcohol consumption that's causing you to age quicker and altering your decision-making capabilities. Sacrifice that last hour of entertainment TV for an extra hour of sleep to help you recover and reach optimal functioning. None of these decisions require significant effort or financial means from you but they have the power to change your life forever. It's these small, daily decisions and sacrifices that separate a fulfilled, successful life from an unfulfilled life that falls short of your definition of a successful life.

The areas of your lifestyle that you view as cheap and insignificant today have the potential to cost you greatly later in your life and have a significant impact on the quality of your future life. Poor physical health knows no limits and mercy when it comes to the impact it can have on your life. If you aren't mindful and making your physical wellness a priority, you could end up paying through crippling means later in your life. Some even pay for their poor choice of habits and neglect of taking care of their physical health with their life itself, which is an absolute tragedy.

Nothing in this world is worth inflicting these difficulties or death on yourself. You've already made it this far, what good is it if you can't enjoy it? If you don't prioritize physical wellness and make an effort to establish it in your life, it will make no effort to establish itself in your life. Take care of your physical wellness and it will take care of you along the journey.

The habits that you implement to develop these parts of yourself will look different for everyone and there is no universal formula for guaranteed success. Like most everything else related to human lifestyle, it's a matter of trial and error. You try different things until you figure out what works for you and what doesn't work for you. Once you find what works best for you, remain consistent and never stop doing it. It doesn't have to be complex or stressful. Most of the time, it takes very little time or effort to do something that your future self will appreciate you for. It's simply showing up for yourself and remaining consistent, no matter how big or how small the impact may seem in the moment.

Developing better habits largely consist of consistently doing small, simple, and oftentimes boring tasks at a high level and with intentionality. It's not rocket science or some secret formula that only some people were given access to that separates the successful from the unsuccessful. It's a decision to consistently show up for yourself day in and day out. This is a decision that most people neglect to make for themselves, which is why only a small percentage of people reach the success that they're capable of reaching in their lives.

I believe Darren Hardy's outlook on forming habits sums up the power of building good habits beautifully. In order to attract the people you desire, the opportunities you desire, and all your other desires in life, your daily habits and decisions must reflect those that would attract these desires to you. This isn't the rule of magnetism that you so often hear when people try to explain why a gorgeous, "life-of-the-party" type of woman is with an unattractive and socially awkward man. Opposites do not attract in this case and your money and wit can't buy you good habits. Only your effort and intentionality can buy you good habits, which is why building good habits holds all the value in the world but costs little to nothing compared to the material things we value in life.

You must become someone that the person you desire a relationship with would be happy to be in a relationship with. You must become a candidate that meets the qualifications for that great opportunity for that opportunity to have mutual interest in you. Your dream job isn't going to land in your LinkedIn inbox without you first doing the work to make yourself attractive to the person responsible for hiring the very best prospects they can find. This is the beauty of life. You can have anything you desire in your life, if you're willing to become someone who attracts those desires through your actions and hard work.

Who wants anything handed to them? The *work* and who you become in the process of doing the work is the real reward and where the real changes occur in your life. Everything else is a by-product of committing yourself to growth and doing what's necessary to achieve that growth within yourself. We spend so much time focused on the ending destination of the journey that we often neglect to acknowledge the fact that the real reward is who we become in the process of going through our journey.

Without enduring the process, you wouldn't know how to properly cherish and have the genuine appreciation for watching your dreams and goals manifest despite all the challenges and forces of opposition that once stood in the way. You would find yourself lost in a constant cycle of mishandling the very things that you prayed and worked so hard for. This is no knock or personal dig at you, because as humans, we all naturally take for granted those things that we haven't sacrificed our own time, energy, and effort for. The sweat equity and the effort that you apply to changing as a person ensure that you understand the true value of your dreams and are willing to make the sacrifices necessary to obtain them.

As a result of having sweat equity and effort invested into your dreams, you will be someone who has matured and prepared themselves for the time when your opportunities arise. When things come easy to us, they tend to lose their value to us. It is a blessing that your dreams require blood, sweat, tears, discipline, and sacrifice for you to bring them to reality one day. You're too capable and you hold too much value to the world to waste your talents and ambitions on chasing "cheap" dreams– the resistance is supposed to be there! The difficulties that stand in the way of your dream validate its significance and value to you.

I wouldn't be writing this if I didn't believe in the power of these words and have proof that this small principle can change your life forever. I'm living proof of the power of this principle and the shifts that small changes in your mindset and your habits can make in your life. Though I'm still in the process of chasing my dreams and haven't reaped the fruits of my labor yet financially, I've begun to reap the fruits of my labor in the quality of my life and witnessed true transformation in my thoughts and habits over this period of transformation in my life.

I'm now chasing true substance and meaning in my life, not just the closest substance I can get my hands on to "escape" from my difficulties and struggles in life. I give all the credit in my life's turnaround to God for not giving up on me. His wisdom and virtue have allowed me to become committed to showing up for myself every single day in a way that attracts the things and people that I desire into my life. Small changes and consistency have changed the trajectory of my entire life and I have no doubt in my mind that they will do the same for you.

I'm mindful of my environment and only desire to be around the things and people who inspire me and push me to improve and elevate. I've put in time and effort into developing my spiritual wellness, mental wellness, and physical wellness. I've gone to great lengths to ensure that I'm in an environment that fits what I want my environment to look like, despite what environment others may have wanted for me. I've put myself in the situation I used to dream about through hard work and focus. I don't have everything I desire in life, but I'm slowly developing the mentality and attention to detail that'll allow me to take what I desire from this life.

I haven't reached my breakthrough success yet, but I've broken through so many barriers and distractions that once had a firm hold on my life. Those breakthroughs that seem invisible right now will pay huge dividends later in my life because they've allowed me to focus and start the work that has led me to see myself and my potential in a completely different light than ever before. I've become a much better representation of the success that I desire for my life through my actions and the daily habits that I have built for myself. For this reason, I wholeheartedly believe I will attract everything that is meant for me in due time.

I'm a human being and I go through the same struggles that any other human being goes through. Admittedly, I have setbacks and bumps in the road where I catch myself going back to thoughts and sometimes even actions of my old ways. Temptation is real and it takes great strength to resist those harmful behaviors that were once so familiar and comforting to us. I'm still at war with my sinful flesh each and every day just like every other human being, but I'm now aware of this spiritual warfare and doing my best to better equip myself for victory with each day that I lean into focusing on building good habits to live a more disciplined, virtuous life.

I now understand that a tested spirit is a strong spirit, so I look at every test, whether I pass or fail, as an opportunity to learn, grow, and build a stronger connection to the good that lies within me. When it's all said and done, you will never be perfect and I will never be perfect. The most that we can ask for is that we're able to learn from and grow through our imperfections. I don't look anything like some of the poor choices I've made or some of the things I've been through in my life– I thank God and the love and support of my family and friends for that.

I will be prepared to reach for my dreams when the opportunity to grab them arises, not because I'm any more deserving than anyone else or because I've completely mastered myself and all my own foolishness. The only distinguishing factor between what I've done and what the masses do is that I took the first step and decided to take *full* responsibility for the one person that I can control in this world– myself. I don't have it all figured out, and I never will have every solution to every problem in the world. Not only have I accepted this truth, but I've also found comfort in this. I don't have to be perfect to become the best version of myself that I can be and to live the life that I desire.

I must simply maintain good habits and be better today than I was yesterday. If I commit to following that standard for the rest of my life, the future has no choice but to be brighter than my past and the times in which I was living without direction in my life. One great thing about finding yourself in a horrible place in your life is that there's a whole lot of room for improvement! There is nothing beneath that place at rock bottom, where you're on your ass and staring up at the sky above you– the only way you can go is up! Eventually the bottom gets uncomfortable and you get back up on your feet and try again.

I didn't start out reading my Bible every day consistently, working out rigorously five times a week, or reading a new book every single week. I would be wrong to tell you that I did. My process started with very small changes. As I grew more comfortable with change in my life, I began to do a little more until I was eventually living with completely different habits and philosophies on life. Improving my habits allowed me to focus inward and to see the world and this life differently, which helped me understand the magnitude of doing all I can to put myself in a position to reach for my goals and aspirations with everything I have in my being.

Before I got into the habit of reading my Bible and doing devotion daily, I first got over the shame I was feeling and found the courage to open my Bible once and ask for forgiveness. Before I was in a consistent gym routine, I would get in the gym on days I had spare time and found myself bored. Before I was reading a new book every week, I went through periods of my life where I couldn't even tell you what the last book I read in full was. In fact, the last book that I read in full up until I was in college was most likely the Harry Potter book I "read" in middle school to give me enough points to not miss the pizza party they would throw for the kids who had earned enough reading points for the month.

Back on topic, I first picked up a book and started skimming once every few days, then eventually I rediscovered my love for reading. More importantly, I found the *value* in reading and educating myself. It didn't all happen overnight, and my process is still happening as you read these words, but small, deliberate actions and a strong desire to improve my life started the change of the tide in my life that has resulted in the person I am today. Small, deliberate actions led to the first page of this book and the consistency in those actions eventually filled the remaining pages.

As I've said throughout the course of this book, it was done for me so it can surely be done for you as well. You simply must want it for yourself more than you want the comfort of remaining in your bad habits and vices. It's fine to be in a dark place in your life and unhappy with where you are, but you owe it to yourself to crawl out of that dark place and find the light again. Where you start or the mistakes you make in the beginning in life aren't how your life's legacy is defined, but where you finish and how you bounce back from those mistakes that you made in the beginning to finish strong is what defines your life's legacy.

Stop beating yourself up about the mistakes you've made to end up with the life you have now and focus on showing up for yourself out of love and appreciation for yourself to create a better future. If you've made mistakes in your life, and I know you have, it's not the end of the world. In fact, you're in great company! You have something in common with not only every other human being but some of the most influential and successful human beings to walk the face of the earth. Every single human being makes mistakes, but not every human being *learns* from their mistakes. Learning from your mistakes and being willing to change is the response that will develop good habits and allow you to create a better future for yourself moving forward.

Good habits often seem like they grow legs and run away from us. Everybody claims they want good habits in their life but there's not too many who are willing to sacrifice their bad habits. While implementing good habits is a challenge, I know from personal experience that living with bad habits comes with its own challenges as well. The only difference is that one group of challenges contributes to living at your full potential and building you up and the other group of challenges breaks you down.

It goes back to the fact that life is a game of suffering and sacrifice. You suffer for something either way. What you aren't willing to suffer for becomes the sacrifice. Will you choose to suffer for positive changes in your life and sacrifice the things and people that are holding you back, or will you choose to continue to suffer living the life you have created for yourself by remaining in your poor habits and sacrificing the better life that you desire and are fully capable of building?

If you're struggling to wrap your head around letting go of your bad habits, try thinking about it from the perspective that you're sacrificing your dreams and goals each time you give in to your bad habits. Go ahead and delete the idea from your head that a life without suffering and sacrifice is possible because it's an illusion that is causing you to remain stagnant in your life. For new opportunities and abundance to come into your life, you must make room for them.

Some sacrifices are necessary for you to become the person that you're meant to be and for you to experience all the love and fulfillment that is destined for you in this life. Sacrificing things and people you love is one of the hardest decisions you can make in your life, but it is also one of the most important decisions that you *must* make in your life. It is imperative that you shed yourself of the weight that is holding you back if you want to live in freedom and reach your potential.

That weight must go, and you must begin moving towards building better habits and a better lifestyle, or you will continue to be anchored in the same places you currently find yourself in life. The very captain that can free your ship from its anchor is right there in front of you every single time you look in the mirror, and you'll be surprised at how much skill that captain possesses when he (or she) is at his (or her) best.

In fact, you will likely find that the anchor wasn't the main factor of the environment that was holding the ship stagnant. It was the captain's *belief* that the anchor was capable of stopping him from putting the ship back into motion that kept his ship stagnant. Locate the anchor, remove the anchor from underneath you, and learn to set sail again. If only you knew what awaited you if you just got back going, you'd be racing to release that anchor and discover all the great things that are meant for you on your journey.

You are capable of becoming the person you've always dreamed of becoming. You are capable of building the life that you've always dreamed of living. The steps to doing so are fundamentally simple, but they will not be easy. This is your dream self and your dream life that we're talking about. Surely, it's worth enduring a little suffering for life-changing growth, right? This is exactly how it will happen. You will achieve becoming both the person you've always dreamed of becoming and building the life you've always dreamed of living through your *good habits*.

You will suffer for short intervals, and you will find yourself uncomfortable and questioning your decision to be different from your friends, family, and the rest of the world. On the other side of that discomfort and uncertainty, you will experience growth and form an identity that allows you to be confident in the person that you're becoming. Suddenly, that short-term suffering will be viewed with a little more enthusiasm each time it forces itself onto you, because you now realize that short-term suffering tends to bring massive gains into your life.

In the same way that short-term suffering yields growth on the other side of the pain and discomfort, building good habits yields a better version of yourself that can do anything you put your mind to in your life. Show up for yourself with the intention of showing up better than you were yesterday and you will slowly but surely become better today than you were yesterday. By getting better each day, you can only get closer to the life you desire. Although it can feel lonely at times, you're not alone in your suffering and on your journey. We must experience the suffering before we can experience the breakthrough, so learn to look forward to your sufferings. They are the tests that qualify you for your promotions in your life.

I've shared with you some of the things I was battling before changing my habits and seeking direction in my life. No matter how I was choosing to live my life, I can honestly say that I always felt there was more out there for me in the world. When the girls left, the smoke cleared, and the liquor had been slept off, I was always left feeling even emptier than before. I didn't want to live my life like this and I eventually found an obsession with discovering my true purpose and ambitions in life that saved me. It took courage, losing friends, and making decisions that invited unfamiliar feelings and emotions into my life and the lives of those closest to me.

I felt alone throughout the process at times and misunderstood by people I was begging to understand me. You will lose a lot and you will view important people in your life differently in some ways. It will be difficult at times to work towards a vision that it feels like nobody else can see. If no one else in the world does (which I can almost guarantee is not the case), I want you to know that I believe in you to make the small, daily changes necessary for you to become who you want to become and to live the life that you want to live! I believe in you to just start *somewhere,* and that by staying committed through your process, that you will become someone who can go *anywhere* they desire and win with any hand they've been dealt.

201

Chapter Eight

Principle #8: Exercise is free medicine– medicate at least 3 times a week.

Let's face it. Right now, you are the oldest you have ever been in your life at the very moment that you're reading this. You're now even older than you were from the time you read the sentence before this. From this point on, you will only continue to get older and older. This may seem like a change of pace from the positive, encouraging tone of this book so far, but I'm only saying all of this to say this– you aren't getting any younger and your body is only deteriorating with each day that passes. Now that I've gotten that out of the way, we can go back to being positive and finding the solution to slowing this process of aging and deterioration down, which will help us enjoy our lives a lot longer.

Your body is in fact getting older. There's nothing you can do about this obviously because "Father Time" is alive and has never been defeated throughout the course of history. However, it can be slowed down tremendously. Through constant use of the muscles and taking care of your body, you can remain strong, able-bodied, and feeling up to par for the entirety of your life. While getting active and living a healthy lifestyle does come with its challenges and lots of soreness at times, there are endless benefits to getting your body moving and consistently working your muscles. Choosing the more challenging route to produce better, more fulfilling results has been the theme of this book and this principle is no different.

We just spoke about the importance of your daily habits in the previous principle, and getting into an exercise routine is one of the most beneficial habits you can develop for yourself. Contrary to popular belief, personal fitness is a way of life for many people for many reasons other than the increased physical attraction that often comes from consistent exercise. The physical benefits are nice and help to keep you motivated on your fitness journey, but there's a much bigger picture to personal fitness and the reasons it has become an important part of so many lives. These reasons vary within all of us, but the main driving force behind adopting good personal fitness habits is the simple fact that you only get *one* body and *one* life.

There are no "do-overs" if you don't take care of your body properly. For this reason, some people tend to take their physical health and wellness quite seriously. You may not be included in this group of people who make their physical health and wellness a top priority and that's perfectly fine. Regardless of who you are and what you give priority in your life, you should find at least three days to exercise in some form for at least 30 minutes throughout any given seven-day week. This isn't just my suggestion or opinion– this is *science's* suggestion. You can ignore me all you want but please don't ignore the facts and science.

Exercise's impact on your life starts with building a stronger and healthier body for yourself, but your journey into developing and mastering your personal fitness will also teach you so much about yourself and life. You're probably wondering how in the world exercise could possibly teach you about yourself and life. It's just a series of movements that cause you to sweat and feel better about yourself, isn't it? You're right, it is a series of movements that produce sweat. However, it takes a certain level of discipline and love for yourself to make the commitment to get these daily movements in. You will come to find that these increases in self-discipline and self-love are the real benefits of exercising and getting active, not the six-pack abs that you get to run around the beach with.

For example, from the surface, a back squat is a simple exercise that helps increase strength all throughout your legs by resting a barbell with the weight you choose on the backside of your shoulders and squatting until your thighs and butt are parallel with the ground, while keeping your chest up and tightening your core to keep your lower back flat to support the weight of the barbell that is on the backside of your shoulders. Back squats are a staple of "leg day" for many lifters and have proven to be very beneficial in developing leg strength, core strength, burning calories, and even assisting in injury-prevention. They're one of the best all-around lifts you can do to target multiple areas of your body, building strength and definition in multiple parts of your body. Based on the information I've given you, it sounds like back squats are relatively simple to do and they produce great benefits. Why wouldn't people do them?

Though back squats are relatively simple to do and produce great benefits, they become harder to do with each rep. It's important to keep in mind that the best results only come as a result of doing reps consistently and correctly. Due to the fact that they use so many muscles and target different areas of the body, they're one of the most demanding exercises available in the entire gym. They demand more energy and focus than most other lifts because that chest must stay up and that core must remain tight and engaged to support the lower back as it's supporting the weight of the barbell– every single rep.

The more reps you get through, the more your legs start to burn, abs begin to contract, and energy levels dwindle. This is where focus and grit become key factors in pushing through and getting the most out of the pain you're experiencing. When you no longer have the same physical energy and strength that you began with, pushing through a set of back squats becomes dependent on pure focus and mental toughness. No matter how strong you think you are or how strong you may look, that barbell and its weight are going to test you with every rep.

Life is also like a tough set of back squats. The direction and the success of your life becomes dependent on pure focus and mental toughness when you've become worn out and feel your energy and passion dwindling. An overlooked area of strength that exercise works to improve has nothing to do with height, weight, strength, speed, or any other physically measurable attribute. Exercise provides mental strength that instills core components that translate directly into all other areas of life. Better discipline, newfound mental toughness, learning to finish what you start, becoming tolerant of pain for a greater good, changing your self-image, and gaining confidence in yourself are all possibilities that you open yourself up to when you get active and exercise on a regular basis. These are areas of your life that upon diligently working on them and improving them, will lead you to see improvement in how you view yourself and your life.

When your legs are burning and your abs feel like they're about to split your body in half, but you still have two squats to go to finish your set, it doesn't matter how physically gifted or strong you are at that point. You're faced with a decision at that moment, to give up on the set and rack the weight two reps shy of completing your set or taking a deep breath and enduring a few more seconds of pain to complete your set. The first option almost immediately relieves the pain, but you're left with the dissatisfaction of not reaching your goal for yourself. The second option involves willingly throwing yourself right into the pain and discomfort to feel even more of it, but you endure those few seconds of misery and are left with a sense of pride in yourself for the rest of your day for not giving up on your goal.

No matter which option you choose, the physical pain you were feeling fades away almost as soon as you rack the weight and step outside of the squat rack. However, one option gets the job done and one doesn't. A few additional seconds of pain and discomfort separate the man who finished the job from the man who left the job incomplete. Both men were capable of completing the job. Deep down, the man who gave up and left the job incomplete knows this truth.

After all, he was *seconds* away from achieving his goal and not having to carry the guilt and shame of racking his weight prematurely. He allowed the pain to convince him that he didn't have anything left in the tank to give, and this is one of the first lies that the mind will tell you when you're going through something that's uncomfortable and unpleasant. It is at this moment that you are faced with the choice to endure the pain and get through it, or you can make the choice to find the quickest path away from the pain and discomfort you're feeling. It is often these moments, usually a matter of seconds, that separate the strong from the weak.

This doesn't only apply in the world of back squats and exercising. This same concept also applies to life. This is what I mean by exercise will teach you about yourself and life. Exercise will make you aware of your weaknesses beyond your physical capacity, while helping you strengthen those weaknesses. You will have a stronger body, but more importantly, you will become a stronger *person* in all areas of your life by challenging yourself and fortifying your mind to avoid shutting down when you're going through pain or a difficult experience.

It may appear to just be a set of back squats at the gym, with nobody's life or well-being on the line. However, those tough nights in the gym when it's just you, your headphones, and your thoughts, can put you in an entirely different headspace than you were in before those tough, lonely nights in the gym. Constantly enduring the pain and learning to speak to yourself in a way that's encouraging and empowering builds confidence and fortitude within a person beyond the gym and that squat rack. These positive habits stick with you in all other areas of your life and they begin to introduce you to the true potential and strength that you possess. They introduce you to the real you, which is oftentimes someone that you never knew existed within you. You find out in time that it was always in you– you just had to train your mind and your body in a way that would bring the best out of you.

In a world where much of your focus goes to other people and outside obligations, exercising and personal fitness are times to focus on *you* for a change. It's your *personal* fitness, not anybody else's. Time spent taking care of your body and improving your fitness is time unplugged from the world and instilling love and appreciation for yourself and your health into you. This time isn't about anybody but you.

It's time to acknowledge an important truth of life. It's you versus you every single day. You are your own greatest adversary. Every single rep you push through or don't push through counts and it's up to you if you grow stronger or if you become weaker. Your physical body and your health are your greatest physical assets and this time moving your muscles allows you to protect and cherish those two things in a manner that will allow them to take you the distance. Nobody else can do it for you.

Once you begin exercising and focusing on your fitness, you will notice some changes within yourself physically and mentally. People love the benefits of exercise and the time to themselves but let's be honest– all exercise hurts in some shape or form. The difference is that to some, the pain is worth the benefits. Therefore, the pain is associated with a positive experience. By going through that pain and reaping the benefits consistently, you're gradually strengthening both your mind and body. Once again, this concept applies to more than just exercise. It applies to the rest of your life as well.

By putting yourself through small intervals of suffering to see improvements in your health, you become willing to put yourself through intervals of suffering for improvements in other areas of your life as well. The pain is temporary, but the results are everlasting with the right mindset and maintenance. The body is resilient and the more it becomes repeatedly exposed to a feeling or sensation, the less that feeling or sensation is able to have the same effect on the body that it did when it was first exposed to it. The more your body is exposed to these brief intervals of pain, the less the pain is able to affect you and take you away from your focus on the task at hand.

That confidence to withstand pain from exercising for physical and mental wellness also builds your confidence in yourself to do the other hard things in your life that may cause you pain and discomfort. Now that you know there's a reward on the other side of going through that pain, you're less likely to continue to shy away from that pain and allow your fear of experiencing pain to have control over your life. The bottom line is that the feeling of working hard and overcoming challenges produces healthy sources of dopamine that you need to stay inspired and engaged. You begin to crave it in other aspects of your life outside of your personal fitness.

Life is an event that requires mental toughness to find success in. Challenging your body daily to maintain a standard of fitness and health not only prepares your physical body to endure the physical demands of life, but it also prepares your mind to take on the challenges that life will bring your way mentally. Having a strong mind and being able to control your thoughts and reactions to what happens around you is just as important as having the ability to demonstrate physical strength when called upon, if not even more important. Over the course of history, there have been many who mastered their abilities physically but ultimately fell victim to their inability to *think* effectively.

Your exercise journey is no different from anything else in life. It's very important to put yourself in the right environment to be successful and to find fulfillment in what you're doing. The environment that you choose to exercise in is completely up to you and your personal preference. Doing 25 pull-ups on a bar hanging from your doorway in your bedroom is the same as doing 25 pull-ups in an award-winning gym that is owned by an Olympic powerlifter. The work is the same anywhere and everywhere. Find an arrangement that you feel safe in and that works for you.

While a public gym is not a necessity, I'm an advocate for public gyms personally. I'll tell you exactly why– public gyms allow you to be around a fitness *community* and other people with like-minded goals and intentions while working towards your own personal goals. The only thing that's better than one person trying to change their life is a group of people trying to change their lives in the same room. In my eyes, that's exactly what a public gym is– a community of people willing to put in the time and effort to live well and discipline themselves.

We all need support, advice, relationships, and love to get through our personal challenges in life. That mountain of work that you must do to reach the goals you have for your personal fitness may seem intimidating. I promise you that putting yourself around others who are also climbing their own personal mountains will inspire you on another level to keep climbing and encourage those climbing with you. There is strength in numbers and surrounding yourself with like-minded, goal-oriented people.

My love for public gyms has nothing to do with going in and recording Tik-Tok videos or posting on my social media that I'm at the gym. It has everything to do with surrounding myself with a community of people who are pushing themselves to be more than they currently are. Nobody is holding a gun to these people's heads to force them to go to the gym and put their bodies through some strenuous activity. These people make that choice for themselves because they're on a personal mission to become stronger people and live healthier lives. When you're pushing yourself to become a better version of yourself and enduring new challenges, these are the types of people you need around you to keep you inspired and accountable for your ascendance into a new and improved version of yourself.

The fitness community is one of the most positive communities in the world. If all communities were like the fitness community, the world would be a much better place to live in than it is. In fact, there are many things that the rest of the world could learn from the fitness community to bring back peace and prosperity. That's a strong statement to make because the world has some major issues that are very complex to work through. However, this is the admiration I have for the fitness community and the confidence I have in my personal belief that people respond positively when treated positively.

You may be wondering how everyone approaching the rest of the world as the fitness community approaches one another possibly correlates to more peace and healing in the world. Well, in the fitness community, you come as you are. Nobody joins at their peak, and everyone is working to improve *something* within themselves every single day–

whether it be physical, mental, or just improvement in their overall health in general. Nobody has *arrived*, so everybody is constantly working.

Of course, you'll always have people who carry themselves as if they're better than everybody else. For the most part, this is not the case in the fitness community. Everybody is welcomed with open arms to pursue a better life for themselves. Can you only imagine what the world would look like if everyone acknowledged that they will always have room for improvement, worked towards improving, and treated everyone else with respect in their process of improving themselves? It could just be me, but it sounds like there would be a whole lot of improvement going on and not a whole lot of conflict. Where there is meaningful and intentional work taking place, it is rare that trivial and meaningless quarrels will disrupt that work.

It's also common for you to set goals for yourself throughout your personal fitness journey. The more acclimated your body gets to exercising, you generally tend to want to do more as you get comfortable with pushing yourself and develop the confidence in yourself to strive to do more. You see others around you pushing themselves and reaching towards their goals, so you become inspired to push yourself towards your own goals as well.

It's much easier to get on the stair master for 20 minutes on that day when you aren't feeling it, when you see three other people pushing through and getting their work in for the day. Iron sharpens iron, and being around goal-oriented people who are working towards their goals, can only inspire you to find the strength within to continue your pursuit towards your own goals as well. Can you imagine what the world would look like if we all adopted this practice and allowed our competitive spirit to push us towards our goals *together*?

Once you've joined and set your goals, the most important part is that you now have a healthy and supportive environment that is inspiring and encouraging you to reach those goals and become the best version of yourself that you can possibly be. People who are in the gym are committed to improving and living a life of higher quality and they want to see others do the same for themselves. They understand that health and moving the body is important and believe me– they wish *more* people would stop neglecting their bodies and their health so they could also reap the benefits that taking care of your body provides.

For the most part, gym-goers are extremely supportive and uplifting. I can't tell you how many people have come up to me in the middle of a workout and complimented the way that I do my work or maybe even provided some advice on how I can get more out of my workouts. The bottom line is it's all positivity and coming from a place of wanting to see me do well. This is the spirit that most of the fitness community has towards one another. Small compliments or even just small acts to acknowledge people's progress and their commitment to that progress can go a long way. You never know what someone may be going through, and if you have the opportunity to lift someone's chin, you should always take that opportunity.

I don't blame the struggles I had with my identity throughout my childhood on anybody but myself for believing the lies and ignorance of others, but one thing that I do know for certain is that I have encountered strangers in the gym who have shown me more love, compassion, and made me feel more human than people that I share blood with ever even tried to show or make me feel. Perhaps, this is the main reason that I hold fitness and surrounding myself around the right fitness community in such high regard in my life. In many ways, I think these people helped me keep my chin up when it felt impossible to do so. Through these people and the work, I was able to find a love for myself that I never knew prior to their kind words, gestures, and the eventual confidence in feeling a sense of belonging to move forward from trauma that had left me feeling "less than" for much of my life.

It's a great thing to be surrounded by people who are trying to succeed but also want to see others succeed as well. Those are the truly successful people because their hearts remain pure on the journey towards success. There's enough success for all of us in this world that are willing to go after it because the majority don't bother going after it. We don't have to compete against one another as if opportunity and abundance are scarce in this life. Rather, competing *with* one another makes all parties stronger and creates more opportunity for everyone.

More so than anything, this is what makes an investment in a public gym worth it in my eyes. Building relationships with those with strong work ethics and pure hearts means building relationships with some of the best people you'll ever meet. Competing everyday only makes you sharper. Constantly being surrounded by positive energy and people who have a passion for improving and helping others makes the small monthly payment and daily commute well worth it in my eyes.

Just imagine what type of world we would live in if we all lived with purpose and intentions of improving but also possessed the humility and compassion within us to help encourage others along their journey as well. Imagine a world where love for one another and a genuine desire to see others succeed pushed us to work harder to do our part in inspiring the next person to find it within themselves to succeed. Imagine a world where we worked together to find true substance in life and encouraged others along the way.

Once again, the environment you choose is totally up to you. Getting active is the most important thing. I just wanted to give you some insight as to what joining a gym could potentially do for you because I know what it did for me and my life. However, I am also understanding that what worked for me will not be what works for everyone else, and I wholeheartedly support whatever is best for you and makes you feel the most comfortable.

All I want is for you to find whatever it is that works best for you and provides you with the results that you're looking for. I want the best for every set of eyes reading these words, not only in your fitness and health– but in all aspects of your life. Whether in a public gym or just using free weights in your bedroom, it only takes 30 minutes to an hour of your time, a few days out of the week, to invest in yourself and your physical well-being.

One's quality of life and success in life is largely dependent on one's investments throughout life. Smart investors only invest their time, effort, energy, and money into the things and people that they feel will give them the greatest return on their investment. In some cases, you have the right intentions but still make a poor investment. This will never be the case in your investment into your fitness and a healthier lifestyle, because you will always get a positive return on a small investment.

As we all know, there's 24 hours in a day. Even if you spend one full hour exercising, you're still left with 96% of your day. Even better, you can even be assured that *at least* four percent of your day went towards improving yourself! We all have the time to invest but we don't all have the right priorities in regard to how we invest that time. Will you make the decision to commit to using your time wisely and allowing it to work in your favor or will you find yourself wishing for more time later in your life? Your answer to this question is what it all boils down to.

The greatest love you can experience is self-love. The way you talk to yourself, feel about yourself, and respect yourself sets the tone for how everyone else treats you. Setting boundaries and growing confidence in your ability to do difficult things in life starts the evolution of a lifetime. All other love in your life is affected by the way that you love yourself and show up for yourself. We often think we will come to love ourselves more by being loved by others, but there is nobody who can give you the type of love that you can give yourself. There is no love like self-love. As difficult as it can be, it is vital that we learn to love ourselves so that we can eventually love others.

The people who mean the most to you deserve to experience your love, kindness, and compassion to the fullest extent without any limitations. This is why it's so important to heal, become aware of your triggers, and work on your responses to life. You need yourself to be at your best, so that you can develop fulfilling relationships and be limitless in your ability to express your love and compassion for those who mean the most to you. You must learn to love yourself properly, so that you can love the world and the people who keep you going properly.

A major component of self-love is getting active and taking care of your mental and physical health. You should never give up on yourself under any circumstance because you're the one person that you're guaranteed to have by your side for the entire duration of your life. Lord, forbid it happens, but something could happen at any given moment to the people in your corner and anybody could walk out of your life at any given moment with no explanation.

Of course, there's no bond or relationship that you can develop that is immune to tragedy and unfortunate circumstances. You've built strong relationships with these people and have developed a bond with them that adds value to your life but there's no guarantee that this bond will always be there. It is our human nature to provide attention and love to others, but we also crave to receive that same attention and love back. This is why humans open up to one another, despite knowing deep down that it makes us susceptible to experiencing grief, loss, heartbreak, and several other emotional experiences that come with losing touch with someone we love.

It is without question important to take the risk that comes with developing human connection and to love these people wholeheartedly, but it's also important to avoid dependency on anyone and to learn to stand on your own. A cold reality of life is that you can't realistically depend on *anyone* outside of yourself to be there for you because you never know what the future holds. This is why it's vital that you love yourself and take the time to invest in yourself, because you are the one person who is physically unable to leave you.

You could execute all other 11 principles in this book to perfection, along with every other self-help technique and model that lines the bookshelves. If you feel miserable and dissatisfied with your state of health when you're older and living that "better life", it's all for nothing. No amount of success, money, or material possessions will ever be worth your health and how you feel about yourself.

The ability to pump breath in your lungs is not affected by success, money, or material possessions. These things cannot save you from poor health and a poor self-image. You can't take these with you to the grave. Don't be so focused on all the external pleasures of life that you forget to prioritize what matters most internally– you and your health.

My last key point on prioritizing exercise and a healthy lifestyle is that taking care of yourself puts you in a position to take care of everything else and everyone else that matters to you for longer. By keeping yourself in good health, you will feel better and you will live better. You will also be able to function at a higher level, which will help you accomplish more and work towards the biggest goals you have for yourself, without your body working against you.

That increased functioning, paired with the mental and physical benefits of consistent exercise will work together to create a much more productive, confident version of yourself. You will be able to do what is required of you to become the person you want to become and you will feel good about yourself while doing the work. This new side of you that's been uncovered will transform your relationship with yourself, your loved ones, and the entire world around you in ways you could've never imagined.

It all goes back to knowing and understanding your why— if it's not enough for me to tell you that you should take care of your health out of love and appreciation for yourself, think about all the other people who love you, care for you, and wish to see you live a long and prosperous life. Think about how slacking on your health could potentially affect these people one day. Everything you do in your life comes with a consequence, whether it's a big or small consequence. Your actions affect more than just yourself. Don't make the people you love and who love you suffer as a result of failing to control what you can control in terms of your health and well-being.

We all have people that we want to be there for in life, whether it be in family, friendship, a romantic partner, or even the random person on the side of the street who could use some help getting a hot meal. That's what life is all about, being able to change lives and impact others through the way that you evolve your life and the way that you love others. Think about the people who want to see you become the best version of yourself.

When your love and appreciation for yourself is running low and you don't feel like making the small sacrifices for yourself, think about those people and allow that external source of motivation to carry you through.

As I mentioned earlier in the book, that external source of motivation for me personally, came from my younger brother Preston. I was at an all-time low in my life and didn't even want to get out of bed most mornings. I regularly slept through my alarms and showed up late for work. I was drunk and high throughout most of the weekend on a regular basis. I was ruining my sensitivity to my emotions and exposing myself to all kinds of different energies with one night stand after one night stand. I was living for the world with no regard for my future or greater purpose in life. I was down and out, a lost soul. I had constant thoughts about death because there were times I thought I wanted out.

My brother gave me a reason to keep my head up. At my lowest, he was always there for me. He never failed to put a smile on my face or make me laugh. He always encouraged me to look forward and not to the past. He was always there to hang out with on the late nights I couldn't sleep. When everything around me seemed to be going dark, he was the light that never faded and kept me going. When I felt like I had none, he was always my reason to keep on living. I needed him at the time but I knew he needed his big brothers as well- the fight for my life became about so much more than my own emotions and feelings.

Sure, I enjoy seeing my progress and developing more confidence in both the way I look and the way I feel. That's not the main thing that drives me any more than the next man. I know what it feels like to feel dead inside. I know there's people who feel this way every single day and the unfortunate reality is that some of them won't be as fortunate as I have been. I must be here and be at my best in order to leave the biggest impact that I possibly can and to be a voice for those that are struggling. God didn't put me through these experiences for me to keep silent about them and He didn't deliver me from hell on earth to not show love and compassion to those that are in similar situations.

My health is important to me and my self-love is growing stronger by the day. What really motivates me is that the people that drive me the most in life deserve to have the healthiest, wholesome, happiest, and successful version of me as possible. Yes, I do the work I do to develop and improve myself, but I also subconsciously do it to become someone who is capable of impacting lives beyond just my own. Maintaining a disciplined lifestyle is just one of the ways I try to inspire others to reach for their highest self. If I can't motivate, inspire, and help the people around me– success, money, and whatever other accolades come from this life mean nothing to me.

No matter who you are or what level of health you currently find yourself at, you can make the decision to be more conscious and intentional of how you move, nourish, nurture, and appreciate your body from this moment forward. I can't guarantee that you'll have six-pack abs rippling through your stomach but I can guarantee that you will feel better than ever before. All it takes is committing yourself to loving yourself more and taking advantage of the world's greatest free medicine– exercise, accountability, and hard work.

I've seen myself when I have good habits of exercise and value my personal fitness, and I've seen myself at times when I didn't have good habits of exercise and didn't value my personal fitness. Every single day of the week, I will take the temporary pain of exercising and stressing my muscles over the long-lasting pain of lacking confidence in myself and having a poor self-image. The person I am today, the confidence that I possess, the love that I have found for myself, and my appreciation for my overall health and wellness is worth every minute and hour of hard work and sacrifice that it takes to maintain.

Through the blood, sweat, tears, and the many challenges, you will find a version of yourself that you never knew existed within you and this person will begin to show up in all other areas of your life as well. Not only am I suggesting that you exercise and move your body, but I'm also telling you that you will never be at your best without prioritizing this key component of your life. Stop wishing you looked like everyone else and put your head down and work to become a better version of yourself, one that is holistically well and thriving.

I have developed myself so much further mentally from a standpoint of fortitude and resolve through prioritizing exercise and personal fitness, and I am a living testimony of the changes it welcomes into your life. It won't be the easiest thing in the world, but your quality of life and how you feel about yourself are without question worth fighting for. Everything that's needed for you to reach whatever goal you've set lies within you. The only question that remains is how much work are you willing to put into reaching your goals?

Get moving and stay consistent. It will take you places you never imagined! No matter how high or low the goal, I want you to hear it from me personally that I *know* you can reach your goals and I believe in you wholeheartedly, if you can find it within you to believe in yourself.

Chapter Nine

Principle #9: No empire is built in favorable circumstances– the test always comes before the promotion.

As human beings, we have an innate tendency to look at things, people, and situations in their current state of being and assume that they've always been in that state. That is, we often fail to consider the *history* of these things, people, and situations. We often neglect to remember how they came to be in the first place and what they looked like before they became what they are today. This is especially common when we look at the modern-day empires of strong, developed nations. If you look at any of the modern-day powerhouses, it would be easy to assume this power has always been in the same hands. After all, they have access to *everything* and are developed well beyond other surrounding nations. However, I can assure you that a brief visit through history will reveal that these empires didn't start out as empires– rather, these empires were forged through sacrifice, hard work, surviving difficult times, and becoming trailblazers in the business of providing lives of higher quality to their citizens.

In more cases than not, war was involved at some point during the transition from a pawn in the world to building an empire, because success and freedom are two things that are never given. These are two things in life that hold tremendous value worldwide to us as human beings, so there is a price to be paid to attain them amongst the competition. This is why people are willing to kill and to be killed in their pursuits of success and freedom.

They have been willing to kill in the past and they will continue to be willing to kill for success and freedom for as long as mankind exists. Empires are not a natural occurrence. They're built through intentional actions, a relentless pursuit of liberty, and a fierce competitiveness that prioritizes the mission over fear and the obstacles that stand in the way of completing the mission.

If you're dealing with some unfavorable circumstances in your life, I'm here to tell you that you very well could be in the beginning stages of building your life's empire. However, I'm also here to tell you that your life will not become an empire as a result of natural occurrence. The wars aren't going to be fought for you. You must become intentional in your actions, relentless in your pursuit to create a life of freedom and abundance, and fiercely competitive to separate yourself from the billions and billions of people who are also competing for the exact same things in life that you are competing for.

The competition can get stiff but it's key to understand that competition only exists to push you and make you compete at a higher level. The truth of the matter is that there's a table long enough for all of us to eat at, but only those who are even willing to pull up a chair in the first place will find a seat. It's not favorable circumstances that separate those that have what they need in life and those that do not. This can be a factor in achieving success, but there is no hope to maintain that success in favorable circumstances alone. What separates those that have what they need and those that do not in the world is effort, consistency, and a strong desire for a seat at the table which provides the opportunity for growth, success, freedom, and abundance in life.

Look at Bill Gates, who is a co-founder of one of the most successful companies known to man and one of the wealthiest men in the world today. The world has Mr. Gates to thank for his contributions to the creation of Microsoft and the Xbox gaming console, among many other smaller companies and contributions. This lucrative business has made Mr. Gates an outlier in his industry and earned him a net worth that is estimated to be valued at approximately 109 billion US dollars. Seeing his massive success and the fortune he has accumulated throughout his life, it would be easy to assume that Mr. Gates was always extremely successful and wealthy throughout the course of his life.

However, Bill Gates was a college dropout and many people close to him initially considered him crazy and incompetent for "wasting" his opportunity to attend Harvard. Harvard's reputation speaks for itself and I'm sure I don't have to tell you the courage it must've taken for Gates to walk away from an all-but-guaranteed degree from an institution that holds the weight that Harvard holds in the market for job-hunting and landing high-income careers fresh out of college. He was cruising through one of the most prestigious business curriculums in the world and over halfway to completing his degree! It's no wonder those closest to him were hesitant to accept his decision to drop out and pursue a risky, unproven business venture.

It didn't matter what anyone said because Gates saw the bigger picture. He understood that a degree from Harvard would afford him opportunities to become successful and wealthy over time, but he also recognized a need in the world and believed he could play a major role in finding a solution for this need. While he did come from a successful, upper-class family that was generous and supportive of his business' startup, Gates started out in unfavorable circumstances. At the end of the day, he was a college dropout who was dependent on financial support from his family and friends to get a business off the ground that he left the world-famous and award-winning business school at Harvard for. It sounds like a ton of pressure and even more uncertainty because that's exactly what this situation was for Gates. Failure of this business could've set him back years and millions of dollars, but he held onto his faith in the small chance that he would be able to get this business running and make his leap of faith pay off.

Gates worked relentlessly, not knowing if he would ever be able to develop a software that would yield him a return worth all the risks he took and the investments he made along the way. As we know today, his hard work and his sacrifices ended up well worth the risks he took, and he has been compensated well for his troubles. However, it's important that we acknowledge that Microsoft and Xbox didn't become giants in the technology industry overnight, by natural occurrence. There was a process and a method to his madness. Gates was intentional in his efforts to develop a software system that could enhance the experience of using computers for all users, relentless in his pursuit of his vision that he knew had the potential to change his life forever, and fiercely competitive in his work ethic to deliver a high-value product to a high-value market.

I tell you this brief story of Bill Gates' life and massive success to tell you this– you're going to be waiting for forever if you're waiting for all your circumstances to be favorable before you take that risk. The greatest empires and successes in the world have historically been created in the midst of uncertainty. These leaders saw a small window of opportunity and risked the lives they were living for an opportunity to provide a better life for themselves and those in close association with them.

If there's one thing you should know about history, it repeats itself. It always has and it always will, because though the times and the layout of the world change, human nature remains the same. Empires of great success and power have been forged amid uncertainty and chaos for as long as empires have existed, because times of uncertainty and chaos create stronger, more resilient people. These people are the ones who are willing to lay it all on the line to create a better life for themselves and their loved ones.

All too often, I believe we as humans tend to want to "play it safe" and avoid risks as much as we possibly can. This ideology makes sense because risks *are* scary and they do have the potential to ignite setbacks in life. The masses see this potential threat to their security and their progress, and they naturally shy away from putting themselves at risk of any form in their lives. As a result, most people play the cards they've been dealt with the intention not to lose, rather than playing their cards courageously and with a will to *win*. They consider and take into account the potential to lose everything they've worked for, but they do not give equal consideration to the potential to *gain* and multiply that of which they've already worked so hard for.

Essentially, much of the population is controlled by their fear of what could go wrong and what they could lose, rather than being driven by their faith in the possibilities of what could go right and what they stand to gain. This is why the masses are stagnant and dissatisfied with their lives. They're searching for ways to grow and add to their lives, without being willing to forfeit the comfort and security of the lives that they currently live. You cannot experience both the comfort and security of your current life and the discomfort and uncertainty that come with growing as a person and creating a better life for yourself at the same time. There is no "best of both worlds" in this scenario. You simply must choose one or the other and your actions must reflect this decision or the choice will be made for you.

Life itself is a risk. From the time you were born to now, your life has only become riskier by the year and this will continue to be the trend for the remainder of your life. It's the cycle of human life. A life that provides meaning and fulfillment will always come with a healthy number of risks and it will require you to consider new thoughts and ideas as you seek ways to improve yourself and grow as an individual. There must be a certain risk of loss and potential for gain for something to have meaning to you or for you because if there isn't, it's of no value to you. You're just going through the motions and there's no positive or negative consequences for your success or failure in obtaining whatever it is that you desire.

I think one of the biggest misconceptions that we hold onto as a society is that a "safe" life exists, when this is simply not the case. No matter how much or how little you have, it can be taken away just as fast as it came into your possession. In most cases, it can be taken away much faster than it came into your possession. It may or may not even be your fault. Think about all the homes and property that have been lost at the hands of a natural disaster or some other outside occurrence that these people didn't bring on themselves.

There are always risks associated with life. Those that conquer their fears and take the risks that present themselves in life often tend to capitalize off those who allow their inaction to keep them stuck and living in their fears. It's been this way throughout history and the landscape is still the same today. If you aren't the one taking the risks to improve your life, you're helping someone else's risk pay off and supporting someone else's dream while hiding from your own. Then, you likely find yourself wondering why some people are living the lives they want to live and you aren't. It's not because those people were predestined to live a better life than you or that they have abilities and qualifications that you don't. It's the simple fact that you won't pull the trigger and take the chances that your better life requires you to take.

To give you a visual of this, I want you to think about when you first learned how to ride a bike. You most likely first began riding bikes on a tricycle, unless you were like me and didn't learn how to ride a bike until you were too big to ride a tricycle. If you did start out on a tricycle, it took a considerable amount of time before your parents felt comfortable enough to graduate you onto the bicycle. They wanted you to get the mechanics of pedaling down and to understand the concept of how the tricycle worked before putting you on the bike.

Eventually, they started teaching you how to ride the bicycle, but you had better have on your helmet and it had better be strapped up and buckled tightly directly under your chin. I remember my mom wouldn't even go outside and watch me ride my bike until my dad assured her that I knew how to ride because she didn't want to see me fall onto the pavement and scrape myself up. My dad's approach was slightly different from hers, which was the typical approach of a dad– something along the lines of, "If you fall off the bike enough times, you'll eventually figure out how to stop falling off the bike." He knew somebody had to teach me how to ride my bike and sit through the process, so he was right there and doing his best to teach me.

Though your parents were fearful you would fall, they went through with the process of teaching you how to ride your bike and letting you learn from your own mistakes. Suddenly, using the pedals of the bike and maintaining balance all made sense to you. Eventually, you no longer needed parental supervision to ride your bike and you left that helmet in the garage as soon as your dad let you get away with it. That matter wasn't even discussed with mom because she wasn't having it. Riding your bike eventually became so natural to you that you sometimes wondered how you *didn't* know how to ride a bike at one point in time in your life. You could now join all the other kids riding their bikes up and down the streets of the neighborhood and save yourself all the walking. Life was good.

I don't know about you, but I remember that very first time that I was ever allowed to go outside on my own and ride my bike without supervision and without a helmet. I raced up my driveway that sat at the top of my neighborhood and down the hill straight towards my friend's house. It was a summer afternoon, so temperatures were scorching and accompanied by the deep south's notorious humidity. Yet, riding down that hill and racing towards my friend's house, I remember pedaling straight into the humidity and feeling all the heat from the sunshine beaming down on my face.

I felt truly free and wouldn't have rather been anywhere else at that moment in time. The risk of me falling off my bike and getting injured was always there, but in that moment, I knew that I had made the right decision to take that risk of falling or getting injured. Maybe it was the potential of falling and getting injured that made me feel so alive, or maybe it was just a moment that was long overdue in my life. All I know is that by taking that risk and opening myself up to the potential for failure, I created a memory that I still remember over 16 years later in my life.

Though a memory as simple as riding your bike into the wind without a helmet for the first time can seem inconsequential to your life now, I believe looking back on experiences like this from time to time and recalling how those experiences made you feel can serve you well. You've been hearing it your whole life but it's because the saying is true: *Life is short.*

For you to make the most of your time here and to enjoy your life to the fullest extent, I believe you should strive to fill your life with as many moments of freedom and pure bliss as you possibly can. Don't be afraid to bring the kid that still lives within you along on your journey sometimes because some parts of the journey will require the curiosity and excitement that kid will be able to bring out of you. It's so important that as we age and mature, we never lose that child-like curiosity and faith that we once all possessed and life so often beats out of us.

As much as we despise hearing it at times, these moments of freedom and bliss are often directly on the other side of our fears, insecurities, and all the other negative things and experiences that we associate with being potentially harmful to us. We are more controlled by the fear of what *could* happen than we are controlled by what *does* happen. As backwards as it sounds, the best way to overcome your fear is to run directly at whatever it is that's bringing you fear and discomfort. You cannot experience freedom or bliss without first being set free from something that is making you feel restricted and bringing you feelings of discontent.

In other words, those great feelings in life, the "highs", come from doing difficult and fear-inducing things. The pathway to increased fulfillment and happiness in your life runs directly through doing difficult things and solving problems that have haunted you and held you back in your past and current life. There is no experience of a high in life without first experiencing a low, because without the lows and the fear of the lows, there's nothing to be set free from.

Look at the United States of America, which is now the home of nearly 335 million citizens and one of the most affluent and respected nations in the world today. Made up of 50 states and a few US territories, spanning almost four million square miles in total area, the nation has laid claim to much of the continent we know as North America. It is one of the few existing empire's today– a nation that prides itself on providing liberty, justice, opportunity, and equality to all its citizens. However, this pride and mission is *far* from where this nation once started.

Looking at the success and global influence that the United States has become over the last two centuries, it's easy to forget the humble beginnings of the United States. Originally consisting only of 13 small territories along the east coast of the present-day United States, colonized and tightly ruled by the then-almighty British empire is where the United States got its start. The British were no friendly "big brother" to the American colonies and their colonists either. British law imposed many intrusive, demanding laws on the colonists such as requiring them to pay levied taxes on common, everyday goods, housing and feeding British soldiers within the confinement of their own homes, and giving the colonists no representation or say in their government and government decisions that directly affected them.

Though the British were powerful, they found themselves in debt from previous wars and believed the colonists were a viable resource to help close this margin. The colonists eventually realized that the taxes became more and more unforgiving as the British's ambitions to repay their debts grew and they knew there would be no reason to expect any changes if they didn't take action to create change. Taking action to create change– it was important in the story of the American Revolution and it's important in your transformation and transition into a better life. Without first making changes in your actions, you would be foolish to expect changes in the results that you get.

Fed up with being forced to help the British parliament repay their debts through extreme taxation, the colonists eventually took the bold first step towards building their own empire. That is, they took a stance by protesting the unjust laws and sanctions that had been placed on them by the British government and made it clear that they would no longer stand for such an unfair "partnership" with the British. The colonists knew this rebellion wasn't the ideal situation for them, but they also knew for certain that continuing to tolerate being mistreated by the British only guaranteed further mistreatment in the future. The colonists had reached their breaking point and this would no longer be a way of life that they accepted for themselves.

One of the most famous and monumental protests that the colonists organized was the Boston Tea Party, in which the Sons of Liberty united the colonists and they agreed to dump over 300 chests of tea that were imported from Britain into the harbor– directly in the face of the British! The British government had already gotten wind that there was a movement forming against them in the colonies, but the Boston Tea Party publicly marked the end of the colonists' tolerance and willingness to be the defenseless "little brother" to the British.

The message was bold, strong, and increased tension between the colonists and the British greatly. The colonists no longer voiced their displeasure with Britain's rule over them amongst themselves in the safety and privacy of meeting halls and personal properties, but they now voiced it directly to Great Britain themselves and cost them a sizable amount of money in the process. Any rumors that the British thought they may have been hearing about a movement of rebellion coming their way from the colonists could be put to rest. The Boston Tea Party was proof that they had a serious situation on their hands, yet they still didn't fully understand the severity of the problems that were to come.

As you can imagine, the British responded by trying to regain control over the colonists through harsher laws and sanctions. They had to reinforce their dominance over the colonists before they allowed them to gain confidence and momentum in their movement and uprising against the British Parliament. Little did the British know, they could've imposed whatever laws and sanctions that they wanted on the colonists and it would've made no difference. The colonists continued to protest and let their frustrations and intolerance be known. They feared the retaliation of the British, but they would no longer tolerate living their lives solely for the advancement of the British Parliament's financial accounts and to stroke the ego of the British.

These brave colonists had already made up their minds and there was no talking them out of their decision. They were going to set themselves free from Great Britain's unjust colonization or die trying– with or without confidence and momentum. There's something about a group of people coming to a decision and giving their full commitment to that decision that has this extreme power to create change and bring about desired results. This phenomenon has created some of the most important moments in history and has been the turning point in many individual lives. Needless to say, the colonists' refusal to obey the demands and laws of the British didn't sit well with the British.

It became apparent that the colonists and the British were on a crash-course towards the inevitable– war. The colonists desired their freedom from British colonization and to create their own nation, but they knew that this would be impossible without first *earning* this freedom from the British through decisive action and bloodshed. For them to have a chance to build their own empire, the colonists had to defeat the almighty Great Britain in an all-out war for their freedom. It was a tall task, one that would require near-perfect strategy and execution for the colonists to even have a chance at successfully defeating the strongest military in the world at the time.

On paper, the British had every advantage in this war, and you would've thought they would've beat the colonists into submission within a few months' time. However, the colonists had more of one particular thing that doesn't always show up in the analytics and statistics of human capacity than the British did. They had a surplus of *reasons* to risk their lives for a cause that meant more to them than the fear of death or defeat meant to them. This was an issue for the British because no amount of training, machinery, weaponry, or strategy could account for the chip that the colonists were fighting with on their shoulders. It made the difference in the war, just as having enough reasons will make the difference in your life that will spur you into action.

The world-famous personal development mogul Mr. Jim Rohn once said, "If you have enough reasons, you can do anything you put your mind to. You've got enough intelligence– you don't have enough reasons." He went on to say that reasons are what will change one's life. You must have reasons to change before you will do the deep, difficult work that is required to change yourself. Once you change yourself, your circumstances and your life begin to change. The colonists' reasons for fighting the war made the underdogs of the American Revolution hungrier than the favorites and the underdogs ended up outgunning the mighty empire in a war that lasted eight years and is regarded as one of the bloodiest wars in human history.

The war entailed loss of life, destruction of land, economic strain, and severe depletion of resources. The colonists nearly lost it all, and yet, the colonists simultaneously had gained everything they desired because they had done the deep and difficult work that was required of them to win a war that they were never supposed to win. Their *reasons* for fighting the war and their resilience had earned them the opportunity to build their own empire in a manner that would provide a better life for them and their families in the future. By coming together and fighting for reasons that were bigger than any one individual, they changed the trajectory of their lives and the future of the United States forever. If the right reasons forged an entire nation's pathway to power, imagine what having the right reasons to overcome the opposition in your personal life would do for you.

Most of us know the story of the American Revolution but I don't think that we all quite realize the power that's in the story. There's a very valuable takeaway from the story of America's founding and it's a very simple takeaway– we have the power to change *anything* about our lives and our circumstances when our desire for change outweighs our fear of the unknown. Be more like the colonists! Become fed up with whatever it is in your life that is taxing too much of your time, energy, and well-being. Make the commitment to take whatever decisive action is necessary to ensure that these things and people are no longer given power over you and the life that you live.

These forces may currently be the "empire" in your life. They have most of the control in your relationship with them and you are the subordinate. This doesn't have to continue to be the case. With enough of them and the right ones, your reasons for seeking to reverse this relationship can be what gives you the edge to overcome these things and slowly start the process of building your own empire in your life. *You* have the power to change what you tolerate and give control over you in your life and only you. This is one of the most important realizations you must come to understand in the process of this journey, or you will never understand your true power to take from this life whatever you demand from it.

Speaking from experience, I know there's so many times in life where we feel unfulfilled because we know there's more out there for us. We have that voice in our head, that gut feeling that we could be doing more with our lives. Yet, we simultaneously tend to naturally resist seeking out those opportunities and doing more than we're accustomed to doing because doing so would require us to get out of our comfort zones and open ourselves up to new risks, failures, and possibilities.

We've discussed it multiple times throughout the book. Creating change requires us to do everything that is opposite of our natural instincts as human beings. It's natural human tendency to resist changes in our routines, habits, and thought processes, but I'm here to tell you once again that you must go against the grain of your natural human nature if you desire to become all that you can become as a human being. Your human nature doesn't welcome the excitement and unknown that comes with running your race to the fullest and fearlessly, so it must be reprogrammed through deep work and intentional actions to get into the habit of accepting discomfort and the unknown.

Growth is painful and scary because it requires you to go places you have never been before– both mentally and physically. You must shed the parts of you that are holding you back and preventing you from living a life of fulfillment and replace these layers with layers that will serve you in the future. The process of shedding can be painful and it does leave behind a mess for a while, but you're shedding for a reason. The new and improved parts of you that are going to help you out of your bondage cannot and will not coexist with the parts of you that were keeping you in that same bondage.

There is no such thing as forging an empire within your comfort zone that is full of your preferences and everything else that has caused you to become "colonized" by the stronger powers in your life. If you want to build a life that brings satisfaction and success, you must first feel dissatisfaction and failure that push you towards pursuing the discomfort that is growth. Only once you have experienced and endured the discomfort of growth will you be able to experience comfort with who you are and the life that you live.

The United States as we know it today would've likely never been formed if the colonists didn't go against the grain and step outside their comfort zones to pursue the lives they dreamed of living. They weren't even sure that the lifestyle they desired was possible for them, but they were so curious that they had to find out for themselves. One of the most powerful and respected countries in today's world was born in some of the most unfavorable circumstances imaginable. By going against the favorites and having a healthy dose of curiosity, the colonists rewrote the history textbooks in ways that many of that time never would've thought possible. What's stopping you from having faith in yourself to rewrite what the world has said about you up to this point in your life?

This is just one of many historical examples that show there's power in unfavorable circumstances. Believe it or not, there is significant power in *not* being where you want to be in your life! If you're experiencing these feelings, I want you to know that this is a positive sign because it means that you genuinely want a better life for yourself, to the point it's causing you pain to not be at the point yet. That pain you're feeling is placing you into a beautiful place in your life that has the potential to change the entire outlook of your future. These very feelings are what give you the *reasons* to make the necessary changes and allow you to make the transition from being a victim of the hand that life has dealt you into an individual that has developed a greater understanding of themselves and learned how to effectively play the hand that's been dealt to them as a result of their life experiences.

The very things that feel like they're meant to stop you or knock you off course are the very things that will strengthen your character as a person and create a resiliency within you that will prepare you for your ascent towards the higher calling on your life. The colonists weren't dealt the best hand that the deck had to offer but they took what they were given and made effective use of it. They had to go through the mighty British army of redcoats to win America's independence, but this uphill battle made this future nation stronger, more connected, and resilient than ever before. Thus, they found the strength to build their empire amid great resistance and difficulty. You will also meet opposition on the journey to your calling. The truth is this opposition is never meant to stop you, only to make you stronger and prepare you along the way.

In its natural state, metal is extremely stubborn and lacks the flexibility that would allow it to be useful in most places. There are some places where metal simply won't fit in its natural state. However, once put to the fire, metal is able to loosen up and expand itself– it becomes more flexible, and as a result, becomes more useful and valuable to the world. Like metal, we are also naturally stubborn and unaware of our ability to become more flexible, useful, and valuable to the world around us.

The only way that we will loosen up this stubbornness and become more aware of our ability to become flexible and serve a greater purpose in this world is to first be put to fire. The only purpose of the opposition is to challenge you and to prepare you to fulfill your purpose in the world but we as humans have a habit of getting stuck in these challenges and allowing them to stop all forward progress completely.

Why do you think people settle for an average view from the middle of the mountains, knowing that there's a greater view at the peak of the mountain? It's no coincidence that the roads that lead directly to the peaks of mountains and provide the most beautiful, breathtaking scenery are the roads least traveled, the roads that only the courageous and those willing to endure the ride get to see and experience. They're more narrow, icy, and dangerous. The views they lead to are unbelievable but the trek up the mountain is tumultuous.

242

The only way to reach these beautiful roads is by navigating all the twists and turns and slowly making your way up the steep incline. As you ascend the mountain, the number of travelers around you gets thinner and thinner. Eventually, you realize you have reached the point beyond where most of the other travelers were willing to go. It's uncomfortable continuing the ascent in the absence of everyone else, but the only way to reach the peak of the mountain is by seeing where the majority stop and enjoy themselves and making the decision to be the exception and press on.

There's a reason the parking lot at the bottom of the mountain is full of people. The majority are willing to pay the price of general admission and enjoy the same experiences and sights that the majority have access to. Yet, the top of the mountain is designed to come to a peak. That peak is a point, which is very narrow and lacks the surface area to support the same capacity as the large parking lot located at the bottom of the mountain. The difficulty of the climb to the peak will disqualify the vast majority from reaching the peak.

The majority of us understand this concept when it comes to visualizing the shape of a mountain but the important question we must identify and answer is what separates those that settle for general admission at the bottom of the mountain and those that are willing to pay the greater price to experience the peak? What separates those that accept the average views from those that press on towards the finer views? The answer is that the only thing that separates these people is that those that reach the peak and unlock the finest views have the courage to endure fear, difficulty, navigating unfamiliar terrains, and the longer, more time-consuming process that is required to reach new heights in human achievement.

The way towards the life you want to live and building your empire is *through* whatever is in your way. The circumstances don't have to be favorable, and they likely won't be at first because life's circumstances don't adjust until we first make adjustments within ourselves. These adjustments take some time but they can be made to your benefit. Changing the circumstances in your life is simply a decision to make a commitment to yourself to rise above your current circumstances until you reach a point where your circumstances can no longer hold you in confinement and prevent you from pursuing the desires you have for your life.

There's a phenomenal book titled *The Mountain is You*, written by Brianna Wiest and her message in this powerful book is this: You will come to realize that the "mountain" you've been so focused on conquering your entire life is and has always been you. That's the purpose of all these principles and this crazy journey called life in a nutshell– self-mastery. The purpose of it all is to understand that you control the life you live by controlling the person that you become. It is when you realize that you are your only threatening adversary and source of opposition that is limiting you in your life that you will be set free from limitation and understand the true power that you possess to make this life everything you desire and more.

You will never experience true freedom and glory over your circumstances by trying to go around them and minimize the limitations they bring. These patterns and approaches have held you back for far too long and it's time that you find the solution to them once and for all. It's time that you break right through them and do the difficult work that is required to put yourself back in control of *your* own destiny. It won't always be easy, and it will be uncomfortable, but it will be well worth it in the end. You will be relieved to be back in the captain's seat of your life where you have always belonged.

Thinking back to the story of the colonists and their bravery to fight for their independence from the limited lives that colonization provided them with, I make the notion that we all have a bit of the colonists' fire and willpower to create a better life within us. It's obviously no longer the royal government in this day and age, but what types of people, habits, and decisions are you choosing that are holding you back and causing you to live at a fraction of your full potential? What things and relationships in your life demand a tax of you that you know deep down you can't afford or are no longer interested in paying? Perhaps most importantly, are you willing to go to war to separate yourself from these people, habits, and decisions to experience a life of freedom from these sources of unhappiness and limitation in your life?

Whatever the answers to these questions were for you personally, I want to challenge you to remove the seeds of lies, doubt, and bondage in your life from their *roots*. These seeds are no longer serving you and it's time that you no longer give them the power to continue to limit you and hold you still when you so desperately desire to go forward. You're not stuck in your present life and present circumstances. There's a fed-up colonist with the courage to take a chance to create change and seek a better life within all of us.

You must dig deep enough until you find that colonist within you amongst all your fear and self-doubt.

Once you find that colonist, replace those seeds of fear and doubt with the colonists' seeds of faith and courage. Don't just replace them– water them thoroughly and see to it that they grow until they can no longer be contained. These seeds of faith and courage changed the course of the colonists' lives and the entire future of present-day America. What is it again that makes you think the same won't happen for you in your life with some faith and the persistence to create change in your circumstances and your life?

Though the illusion of fear holds more people captive than any institution in the world, fear was never meant to control your thoughts and prevent you from taking action towards living the life that you were called to live. If anything, fear, anxiety, and all the other emotions that we experience along the way serve as "nudges" that signal we're pursuing something worth pursuing. They're not so much factors of resistance as they are confirmations that we're working towards something purposeful and meaningful in our lives. It's a privilege to feel pressure and to feel small doses of "fear" because on the other side of these mental hoola-hoops lies the real you and a stronger version of yourself. The best version of each of us is called to authentic greatness and achievement that knows no limitations.

My goal is for each and every eye that reads these words to establish a clearer vision of the empire they want to create for themselves. Then, I want you to take small steps towards that vision every single day, despite your worries and fears. Acknowledge your fears and allow yourself to feel your emotions. Still, take a deep breath and understand that it is within you to feel these emotions, decide which ones serve a purpose in your life, and to let those that serve no place in your life pass into the abyss. It is within you to feel these things and use them to your benefit to design a life of abundance and fulfillment.

Overcoming adversity and difficulty has played a role at some point in forming every single elite empire that the world has ever seen, so don't look down on these challenges that come along the way as fatal to what you're working towards in your life. Look at these challenges for what they truly are– growing pains towards a greater future. These growing pains are something that every great empire has gone through. Last but not least, remember that unfavorable circumstances do not determine the course of one's life. It is who one becomes amidst their circumstances, favorable or not, that determines the course of one's life. Become all that you were designed to be and there is no circumstance that can stop you from building your empire and taking this world by storm.

It takes guts, willpower, and sheer courage to go to the places that the masses are unwilling to go but it's within you. It always has been and that faint voice inside of you has been telling you this truth all your life. As someone who is on the ascent up to the peak of the mountain, being put to the fire daily, and still learning to channel the fed-up colonist within myself every single day, I want you to know that I'm with you on your climb. I'm somewhere on the mountain fighting the same uphill battle that you are to get to where I desire to be in my life. You're not alone on your journey and you never will be. You and I are in great company because the greatest empires to ever exist have all had to navigate

their own mountains and unfavorable circumstances on their way to the top as well.

Chapter Ten

Principle #10: "Be like water, my friend."- Bruce Lee

Bruce Lee was a martial artist and philosopher who was well-respected during his brief time here on earth. Mr. Lee was unlike any fighter the world had seen up until his time and you can make the argument that no other fighter has been like him since. His unique combination of brute strength and iron-horse toughness, mixed with his passion for wisdom, tranquility, and inner-peace made him a unicorn on the martial arts scene. He was as physically gifted as any martial artist the world has ever seen but it was his mental capacity to think and transform his mind that truly separated him from the competition. He cultivated an understanding of life and its meaning that made his mind even more resilient than his world-class physical toughness.

On this journey of transformation I've been on, I began to study people who had traits and features that I wanted to cultivate and implement into my own life. I was always fascinated by how well-rounded Mr. Lee was at seemingly all aspects of life. I began to dive deeper into his life, looking for insight and guidance to help me develop the same strength and resilience he was so well-known for. It was during this time that I came across his world-famous quote, which headlines this principle and forever changed my life. In this quote, Bruce Lee says, "Empty your mind, be formless. Shapeless, like water. Now, water can flow, or it can crash. Be water, my friend."

Not only is this a beautiful quote, but this quote also sends a beautiful and powerful message as well. It is my personal belief that this message resonates with the current living generation more so than any other generation of human beings, because there is constant pressure that has never been seen before on our generation to keep up with the trends of the world and to follow the same paths as everyone else.

There's pressure to graduate college at a certain age, to move out of your childhood home by a certain age, and to be successful and living the life you set out to live by a certain age. This generation has a unique way of making people of all ages and backgrounds feel like failures, simply because their timelines aren't aligning with the idea that there is a universal timetable for how things "should" be. These imaginary timelines that society has created have young people panicking and stressed out as if they're running out of time, when time is the one thing that's on their side at this point in their lives.

I will admit that I'm just as guilty as anybody else of allowing these societal timelines to make me feel behind in life or like I'm failing from time to time, if not even more guilty than most. Separating myself from the world and its expectations is still a work in progress and can be difficult for me at times. Perhaps this is why I found this quote to be so powerful, because it addressed an internal struggle of mine and gave me a new perspective on it. Society's expectations cloud the mind and fill our minds with this false sense that there's a universal age of breakthrough for everyone and that is simply not true. Everyone's story is unique in its own way and we all have different seasons of sowing and reaping in our lives.

Holding onto these "one size fits all" expectations fills our minds with pressure and angst that are robbing many of us of our peak years to enjoy ourselves, learn about ourselves, and to make the mistakes that will teach us valuable lessons as we progress deeper into adulthood. The twenties are typically viewed as a decade of discovering one's passions, interests, and self. It is widely considered the most formative and enjoyable decade of human life. These human beings are at an age where they're no longer minors who are fully dependent on the care of someone else, but they haven't yet gained the full experience necessary to grasp the expectations of adulthood in comparison to the childhood they left just a few years ago. They're in an in-between stage of learning how to become self-sufficient adults, while still searching for themselves and maintaining youthful tendencies and interests in the process.

Though difficult at times, it's truly the best of both worlds to be at an age to have the independence to discover oneself and one's interests without yet being put under the same pressures that a more experienced adult is exposed to. Yet, in today's world, these young people with massive potential and capability to impact the world are ridden and bogged down by stress, depression, anxiety, and crippling fears of failure during this *special* time in their lives. Although adult life is just beginning for this bunch, an overwhelming amount of them feel as if they've already failed because their life doesn't look exactly like what society says it should look like by a certain age or exactly like their friends' lives. They feel as though they've failed at life before they even begin living life and formulate a clear definition of what a successful life looks like for themselves in the first place.

Nonsense. Whether you're in your twenties or not, *you* define your own success and establish your own timelines. To empty your mind means to let go of society's expectations for you. It also means letting go of your own expectations of yourself. It means to take a deep breath and allow yourself to just be present. It means not to focus on where you want your feet to be but simply focusing on what you can do to grow wherever your feet are planted at this very moment.

These thoughts and preconditions put you in a box that doesn't even exist. They limit you to a few options and possibilities, when you live in a world filled with infinite options and possibilities. Empty your mind and simply just be, always understanding that focused effort and purposeful action towards the life you desire is always going to be more beneficial in moving you towards that life than playing the role of a spectator and watching everyone else live their lives.

To be formless means to have no definite shape or structure. Rather, formless objects have extreme flexibility and the ability to adapt to become useful. These formless objects become valuable and useful through this ability to adapt and take shape of whatever it is that they're being used to support, because they're able to be used in many different situations and for many different purposes. Their versatility and flexibility allow them to serve many different purposes to the world, which makes them valuable.

In the same way that you can empty your mind of expectation, you can also become formless. That is, you can become more flexible in your approaches to your life. Life is constantly changing and becoming fixed in any mindset or consumed with any expectations can hinder your ability to enter your flow state. The flow state is an important state of mind because it's a state of mind where you are one with your greatest desires amidst all the noise and distractions around you. Despite the noise around you, the flow state quiets your mind and amplifies your focus. In a state of flow, your capacity to create and serve the world is at its peak potential.

Water is an element of *flow*. It always goes with its nature, never against it. This flow is typically not interrupted by the outside elements, as water is formless and shapeless– its elements remain the same. The elements around it are constantly changing but water's elements remain the same. This rare characteristic is one of the main reasons that water accounts for over 70 percent of the earth's surface area and has been the most reliable resource in sustaining all forms of life throughout earth's history. It is valuable beyond words, as it is the element of life that we all must have to function and live.

You are also a being of flow. You're at your best when your mind and body are acting together with fluidity towards a focus, goal, or meaningful acquisition. Life and the elements around you are constantly changing and there will be pressure to change with these elements. However, developing the self-awareness and confidence necessary to discover your own path and remain focused on that path is one of the most beneficial skills to have in this world of influence and distraction. This is how you remain in your flow state, maximizing your potential to create and do meaningful work.

Unlike water, you are a mortal being. Therefore, you will not have the same longevity and resourcefulness that water has. This doesn't mean that you can't stay true to yourself and what you stand for throughout your short time here. Living in your truth and taking a strong stance for what you believe in will still have an impact on the world during your time here on earth. By doing so, you will become an element of persistent value to the world, just as water is.

Now that we've covered how water flows and remains the same, let's address the other capability of water– the ability to crash. While water is primarily an element of stillness and flow, there are certain conditions that stir water and cause it to "crash". Under the right conditions, the same water that sits calm and in a state of flow has the potential to become one of the most powerful forces on the planet. Just as it is capable of flowing and resisting change, water is also capable of adapting and doing whatever is necessary for its survival.

Take a tsunami for example. Tsunamis come from ocean water, which sits in stillness and a flow state of small, controlled waves. Much like in our world, the ocean is full of constants and variables that are constantly changing and applying pressure to the inhabitants to adapt and survive amongst the rapidly changing environment. Most of these changes are small, barely noticeable. Then, there are the changes that create massive changes and shifts. For example, an earthquake violently shakes the ocean floor and causes the ocean floor to rise. Now, the water in the ocean is required to rise with the rising ocean floor. All it takes is a few shocks in the environment to create a tsunami.

These massive waves are composed of the same ocean water that was previously sitting still and in a flow state, but these small waves are now adapting to changes in their environment and being forced to rise with the disturbance to their state of flow. Once sitting still, harmless, and in the calm of the middle of the ocean, these waves have risen into forces of great power and strength headed towards the coast. Of all the elements, water is widely considered to be the most powerful and capable of the greatest destruction when put into the wrong mix of outside sources. The ability to rise from the calm of stillness into forces of great strength makes water rare, an element of great balance that is capable of survival in any environment.

Life is like the ocean. We settle into habits and routines and our daily lives are often filled with repeating the same actions repeatedly. We operate in the form of mostly stillness and small waves throughout most of our lives, at peace and away from the conditions and pressures that we don't desire in our lives. Then, like in the ocean, those outside conditions and pressures eventually find us and there's nowhere to run or hide. We're left with a very important choice in these situations. There's the choice to find a way to rise above these pressures or the choice to remain still and succumb to the pressure.

It's not our goal to be destructive or to pose the threat that a tsunami does, but it is our goal to survive and to do so at the most optimal level possible. Reaching a flow where our mind and body are working together for us and protecting that flow from all the other outside influences and pressures is the goal. It's important to understand that this state of flow is possible for anyone who seeks it out and does the work required to establish it in their lives, but it's equally as important to understand that you're also capable of protecting it once it's established.

Struggle is a part of life. Without it, nothing has meaning because everything comes easily and without sacrifice. How one handles struggle is a major factor in the life that one lives, because a life worth living requires overcoming struggle to accomplish something along the way. For you to find peace, happiness, wealth, success, or anything worth having in your life, there will be a certain amount of struggle required for its attainment. Without the presence of struggle, there can be no hope for long-lasting, meaningful success and progression in life.

The ability to embrace these struggles that come, along with anything else that life throws your way, makes you a resilient being in this life. This ability to embrace struggle makes you a source of energy that persists and adapts as needed for your survival. The presence of struggle strengthens you along the journey, because it requires you to give significant effort and to have faith on the way to pursuing your dreams.

Life is a constant until death. There is no timeout option to stop the opposition's momentum and save the time on the clock like there is in sports. You can go to the bench area and strategize like a coach does, but the clock never stops moving. Time is the one constant in the equation of life. Every other part of the equation is constantly changing and evolving, but these are happening over the time that never stops moving. Nothing else is guaranteed in life, other than the fact that changes and adversity will come along— when they come, you *must* be able to adapt.

I believe a key characteristic of water that we as humans can adopt is water's ability to flow only *with* its nature, never against it. While we do have to go against our own *human* nature and shock ourselves out of our comfort zones to build a better life, we should never be going against our own *personal* nature and our *values* in our pursuit for a better life. The only way to a better life is through unapologetically being yourself and living through your core values. Yet, how many times in life do we know that a decision isn't right for us, that it'll only put us farther away from our dreams and desires? How many times do we make these decisions anyway? *We* keep ourselves stuck in these vicious cycles of self-sabotage by going against what we know deep down is against our nature.

As a result, we're suffering from unnecessary setbacks and resistance on a path that is already difficult enough. We make things harder on ourselves by pursuing things that are not in alignment with who we are and the things that we truly value in our lives. We go against our own nature and disrupt our own flow state towards making the necessary improvements in our lives. We know that these decisions aren't even an acceptable representation of who we are or the lives we want to live but we lack the discipline and self-respect required to draw the line and create the boundaries that allow us to show up for ourselves in a way that adds value and meaning to our lives.

How many times have you known water to just suddenly reverse its stream and go against its flow, to try and flow as if it were going downstream to go upstream? You haven't because water is an element of natural flow. It stays true to its nature and is unfazed by the elements and influences surrounding it. It consistently sticks to the patterns that allow it to flow with its nature, with the least amount of energy required and against the least resistance possible. It never adds any unnecessary resistance because it never gets out of alignment with its nature and its purpose to flow. Instead, water simply exists and flows slowly but surely. As a result, there is nothing that can stop water from flowing and serving its purpose to the world.

Learn to flow with your nature, to be at one with your mind and body in working towards becoming the person that you desire to become and building the life that you desire to live. The external challenges of this journey are enough resistance. There's no need to add yourself to the list of resistance and challenges you will face. Get out of your own way and flow the way you were meant to flow. Nobody can stop you when you're in your element and flowing in the way that is aligned for you, towards the people, places, things, and opportunities that are meant for you. Nobody can stop you when you're flowing in a way that compliments your values and pushes you *towards* the person you envision yourself being and the life you envision yourself living.

Another very important part of this wisdom from Mr. Lee is learning to "empty" the mind and become formless. The unpredictability of life cannot be stressed enough. Becoming fixed in your mindset towards anything in your life is a losing game because life is far from a fixed event. Anything and everything can change at any given moment. By becoming fixed in our mindsets, we make it much more difficult to accept things that happen in our lives when they don't match with how we wanted them to go or believed they were going to go.

It's a great strategy to have goals and to work towards them, but having your mindset completely fixed on how they will come to fruition and how the process *should* go does nothing but set you up for immense mental turmoil, disappointment, and heartbreak. Even when we set goals and reach them, the pathway in which they're fulfilled is often nothing like the one we were originally fixated on. Release yourself from the expectations you have for your journey and allow the journey itself to mold you and show you the way. This is why learning to love life for what it is, a *process*, is so critical.

If you would've told me during my senior year of high school that the next five years of my life were going to go the way they have, to say I wouldn't believe you would be an understatement. If you would've told me that I would survive that five years and come out *stronger* and *better*? I'd tell you there's no way those events led to a better life and a better person. Almost nothing went according to plan. How could I become stronger and better, consider myself to be living a better life?

At this time in my life, I had my own plans, and those plans were fixed in my mind. There would've been no way for me to see how all these challenges and obstacles I've endured over the past five years could redirect my plans for the better. At the time, basketball was my biggest passion and there was no plan B. I had a love-hate relationship with the game, but despite all the troubles and mental struggles, there was no denying that playing basketball for as long as I possibly could was my plan. I wouldn't have seen how giving up basketball and losing myself in the process would lead me to this point. If only I could be 18 years-old and this clueless again.

However, as I'm sitting here writing this today, I can't help but be thankful for every bit and piece of the story. It was hard to see it at times, but it all served a purpose and

259

played a part in this transformation of my life. I am who I am because of this story and because of the things that I've been through. I am who I am because I've learned to *grow* through the situations and circumstances that I go through in my life. The rest of my story looks completely different than it did at certain times in my life, in some of the most beautiful ways.

I'm beginning the work of serving my purpose to the world, of pouring my passion and deep love for people into meaningful acts of service to those in need. Did getting to this point look the way I thought it would look? I would be lying if I said I saw anything in my life going the way it has gone since I graduated high school and entered the real world– both the good and bad experiences. Does the fact that it doesn't look the way I thought it would look make it any less meaningful or satisfying to me? Absolutely not. I'm nowhere near finished running my race, but I take pride in the way that I've adjusted to the path I'm on and refocused my eyes on the finish line that God has had for me all along.

The path to a better version of yourself and a better life is not a straight line. The journey is long and demanding, but it's also the most rewarding and worthwhile journey you will ever experience. You can't fully enjoy the journey while you're still trying to hand-pick every road you take and every experience along the way. Instead, it's best to surrender control and let life and your intuition guide you along your paths. Evaporate your personal expectations for the journey and simply learn to appreciate every part of the journey. The "emptying" of your mind is critical for you to learn how to let go of control and focus solely on your growth and maturation throughout your process, while also learning to appreciate and embrace all parts of the journey of a lifetime that you're on.

Letting go of whatever is preventing you from being happy at this current moment is not an easy thing to do. I want you to know that I sincerely understand that and have had the same struggle for most of my life. I also want you to know that it *is* possible to release these things with the right attitude and mindset. Becoming formless and shapeless, able to adapt and do whatever is not only best, but necessary for you to live the highest quality of life possible for you– it's not an easy thing to do but it is possible. Not only is it possible, but achieving the highest quality of life for yourself is an experience you *deserve*. Learn to let things go and forgive others so that *you* can live in peace and harmony.

Like you and mostly every other human being, I often find myself worrying about my future. I struggle with being present and enjoying where I'm at in my life just as much as anyone else reading this. I'm almost willing to bet that I struggle with this even more than some of you. Some days are easier than others to overcome this persistent worry and source of anxiety. Some days, the anxiety gets the best of me and takes me out of my element temporarily. I'm striving to be better in every area of my life by implementing better ways of living, but I am a human being at the end of the day. I make mistakes and fall short just like we all do.

At the end of the day, we will never be perfect and a worthwhile life will never come easy. All we can strive to be is better than we were the day before and to grow a day closer to the life we desire and the final product that we are meant to finish this journey as. If we can make that simple commitment to ourselves, then we become much more capable of living in the present and within our natural flow. Detaching ourselves from our fixed expectations and controlling our emotions becomes much more realistic when we release ourselves from worry and anxiety about the past and the future.

Learning to simply just *be* in a world of chaos is far from easy, but it will change your life for the better. Flow at your own pace, in your own rhythm, and set out to make the most of this precious gift of life that you've been given. You don't have to move the quickest or do the impossible to live your best life. Simply show up with all you've got, and your path will be forged in due time. Be purposeful, still, in a state of flow, but also always remember that it's within you to rise up, make waves, and crash when it's necessary for your progression and survival. Be like water, my friend.

Chapter Eleven

Principle #11: In a world full of choices, always choose humility and gratitude.

Of the many things that I've learned both about myself and life itself up to this point on this journey, one of the most important things I've learned and am continuing to learn is the importance of the role that humility and gratitude play in bettering yourself and your life. For as long as we've been alive, we've heard the term "building blocks". These often represent certain characteristics, ideas, or philosophies that can be used to build a foundation that all our other counterparts stem from. This foundation greatly impacts the lives that we live and the individuals that we become in the process. Therefore, selecting which building blocks you choose to root your growth and development in is a very important and impactful decision.

Simply put, we have all been through circumstances and situations that have challenged us and changed us along the way. None of us will leave this life the exact same way that we came into it because we change and mature through our experiences. We've all experienced *something* in our lives that changed us in one way or another. We're all living with our own unique scars. My scars may look different from yours, yours different from the next person's– but they're all scars and we all have them. These are marks that have forever changed us and despite the wounds healing over time, we're left with these marks as memories of the injuries and pain that once were there. The pain eventually faded away, but we'll never forget these experiences and the pain they once brought.

As deep as these scars can get, as painful of a reminder they can be at times, these scars are a symbol of strength and overcoming. They tell stories of our greatest challenges in our lives, the times life *almost* got the best of us. However, these scars serve as proof that we have gone *through* these things and come out on the other side. We are left with scars for injuries that inflicted temporary pain and damage that we have healed from– not permanent pain, damage, or a grave. Sure, we'll never be the same as we were before the scars and injuries. Life is an event of progression and constant change, but these scars have made us stronger and tell the stories of how we have found the strength to overcome the difficult, painful times in our lives.

You approach your highest frequency and your greatest potential as a human being when you can put aside your own personal scars and see beyond your own personal traumas to find the humility to realize that everyone else around you is also dealing with their own personal scars and traumas as well. You draw closer to becoming the most dangerous, unstoppable version of yourself when you can look at everything you've been through up to this point in your life, both the good and the bad, and find gratitude for every experience and the role it played in shaping you into the person you have become today and the life that you live today. When you can widen the lens through which you see the world to see beyond your own circumstances, this is when you have the greatest chance to connect with others and leave a lasting impact. Without humility and gratitude, it's very difficult to be of service to others and to fulfill your purpose to the very fullest extent, to reach others and leave a lasting impact.

As contradictory as it may initially sound, putting the needs of others before your own and being willing to help others is the quickest way to discover your purpose and to find your own personal needs fulfilled. Almost all great leaders, both historically and in the present, have found themselves in positions of power and built noteworthy reputations for themselves by putting the needs of others before their own and willingly being of service to others. By devoting their time, energy, and effort into primarily satisfying the needs of others, these leaders have been able to live purpose-driven lives, excel in their careers, and many have simultaneously been well-compensated for their abilities as a by-product of their willingness to serve others.

The world-famous peacemaker, Mahatma Gandhi, famously observed that, "The best way to find yourself is to lose yourself in the service of others." This was one of the many very profound and powerful messages from Gandhi, who was one of the greatest minds and humanitarians that the world has ever seen. Even more impactful than his famous quote and ideology was the fact that Gandhi embodied the words he spoke in his own life. He was arguably the most selfless and humble figure of power and influence that the world has ever seen. Gandhi was the embodiment of "practicing what you preach", as he devoted his entire life to creating peace and used his platform to corroborate civil rights for all.

Though he had the status and individual platform to separate himself from the struggles of others, he never allowed his focus and effort to become an individual focus that would separate him from his mission of serving others. Despite receiving respect and being treated as royalty by some, Gandhi never lost sight of his passion for speaking up for others and fighting for those who did not share those same privileges. He moved many hearts and minds through the means of nonviolent tactics of resistance. He gave the opposition the fight of a lifetime without even raising his hand to throw a punch. Gandhi was ultimately assassinated for the threat his commitment to serving his purpose and serving others posed to the old order of things, but his influence and the important lessons he taught us about the power of a life that's rooted in being of service to others lives on today.

On January 20, 1961, John F. Kennedy officially took his oath to become the 35th president of the United States of America. In addition to swearing himself into office as the chief commander of the United States, Kennedy gave an inaugural address that won him the support of millions of people nationwide. He had just been elected president and was the youngest man to accomplish such a feat at the time, only age 43 when he was handed the reins to one of the most powerful nations in the world– with the expectations of growing that power and creating an even better nation.

He could've easily used the address to boast about his major victory and to attempt to excite the American people with his youthful and progressive plans for the advancement of America, but he did the exact opposite. Kennedy acknowledged that he was still learning, still growing as a leader, and admitted that America needed more than his leadership to continue building itself into a great empire.

Addressing the American public for the first time as president, Kennedy spoke on the importance of sticking together and being willing to be of service to others. Near the end of his speech, he very famously called all American citizens to action when he said, "Ask not what your country can do for you– ask what you can do for your country." He continued to say, "My fellow citizens of the world: ask not what America will do for you, but what together we can do for the freedom of man." These statements were concise, but they were beyond powerful in regard to influencing the public's support of Kennedy and his presidency– not just nationwide, but globally.

Kennedy knew that by living lives committed to service to others and having a willingness to provide favors for others in need, those favors would be returned to the United States and build relationships that would help the United States become stronger both domestically and internationally. He didn't hold himself in too high of a regard to ask the public for their help in making the world a better place through expanding communications, business, and overall opportunity in a way that would bring unity and prosperity. He knew this was a tall task and he couldn't do it alone. It didn't matter what records he had broken or what odds he had overcome to become the youngest man ever elected president of the United States at the time. He understood his limited capacity to bring change without first changing the hearts of those he desired to assist him in bringing change. Therefore, on the biggest stage he had ever been on in his life, he humbly asked the public to join in with him on creating a better future for all people by committing to living lives of service to one another.

The freedom that I have to write and publish this book, to share my thoughts and ideas– it has been protected and defended by brave people who I have never even met in person. Many people have faced the ugliest of evil that exists on this planet– risked their lives and pushed aside all their other personal interests and the comfort of their civilian lives so that you and I can enjoy the freedoms and rights that we're able to enjoy on a daily basis. Despite the problems and negatives going on in their own lives, these people show up to protect other people from the world of problems and negativity that could show up on our own doorsteps if not for their protection. For this, they are heroes and some of the humblest human beings that walk this earth.

Whether you agree with the use of militant force or specific causes the military may or may not choose to fight for, these people are just doing their jobs and they have made significant sacrifices to be able to not only defend their own nation, but also to provide aid to neighboring nations in need. They humbly and selflessly put their lives on the line for a cause that is bigger than themselves, personally making the choice to commit their lives to serving and protecting others. Without their sacrifices and commitment, society, and everything it stands for, is left at risk to invasion and persecution from those who do not hold the same beliefs and wish to enforce their own extreme beliefs and values on the rest of the world. Without security and protection, it's impossible to take the strong stance necessary against what is unjust and what we believe to be morally and ethically wrong.

No matter how you choose to slice the pie, humility is a major piece of the pie in terms of reaching our human potential. We simply can't understand our capacity to impact others and do the work necessary without first recognizing the value of having a willingness to serve others. We must first come to the realization that our individual lives themselves, the challenges and circumstances that we face, are of very little importance to the world at face value. However, how we choose to live these individual lives we have been given, how we *respond* to the challenges and circumstances in our lives to become people of value and positive influence, is of great importance to the world.

We have all been given the same gift of life. Yet, within that same gift, we've all had different passions, interests, purposes, and talents placed within us to put out into the world amongst us. We will all choose to do many different things with these gifts and end up with many different experiences and outcomes, as we all have different paths we're traveling on and different callings on our lives. Therefore, it isn't what's been placed in us itself that makes our lives significant to the world. What truly matters and makes our lives significant to the world is how we're able to humble ourselves and make use of the gifts and talents we've been given to maximize the amount of service and impact we're able to provide to the world.

The word "humility" is so often misconceived to be the equivalent of feeling as though we lack the capability to achieve worthwhile things in our lives, but this is not the true meaning of humility. Humility is acknowledging that we are more than capable of achieving whatever we put our minds to in life. We're afforded full permission to believe in ourselves and our abilities. However, we also acknowledge that these talents and abilities were given to us for a reason- it's only those pursuits that are using our gifts and abilities to impact and create opportunities for others that are worthwhile.

When we're willing to be that pair of ears to hear a hurting human out, to purchase a meal for the homeless person sitting on the ground outside of the grocery store with a smile on our faces, or to invite the new kid who just moved away from his family and is feeling lonely for a night out with our own friends– these kind gestures and small acts of service have a way of removing our focus from what's missing in our own lives and allow us to focus on being a blessing and filling needs in the lives of others. When we can put aside our own wants and needs to be there for others, that is when life changes for us. Not only does our own list of "needs" tend to shrink as we learn to serve others, but we also develop ourselves into better human beings that are more capable of developing the relationships and bonds that will lead us to the people and places that will put us in the position to have our own true needs met at the right time. Through aligning our energy with humility and a willingness to give, our energy is returned in abundance, and we live better, more wholesome lives.

The next essential piece to your life's strong foundation is gratitude. Gratitude is, in essence, one of the most powerful and liberating emotions that we as human beings can possess and express. It is the quickest, most natural high available to you in this life. It's more potent than any other drug or substance known to man. The greatest thing about this high? It's available to you at any moment in your life that you seek it out, free of charge and free of the negative risks and side effects that come with intoxication from any other substance.

No matter what you may be going through in your life, there is always something to be grateful for. The simple fact that you have breath in your lungs and healthy eyes to read these words is a blessing in itself. If you look a little deeper, you will find much more to be grateful for, because the truth is that you can find gratitude for *everything* in your life with open eyes and an open heart. When you're able to effectively do this and to truly show gratitude for *all* your experiences, the experiences themselves lose their power over you.

Instead, you become empowered by what all your experiences have given you. What each and every experience gave you, what they added to your life, becomes the focus– not the things and people that they took away in the process. When you acknowledge and appreciate the value of what's been added to you in the process, it helps you to make peace with and also appreciate what was subtracted from you to allow you to create room for the blessings you have in your life today.

In the world we live in, it's very easy to consume negativity and become bombarded by the negativity that surrounds us all. There is absolutely no shortage of negativity, and negativity is screamed from the mountaintops, while positivity is kept to a whisper to all but those who intentionally seek to hear it. That being said, you must protect your mind from being consumed by negativity in a world that aims to consume your mind with negativity. Negativity sells because it keeps people living in fear– a fear that is essential to maintaining control of your mind and keeping you from the truth that will set you free.

This truth can only be found when you begin to think for yourself and do the work that is necessary to protect your mind from negative outside influences.

Outside of a divine calling and an intimate relationship with your source of faith, gratitude is the greatest weapon in your arsenal of protection against the invasiveness of negativity that has stopped so many from living the lives they were capable of living and is currently stopping many of us from living up to our full potential. Simply making it a point to acknowledge how grateful you are for the many blessings that you have amongst the few things missing from your life– it will put into perspective how fortunate you truly are and allow you to value the blessings over the voids.

When you live your life from a perspective of appreciation and gratitude for the blessings in your life, the voids seem miniscule in comparison. You will later find that the voids are likely for your own protection. Gratitude is about focusing on what *is*, being thankful for those things, and releasing what *isn't*. It's about trusting completely in that strong source of faith to provide for your needs at every moment, accepting that God has your life in the palm of His hand and His plans for your life are greater than anything you could possibly imagine or accomplish for yourself on your own.

It's not a crime for you to want more for yourself, your life, and the people you care about. If you're truly growing and developing as you age, it's only natural to expect more from yourself as you progress in knowledge, wisdom, and understanding. It's natural to want to live a life that brings you and the people you care about peace, happiness, and comfortability. However, while working towards those things, the process will become much more enjoyable and much less frustrating if you learn to show gratitude for where you are in the present moment and trust the path that you're on, regardless of what it may currently look like.

Your life will never be perfect, and it will never go precisely as you may have planned it to go, but that doesn't mean that there isn't still beauty in your life. In fact, the moments that alter your course and throw a wrench in your personal plans are very often the moments you will look back on and be most grateful for in the long run. It's the moments that cause you to dig deep and fight through something that transform you the most, because these moments reveal strength and courage within you that can only be revealed to you through certain stresses and tests of faith. These moments mean the most because there is meaning behind the suffering. The suffering was temporary, but the newfound strength gives the suffering meaning and translates to the rest of your life. When you discover this model of temporary suffering to produce growth and strength that remains for the entirety of your life, you discover what life is all about and the important role that perseverance plays in life.

I've intimately shared with you some of the darkest moments of my life. These are moments that up until this book, I hadn't disclosed to anyone outside of close friends or family, if anyone at all. I was just as lost as any of you reading this book, if not even more lost. There were times in my life where I completely lost my way and forgot about the many good things and people I had in my life. I speak on these struggles, because I know that they're real struggles and I've looked every single last one of them in the eyes– but you're reading my testimony and not my obituary for a reason.

It was this idea of gratitude that helped me begin the process of rediscovering myself and picking up the broken pieces. Amid all the darkness, there was still plenty of light to hold on to. There's *always* a way out, and sometimes it's as simple as finding it within you to find appreciation for one thing in your life that you're grateful for that will help you realize the many other things you have to be grateful for in your life.

Gratitude is about much more than being grateful. It's about giving yourself permission to enjoy your life, whether you find yourself in the peaks or in the valleys. It's about learning to take the pain and reframing it in a way that leads to purpose and prosperity. It's about redefining the meaning of your life and all the experiences you've accumulated along the way– holding onto what is good and useful and allowing yourself the grace and forgiveness to release what simply brought pain, confusion, and anything else into your life that was a hindrance to your growth and progression.

It's about learning to appreciate the present moments even in the midst of pursuing a better future. It's all about understanding that there is a source of strength within you that you can always tap into, regardless of how low the present moment may feel or frightening the future may look. Life itself is good and there is *always* the opportunity to learn better, love better, earn better, and live better today than you did yesterday. That will always be empowering and something to be grateful for.

When you can accept everything for what it is, even those moments in your life that felt like or may currently feel like the lowest of the lows, and find appreciation for them, this is where the weight of these experiences begins to loosen their grip on you. This is where you get your love for life back. This life and the situations that you have gone through, are currently going through, and will go through in your future– they're bigger than you and you won't always understand them or be overwhelmed with excitement when faced with some of the things you will be faced with in your life. You don't have to fully understand these situations and moments in your life to be grateful for the lessons they've taught you, the people they've added or removed from your life, and the strength they've revealed within you.

The most important thing to remember is that these moments don't have to tell the full story. The stories that we hold onto and cherish the most are not those that are predictable and filled with nothing but positivity. Those are fairy tales that we save for the kids because the innocent world of children is the only place that those types of stories are valued. In the real world, we cherish the stories that require the characters to go through challenges, to evolve and develop knowledge and skills, to *overcome* what is standing in their way, and most of all, to learn valuable life lessons along the way.

Why don't we allow ourselves to cherish our own challenges that have put us through difficult times to develop us as human beings and evolved us into wiser, stronger versions of ourselves? Why don't we focus on the many things these challenges have equipped us with and given us with the same intensity that we focus on what was removed

275

or taken away from our lives? There's a hero's journey at your fingertips, but it's going to require you to get through some difficult challenges, while learning to be grateful for those challenges that help you find the strength and courage within you that will help you find your life's greater purpose and meaning.

On my own journey, I've had to check myself and find gratitude for many moments throughout my life. There's been many moments where the positive turning point seemed out of reach because I was unable to see past the way I was feeling in the moment. With all these moments in my life, there's a particular pain attached to their memories that took something away from my life, but if it weren't for these moments, the person that I am today would not exist. I had to go through every single loss and setback to experience the feelings of grief and pain that pushed me to become a better, more devoted human being.

To this day, I don't understand everything that's happened in my life, and I never will. I'm learning to make peace with this, humbled by the simple fact that life can change in an instant. I'm also grateful for the difficult lessons that life has taught me up to this point in my life. I'm grateful for God's grace and mercy that saved me from self-destruction, even when my actions could've very easily ruined or drastically altered my life in negative ways. I'm grateful for the strong love of my parents, family, and close friends that carried me through when I didn't even love myself. I'm grateful for the things that went well, but equally as grateful for the things that fell apart and the wisdom and self-control I was forced to learn during these difficult times in my life.

As long as I live, I will never forget the day that I received an email that changed my life forever. It was October 28th, 2019, a typical Monday on campus for me in Cincinnati, Ohio. I was 19 years-old and in my sophomore year of college. This particular day was two days after my team and I had played the first game of our season. Most of the team had either transferred in or were freshman, so we were brand new to playing with each other for the most part.

We lost a tough game in double overtime on our home floor to one of the best, most experienced teams in the league. Despite the heartbreaking loss, we had put the league on notice that it would be a dogfight when you came to Cincinnati, Ohio and had to see those white and purple jerseys. It was a tough loss to open the season, but my teammates and I were in high spirits because it was time to do what we loved. We had shown to everybody, including ourselves, that something special was being built between a group of 16 brothers. The brutal preseason was finally behind us and the excitement of basketball season was visible in all my teammates' eyes.

We were there to get an education but pounding that orange ball on the hardwood and hearing it swish through the nylon nets meant something to each and every one of us. You don't make it through the things that we went through without basketball meaning something to you or without having brothers going through the same struggle to your left and right. We had endured six weeks of absolute hell, and it was finally time to line up against other teams and make them pay. There was no feeling back then like knowing basketball season had arrived and a fresh season was underway.

Back to October 28th, 2019, I had gone to all my classes, taken a nap, and was now in the dining hall to eat before practice. Nothing seemed out of the ordinary. The student union was filled with the usual chatter and laughter that it always was filled with. As usual, everybody was rushing to load up their plates before the football players came in and cleared out the pans, trays, and whatever else they could find that had food in it after practice.

I fixed my plate, went to the salad bar to make a bowl of salad, and then finally made my way over to the drink station to grab a drink. I grabbed a plastic cup and I filled it halfway with Fruit Punch Gatorade and halfway with water. This was the only drink I ever drank before workouts or practice because it was the perfect balance of hydration and electrolytes to prepare my body to work. It was a Monday, so I wasn't expecting a light practice and had to make sure my body was hydrated and ready for whatever Coach Lester was planning to throw at us.

Once I fixed my drink, I walked towards the table where one of my teammates was sitting and sat across from him. Ty and I spent a lot of time together off the court, from playing ping pong in the student center, to knocking out study hall together, to playing video games in the dorm rooms. More times than not, we were together on campus or getting into something off campus. Naturally, he was one of my best friends on the team and there was never a dull moment with Ty and his thick Baltimore accent.

Not long after we sat down, the student union became much louder suddenly. Some people were rushing to take their dishes to the dish pit, some calling their parents, and there was lots of other noise all around. One of our friends on the track team came by the table and told us, "Check your email. I can't believe this." I could tell there was some big news in the email, but I could've never guessed the news I was about to receive. I pulled my phone out, went to my school email, and there it sat. I had an email from the CCU Board of Trustees.

The very first paragraph of the email read, "We hope this letter finds you well! You may have heard by now that CCU has made the difficult decision to cease offering accredited degree programs following the Fall 2019 semester," After informing us that the school had reached out to over a dozen accredited institutions that would accept us under the terms of an academic hardship application, the email continued on, "It is CCU's goal and expectation that we will identify one or more teach-out or transfer options for each currently enrolled student," Last but not least, the email ended with "In an effort to maximize funding for the process of a school closure, all extra-curricular and athletic activities have been terminated, effective immediately."

Blindsided. Shocked. Betrayed. These are the best words I can use to describe what I was feeling at the time of reading this email. I had just transferred to CCU two months prior, moved eight hours away from my family, and gotten the fresh start that I wanted so badly after my underwhelming freshman season. In terms of the team, this was the closest team that I was ever part of, and we had a very talented, young roster that had a chance to be something special for years to come. We all came to campus as individuals just two

279

months before we received this email, but we had grown to become a team that loved and cared about one another in a very short amount of time.

To this day, I find myself wondering what could've been from time to time and just missing the guys that I was blessed to share this experience with. I knew that this email meant I would once again be separated from good people and teammates I loved, way before I was ready– even though it wasn't my fault this time around. I knew basketball played a major role in my decision to attend CCU and now I was expected to finish out the semester without it. The only news I had ever received worse than this at this point in my life was the news of my Uncle Wayne's death and my mom's cancer diagnosis.

From the surface, that email was all bad. It took my teammates away from me. It took the game I loved away from me. It added the stress of finding another school to transfer to, having just gone through the recruiting process for the second time and transferring schools the previous summer. Keep in mind, I had been told I wasn't good enough to play in college two years before this time in my life and I was now looking to convince a third coach that I belonged at the collegiate level!

There was a world of negatives that came with this situation. Yet again, I would not be here as the person I am today if it weren't for this experience and the journey it took me on. I felt as though I had just lost everything that I had been working so hard for and it was disheartening to say the least. In many ways, I'll never be the same person that I was when I was at CCU- I'll never get that innocent, naive, and sheltered mindset back that hadn't gotten a taste of the real world yet Amongst all the negatives, this experience helped me realize that going through adversity can only add to you in the long run and that life is a game of evolution. Our lives weren't meant to stay the same forever– we're meant to grow and evolve through our experiences.

It all had to fall apart for me to start over and rebuild myself. This time, I would build myself up stronger and better than the previous version of myself. I had to fall on my face to truly see what I was made of and to learn how to get back up off the ground. If it wasn't for this disruption in my plan, I would most likely still find my worth in how coaches told me I was playing or how many points and rebounds I averaged in a season. I had to lose basketball to find all the other passions and interests that were always deep within me, but that were always pushed to the side for my commitment and love for sport. I had to lose basketball to find *me*.

I would've missed out on the moments that truly humbled me and led me towards filling the voids I had in my life with the right things and people if it weren't for feeling the emptiness of the voids in the first place. This email put into perspective how quickly everything in life can change and it reminded me of the importance of remaining humble and being grateful for every moment. Most of all, the difficult seasons that followed this email introduced me to the *real* me for the first time in my life. I no longer had basketball to distract my mind year-round from the emptiness I felt deep down, and I was forced to do the work that was necessary to find a state of fulfillment and peace.

In the long run, experiencing the school closure at CCU *gave* me so much more in life than it took from me. I went through the roughest two years of my life following the school's closure, but the learning experience itself was one that no college or university could have ever given me if I didn't live out the experiences that I did. To say there wasn't suffering, to say I almost didn't lose it all mentally– it would be a lie to say these things. Life got difficult and then proceeded to only get more difficult from there. Amongst all the suffering and the uncertainty that surrounded my life during this time, there's still so much about this experience that I'm forever grateful for.

I learned how to handle disappointing endings. I learned how to stay hopeful during the storm. I learned how to take small steps forward, to appreciate myself for not throwing in the towel. I learned how to live my life without basketball being the focus, to detach my love for myself from any results in my performance and how others outside of myself felt about my performance. I learned to look forward and make daily deposits of positivity, to see the glory ahead, and to focus less on the pain I was feeling in the moment. I learned to prevail and fight for the things that I desire in my life, even when it all seems to be crashing down.

I was in a living hell it seemed like when CCU closed. I missed class registration for the following semester, so I wasn't even enrolled in school for the spring semester. I had to wait until the fall semester of the next school year to enroll in school again. I went from being a full-time student athlete at a school out of state, constantly surrounded by teammates, and with a schedule so full I couldn't afford to hit the snooze button for five minutes to no classes, no basketball, being separated from my teammates, and a full-time job at a TJ Maxx near my hometown within a span of three months.

I briefly discussed this time period in my life earlier in the book. I felt like I had every reason to be mad at the world. I couldn't see what I did to deserve having everything taken from me so suddenly, but behind the scenes, what God was taking away was nothing in comparison to what he was adding to my life. He was always working for my greater good and I simply had to go through the things I went through to come to understand that. All He needed me to do was have faith and meet him halfway, and it took some time for that to happen, but my life has changed as a result of making the decision to take those steps towards Him.

Having my life flipped upside down was what it took for me to recognize that there was much more to life than sports, that there was value in me as a human being outside of my ability to put a ball in a hoop or block a shot at the rim. I began to learn about myself, my passions, and became interested in finding my purpose in life in the lowest moments of my life, when it looked all bad from the surface. I found my strong desire to help others and to be a voice to those struggling, during my own struggles and cries out for help– in the trenches. I became inspired to become somebody when everything happening in my life had almost convinced me I would never amount to anything.

God took the ashes from a difficult time in my life and He began to show me glimpses of the beauty that would come from those ashes if I trusted the work and kept moving forward. I'm grateful God blew my plans up, because seeing myself on this journey and watching myself develop, evolve, and mature has been the most rewarding process. I wouldn't be the person I am today without the challenges and growing pains

I've endured on my journey. I wouldn't possess the strength and faith I have in my life today, if I hadn't first experienced what it felt like to feel weak and hopeless. I wouldn't be able to relate to as many broken and struggling human beings if it weren't for my own seasons of brokenness and struggle in my life.

Making it back on my feet after being in the places I've been mentally, there's a confidence instilled within me that I can do *anything* that I give my all to. You can't put a price tag on that type of confidence and belief in yourself when you've been someone who's struggled with listening to the limiting lies others have told you about yourself your entire life. This confidence and belief in myself have changed my life and afforded me opportunities in my life that I likely would've passed up or never been aware of in the first place if it weren't for that email I received on October 28th, 2019.

The fact that I currently live 2,000 miles across the country from my hometown in southwest Atlanta, all alone at 23, is a testament to both my own personal craziness and the strength that I found within myself to handle challenges in my life while picking up the pieces and moving on from CCU. My experience with CCU opened my eyes to the growth that occurs when you're forced out of your comfort zone and being strong is your only choice. I never recognized the strength of my mind and my spirit until they were tested to the limit. I owe my experiences at CCU a lot of credit for who I am today and how I live my life.

Through those tests, I've come to realize that I've built this mindset within myself that knows no limitation other than death itself. The world's limitations don't exist in my world. I've been beating the odds and rising above and beyond what the statistics said I would be my entire life. Trusting myself to make that move and learning to survive on my own has just been another victory over the limitations that I once put on myself and my life. The strength to do so is largely rooted in the experience CCU gave me at an early age in my life.

Another defining moment in my life happened about a year ago from writing this. The first time I experienced heartbreak, I did everything I could to avoid feeling the reality of my emotions. I was also the one who walked away the first time, so I felt certain emotions, but they were on account of my own actions and decisions. I had never experienced losing a deep bond before the first one, so much of the challenge was dealing with having unfamiliar emotions for the first time.

This time it was different. I had been through the CCU closure. I knew how it felt to end a two-year relationship. I had felt these emotions before and knew the risks that came with taking a chance at getting to know and love someone deeply. When the emotions came upon me this time, I knew I had to respond better than I did the first time around and I was determined to do so. Being broken-hearted is a powerful place to be in life– you feel like nothing will truly heal the deep ache in your chest, but you're willing to try almost anything for even the slightest bit of relief. The breaking of the heart spurs humans into action like almost no other experience in life.

When the heart breaks and you're going through significant amounts of emotional pain and turmoil, your body is also made aware of the pain you're experiencing and the

285

damage that has been done to your heart. The body can undergo extreme amounts of physical pain and duress, but a heart that is not functioning properly is a direct threat to any human being's life. Therefore, at the signal of your broken heart, the body is naturally thrown into survival mode and makes every effort to make the necessary repairs to the heart. The actions you take to heal your broken heart are due to the signals that your body has sent to you, indicating that this repair to your heart is an urgent matter.

The body fights for you like no other when it is made aware of your pain and suffering, whether it be giving you the adrenaline rush needed to endure a life-threatening situation or resting the brain and sending you into a coma to protect your brain from significant damage in the event of a traumatic experience. If we fought half as hard as our bodies do, we wouldn't have half the problems that we find ourselves faced with. When the body's fight for your well-being is paired with your own fight for your well-being and an intentional focus on healing, healing becomes inevitable. Healing is possible when you believe it's possible, but it doesn't come without a fight.

In the case of most injuries, it's not uncommon to see that repairing an injured area and concentrating on regaining strength in the injured area results in the injured area becoming stronger than it was before the injury. The same is true of a broken heart. The heart is meant to break and rebuild itself stronger. It's constantly evolving to provide peak functioning for you. Make no mistake about it– it brings great pain when it breaks but this pain is nothing that your heart wasn't designed to endure and recover from. I'm still not sure if I'm convinced that the heart that shatters will ever be made fully whole again, but it *will* reach a level of healing that allows it to function again.

I could've never even known it was possible to care so much about a human being that wasn't part of my family before this experience. I had been stingy with my love and emotional attachment ever since ending my first relationship. I honestly didn't care too much if people stayed or if people left at this point in my life, in terms of romantic interests. I valued my family and friends, felt like they were all I needed to be content in my life at this point in my life. I wasn't looking for love and I was praying it wasn't looking for me. It had been this way for a couple years and I didn't see this changing anytime soon.

It turns out that the saying is true. You find love when you stop looking for it and when you least expect it. I won't bore you with the details, but one random FaceTime call from an old friend began a spark that would set my heart on fire for this girl in a few months' time. It started out as just frequent phone calls, checking in on each other, having basic discussions about life, and getting to know each other better.

You know how it goes from there– the phone calls become numerous and you begin to look forward to them throughout your days. You think to yourself, "What has gotten into me?" Before you can answer, the phone rings again and you see her face and hear her laugh over the phone. That important question you just asked yourself suddenly disappears and seems like an intrusive attack on your happiness. You decide to just let the concerns go and allow the moment to take you wherever it's leading you. This went on for a while and

I'll admit, she stole a heart that I didn't even know existed in me anymore right from underneath me.

Once I began to feel my heart opening back up, it belonged to her before I even had the chance to fight for it. When I couldn't physically be with her, I wanted to be on the phone with her. When I was on the phone with her, I was wishing I could physically be with her. No matter how high I built my walls up, she made the climb and toppled right over them. I thought about her constantly and craved her presence in my life unlike anything I had ever experienced before. I didn't realize it until later because the feeling was such a rarity for me in my life, but I was wholeheartedly in love.

We had some ups and downs on our short journey but I genuinely appreciated every moment we spent together. I saw past the fear of loving someone that had paralyzed me for years and I was finally able to take that leap of faith again. Two hours with her felt like twenty minutes, and I was almost certain that I had found the type of love for her that's only meant to be found once in a lifetime. I pushed aside the intrusive thoughts that sat in the back of my mind and my own personal insecurities. I pursued a deeper relationship with her with everything I had to give because it was what my heart told me to do. No sacrifice seemed too big, because in my eyes, she was worth it all.

For a brief moment, it looked like I was going to get a chance at the girl of my dreams and I felt like I was walking on the clouds. A chance was all I needed and the rest would be history. I think that was the hardest part to accept about this situation. I felt like I had shown her that I was serious about her and was moving with a pure motive. My heart was absolutely on fire for this girl and I was thinking about a future together. I knew I was still young and had things to work on, but I didn't see myself growing and working on those things with anybody else. There was nothing I wanted more than a chance to share my life with her because she was *it* for me– the one who made me feel like I understood why no previous relationship had worked out and the one who made me start thinking like a man, no longer like an immature boy.

As we all know, relationships are difficult. You can love someone, but there's various other factors that go into relationships and making that type of commitment to another human being. In this case, it wasn't the right timing and there were other priorities that needed to be taken care of without the distraction or potentially added stress of a relationship. I understood that the timing wasn't the best and that time could perhaps prepare us to meet again one day, but I felt something that I had never felt before and it was almost impossible to just put those feelings on the shelf for later.

I hadn't cared much about anyone leaving my life for years at this point, but watching her walk out of my life stung me more than I could've ever imagined. The feeling I had was similar to the feeling that I had when I would go to gatherings on my mom's side as a young kid and the feeling I had when the CCU news broke– I had given significant amounts of my time, energy, and effort, just for someone else to give up on me and slam the door on something that meant a great deal to me. Rejection had become a bitter subject in my life, and I was facing yet another bitter dose.

I don't say that from a standpoint of any disrespect because there were circumstances that made things difficult and she was just acting in her best interest. To this day, I love this girl with every bone inside of my body and would never ask her to neglect her own well-being or to put herself second at any time. My love for her and my respect for her feelings still didn't change the fact that this felt like another time in my life where things were going well, I was getting used to things going well, and then it all imploded one day. Having respect for her feelings didn't change the fact that I had feelings about the situation too.

The sleepless nights on FaceTime were replaced with sleepless nights without FaceTime or any form of contact for that matter. I would lay in my bed at night, staring at the ceiling and wondering where I went wrong and if there was anything more I could've done. I would relive all the memories I had made with her through the brutal flashbacks in my mind and pictures in my camera roll. I would put my pillows over my ears, trying to drown out the memory of her voice and laughter that had become a source of comfort to me. Despite the distance that separated us, I knew with no doubt whatsoever that I loved her enough to cover every mile tenfold. I had truly come to understand the saying, "Home is where the heart is."

It was through this experience that I learned that having unconditional love for someone does not always guarantee favorable outcomes. One of the purest forms of love is selflessness, which means learning to have compassion for the thoughts and feelings of others above your own. If you love someone unconditionally, it means you're willing to sacrifice and suffer to be there for them, on both bad terms and good. Regardless of the end result, the willingness to personally sacrifice and suffer for what's best for both parties remains the same.

It brought great suffering to my mind and soul, but I realized that I would have to love her from a distance for the time being if I wanted to do what was best for both of us. Of course, I wanted to do what was best for us in my head, but the heart has a mind of its own once it's involved. It was hard to accept then and it's still hard to accept now at times, but I had no choice but to accept the situation for what it was because the love was unconditional and I did only want what was best for her. I had always told her there wasn't anything I wouldn't do for her, but I don't think I had ever considered that there might come a time where that might include letting her go and moving on. Even still, I kept my word– no matter how empty I felt watching the sound of her voice and the feeling of her touch fade away from my life.

I can see her face as I'm writing this, and I can still remember how I felt when the energy shifted and I realized I was approaching yet another tough goodbye in my life. I can still close my eyes and remember the feeling I felt in my stomach when it all evaporated before my eyes and she was gone. The vibrant blue of her eyes that contrasts with her skin so uniquely and her distinct laugh quickly remind me of how it feels to find peace and happiness in the soul after feeling dead inside for so long. Yet, those same blue eyes and that same laugh simultaneously remind me of how it feels to hopelessly long for what once brought wholeness to the heart once it's gone and the heart shatters– like a punch to the gut.

You never forget what it feels like to get punched in the gut because it's different from most other pains that you experience in life. A great deal of the pain of a gut punch is its unexpectedness and the fact that it comes from someone close to you. It can only come from someone who is close enough to reach your gut and it always comes when your guard is down. The pain it brings is insatiable, so no one in their right state of mind would intentionally open themselves up to the torment that comes with a violent blow to the gut. It's an internal pain that must run its course. There is no prescription for an instantaneous cure or even slight relief. The only way through the pain of a punch to the gut is by going through the pain of a punch to the gut.

There's no denying the fact that I was hurting. I was affected by the loss of a presence that meant a lot to me in my life, but I didn't forget the excess pain and suffering I brought into my life through the poor decisions I made when I found myself in this situation earlier in my life. I was done ruining myself over things that were out of my control. At this point in my life, I had been working hard on myself and I was beginning to become somebody that I was proud to be.

The devil was working in my life, telling me all the same lies he used to tell me as a kid and in my earlier years once again. The bitterness of rejection was something I had struggled with my entire life and it was an emotion that he used to keep me in bondage for years. It was a childhood trauma that he used to put the deep-seeded fear into my head that I was *always* the problem and wasn't worthy of love, a lie that I had held onto for so long in my life. I was tired of believing the exhausting lies that had filled my head and that had been taking away from my ability to enjoy my life for years, so I challenged myself to stop listening to them and to instead live out my own truths.

I had simply put in too much to give up now. My life meant something to me now. Despite the pain and my lack of understanding of the situation, I had to do my best to move on with my life and keep watering my own plants. I was hoping to join our plants and water them together, but that wasn't the way things were working out at the moment and I had to accept that and commit to still watering my own plants with the same enthusiasm. The only thing I could do was control what I could control and maintain my composure.

I had a great support system around me throughout the process, but *nobody* put the work in to make the progress that I had made at that point in my life but me. I would be damned if I let anything that didn't build me into the person I was becoming ruin what I had worked so hard to build. Sometimes, everything around you is telling you one thing and you must simply *choose* growth, push into the discomfort, and do the opposite of whatever it is that the mind and body are craving.

Even though this experience didn't have the end result I was hoping for, I can't say that I would trade the experience of growing close to someone and making meaningful memories for anything else in the world. Sometimes, even good experiences have endings we never see coming– this doesn't mean the experience was all bad. I was dealing with the undeniable pain of watching the girl I loved walk out of my life, but I knew I had to turn my eyes and my heart to the multitude of blessings I had to be grateful for in my life.

I have a Creator who sees the good in me, who saved my life from the fate that my actions deserve. I have friends and family who love me and care for me in the times that I'm hurting. I'm employed and have a sufficient source of income to keep a roof over my head and food on my table. I have endless books and podcasts at my disposal, to continue to strengthen my mind and provide me with insight from different perspectives and increase my knowledge and wisdom. I have a stronger sense of self and was reminded of the importance of being my own source of happiness through this experience. I'm a better, stronger man for having gone through this experience and learning how to prioritize logic and discipline in times that emotions want to take the wheel and mislead me.

I now realize that opening myself up to experiencing deeper relationships isn't something to fear because every relationship brings with it a lesson or a blessing. You'll never know which one it is until you find the courage to give it a try, and truth be told, there are blessings even in the lessons. Some of the most beautiful relationships started with nothing more than taking a chance. I believe going through this experience helped me see the value in taking that chance, that even the lessons come with beautiful memories and beautiful human beings. This experience challenged me, but I couldn't imagine missing out on meeting someone so special to me and that means so much to me still to this day. More than anything, this situation helped me grow as a man and gave me vital life experience in learning how to handle my business and uphold my commitments to myself and those that I love most, even when I don't feel my best or I'm not at my strongest.

The end result wasn't what I desired, but through practicing gratitude, I was able to keep a positive attitude and an open mind. I had to see through all the pain that meeting her was still a blessing, because she was someone who came into my life and re-introduced me to the loving, playful, and lively human being that I had always been in my life. As a result, the pain of watching someone important to me walk out of my life didn't tell the full story. I made use of both the loss and what had been gained throughout the experience to make me a better human being. Through it all, I continued to develop myself as a man and to demand the best of myself.

I was able to take that loss and come to better understand myself and find healing in the right ways. Through focusing on the good in my life and all the future opportunities, the stress and sadness of negative results were minimized. I learned to stop looking backwards while trying to move forward, to keep my focus on where my path had led me and not where I wanted it to lead me. Looking back at the parts of the journey you're unwilling to let go of only causes you to miss the beauty of what lies ahead. It's okay to hurt and miss certain parts of the journey, but your pain does *not* justify you losing sight of the end destination and remaining stagnant on a journey that requires you to keep moving forward.

The world has beat into our minds that we need more money, more friends, and more *external* additions to our lives to be happy, but the truth is that all worldly possessions are fleeting and cannot bring true happiness if we are not happy with ourselves and the lives that we live. All we truly need to be happy is the humility to understand that what we do have can be taken as soon as it was given and a heart filled with gratitude for the many things that we do have. Sure, there are things that can be added to life to make it temporarily easier and less stressful, but true happiness and a strong sense of self comes from humbling ourselves to live a life of service to others and possessing a heart that is grateful for every part of the experience of life. These mindsets must be cultivated daily to keep things in perspective when dealing with the disappointments and unjust nature of life.

You will never be happy until you learn to appreciate the people, things, and opportunities that you *do* have in your life. To protect yourself from complacency, comparison, and all other forces that work to destroy your joy and peace with who you are and the life that you live, cultivate a grateful heart that will help you see the good even when you're staring down the endless challenges of life. Those who remain strong in the face of their suffering and disappointments find long-term happiness and fulfillment in the journey.

If you haven't gotten the message already, this life requires strength, endurance, and perseverance to leave the mark you're capable of leaving on this world. Humility allows you to understand the importance of persisting through struggle and strife to preserve and serve others. Gratitude prevents you from losing sight of the many blessings and positives you have in your life at this very moment, despite having not met your full potential yet. Humility and gratitude are the building blocks to a strong human foundation. All of life's challenges and resistances can be defeated through these two critical components and mindsets. In a world full of choices, *always* choose humility and gratitude.

Chapter Twelve

Principle #12: Pay the price– leave nothing to chance.

In one of the most famous and acclaimed pieces of literature on personal development ever written, Napoleon Hill made a statement in *Think and Grow Rich* that was so profound that I will never forget it for as long as I live. Warning against the dangers of "get rich quick" schemes, Hill wrote, "There is no such thing as something for nothing." This statement is very brief and simple, but as you can tell through the earlier parts of this book, it has changed the way I look at all aspects of life.

I spent most of my mornings as a kid watching SportsCenter with my dad and younger brother before school, unless my dad was out of town on business. My dad doesn't like to talk or hear noise in the mornings. Preston and I usually had our faces filled with cereal or French toast sticks, so the low volume of the TV was the perfect mix for my brother and I to enjoy our breakfasts with dad without sitting in complete silence. Even though we didn't say much, I always looked forward to watching all the highlights and score updates with them before school because it just became what we did most mornings.

Like most of us even to this day, Friday mornings were my absolute favorite mornings of all weekday mornings. My love for Friday mornings was partially the excitement for the weekend, but the rest of my excitement came from knowing I was going to be able to buy ice cream at lunch. My school had a small freezer that was full of different kinds of ice creams they would sell to students during lunch, and I would always see my classmates lining up to get ice cream throughout the week when the principal announced that they were opening the freezer up. My deal with my parents was that they would give me money for ice cream every Friday, as long as my chores around the house were done and I hadn't gotten into any trouble throughout the week. Friday meant it was my turn to get in line and get ice cream, and something about having that dollar in your pocket all morning makes a young kid excited beyond belief.

I'm still young, but my time in elementary school was before inflation believe it or not– everything in that freezer was fifty cents. More times than not, my dad would remember on his own and leave the dollar on the kitchen counter. In the instances that he forgot, I quickly flagged him down before my bus came to pick me up and secured my dollar. If he didn't have any singles in his wallet, he would scrounge up four quarters and put them in a plastic bag for me and tuck the plastic bag into my backpack so I wouldn't lose it. My parents never gave me exactly fifty cents– they always gave me a dollar and told me to treat one of my friends. As long as I did what I was supposed to for the week, my mom and dad always made sure I left the house with money for two ice creams on Friday.

Granted, a dollar isn't a significant amount of money and was relatively easy for my parents to come up with. Looking back, they had it easier back then, considering I'll most likely have to link my Apple Pay and be charged a service fee to use the network that my kids' schools choose to collect their payments through. After paying the service fee and the price of inflation for my kids to be able to get ice cream, I'll get an email asking me to rate my experience, leave a review, and asking if I would like to tip 20% to the school for allowing them to reach into the freezer and grab their own ice creams. Jesus, how much simpler times used to be. I was ignorant to the true value of a dollar back then, but it didn't matter to me– it always meant a lot to me that my parents gave me extra money that they didn't have to so I could have something I wanted.

Now, once the long wait was over and my principal gave us permission to get in line, I would walk over to the line and my friend and I would start discussing which ice creams we were going to get. When I finally got up to the front of the line and looked into the freezer to pick out my ice cream, there was a mutual understanding between my principal and I that I was going to hand him fifty cents for each ice cream that I took. My friend and I would pick out our ice creams, then I would hand over the dollar bill and the debt was paid. These were the very first transactions that I remember from my childhood, but I still understood that I wouldn't be able to get what I wanted from the freezer without first paying the price required for what I wanted.

I didn't realize it then, but everything else in life fundamentally follows this same simple model that I familiarized myself with in elementary school. That is, everything in life has a price. If you're willing to pay the price, there isn't anything you can't have in life. Some prices are higher than others because some things are more worth having than others are. Worth is relative to what the acquisition of an item provides the buyer with, meaning the more an acquisition provides for a buyer, the more the buyer will have to pay to make that acquisition.

You wouldn't take your Toyota Corolla to the dealership and demand them to trade it in for a Porsche. If you did, they would ask you where the other $70,000 is going to come from because the Corolla is worth only a *fraction* of the price of the Porsche. If you didn't have the difference between the Corolla's and the Porsche's value at your fingertips, you would be leaving the dealership with the same Corolla you drove up in because the dealership would be losing significant value in honoring that trade. No dealership would be in business very long at all if they got into the habit of accepting Toyota Corollas for Porsches– that's no disrespect to Toyota at all, but they're two different classes of cars.

In the same fashion, you aren't going to get what you truly desire in life by paying a fraction of the price. You must pay the price in full. The "price" is more than monetary– it's going to take blood, sweat, and tears to get the most out of yourself and to become all that you can be. Without great sacrifice, there can be no hope for great reward in life. Paying a fraction of the price more times than not results in a fraction of the desired results.

Many of us understand this ideology from the conceptual level, but we still find ourselves trying to level up to that Porsche while only being willing to pay the price worthy of a Corolla. Don't let that go over your head because I'm not only referring to cars– the Porsche and the Corolla are symbolic of many other things in life than what cars we decide to drive. There are many areas of our lives that are much more important than what cars we drive, but these areas lack the enrichment and fulfillment that we desire because we're not willing to pay the full price that is required to experience better, so we instead settle for what our effort allows us to afford.

Even in times where virtuous living is not as prioritized as it has been historically, making the effort to strengthen our relationship with that Higher power, seeking wisdom, and living within a strong purpose will lead us to living virtuous lives amongst the masses. We can have deeper, more fulfilling relationships by putting our pride, fears, and anything else that is limiting our ability to love others aside and loving unapologetically, without fear of the consequences that may or may not come. We can look in the mirror and be pleased with who we see in the reflection looking back at us, with just a few hours of our time each week devoted to spiritual growth, exercise, physical wellness, and making better decisions about what we put on our plates. We can get out of the boring and mundane jobs that simply pay the bills and step into the work that sets our souls on fire and gives us purpose– after we're willing to first quit serving what is no longer serving us well in our lives.

Whatever it is that you think about when you think about where your life may be lacking, it's our responsibility to become aware that this area doesn't have to continue to be an area that we lack in. It's within you to give more effort, to show up with a different approach. The amazing realization that I've come to understand about life is that you can change *anything* in your life, if you're willing to make the necessary changes. What separates those who have what they want in life and those that don't is the willingness to pay the price in full, to stop looking for cheap shots of dopamine and pleasure along the way to pursuing true fulfillment.

We don't fill our car's gas tank up halfway and expect to get the mileage of a full tank, so why do we get into the habit of expecting our half-hearted efforts and focus to take us the same distance that our full effort and focus would take us? It's a game of insanity, but it's a game that we all find ourselves playing at one point or another in our lives. If you want to reach your full potential and to live the very best life possible for yourself, it's going to require *everything* you have in the tank. The farther you want to go in your life, the more you will have to find in the tank.

Creating this mantra of paying the price has transformed my mind, which has changed the trajectory of my entire life. For so long, everything I desired felt out of reach to me and I was under the impression that my life was going to be this meaningless, gloomy blur. I started the process of paying the price by making gradual payments and it became evident to me that paying the debt required would be a slow process. The process would be slow and challenging, but I gradually built the confidence in myself to believe it was *possible*. I came to understand that nothing is going to be given to me in life, but nothing that I'm willing to work for is out of my reach to take either.

The same is true for you in your life, no matter who you are, where you come from, or what mistakes you've made in the past. There is greatness within you that you haven't yet discovered and it may take you a while to find it. Your life will get better when you get better– the process of making those improvements looks different for all of us because we all have different strengths and weaknesses and are at different places in our journeys. No matter how strong or weak you feel, one of the keys to life is to never stop searching for challenges and growth. It's hard work but this stimulation is needed to keep you sharp and to fill your need for finding meaning in the day-to-day functions of life.

Many of us have been conditioned to believe that learning ends with diplomas, degrees, certificates, or some other form of acceptance from an outside source. This is incorrect, because as we've discussed already, learning is a life-long commitment to bettering ourselves and the world that we live in. For the human being that is making every effort to maximize their potential, learning never stops because there is *always* more to know and understand. Gaining knowledge and applying that knowledge to your life is a major source of how we can grow and evolve as human beings, so for the growth to continue, the act of gaining knowledge must continue.

I'm not downplaying the importance of getting a diploma or a degree by any means. I respect all of you who have gone through your studies and obtained these documents of accomplishment in your lives because it's not an easy task to accomplish those feats. It takes years and years of hard work and dedication to get to the finish line, and it's truly something to be proud of when you finally make it to the finish line and get your hands on the reward you've been working towards all that time. However, I do want you to understand that these documents and certificates don't excuse you from your lifelong responsibility of learning, maturing, and evolving.

Personally, I have yet to finish my degree and have decided to step away from school for the time being. Yet, I feel as though I'm learning more about myself and gaining an understanding of this world that we live in more so than ever before. In a time of my life where the majority of my near future is unknown and very susceptible to change, I feel more at peace with who I'm becoming than I ever did when I had the "safety net" of the future that I always imagined college would give me. Giving up that preconditioned belief that college was the only way towards becoming successful was one of the major mental hurdles I had to leap over to free myself to discover myself and my true purpose in the world. It was a price that I had to pay, a price that I'm still paying every day to live in the unknown and to experience life in ways that I've never been able to experience life before.

If you have your degree or are working towards it, that's great. Whatever you feel is best for you and your situation, that's what you should always pursue. There's absolutely nothing wrong with finding contentment in working towards an achievement that's going to allow you to level up in your life! However, like anything else in life, that path isn't for everybody and that's also okay! Just because you choose a different route, it doesn't mean you're a failure or that you won't eventually make it to where you're headed. I believe it's important to know and understand this in a world where secondary schooling and the idea of choosing a career path in our late teens and early twenties is practically forced down our throats.

School will ultimately teach you how to follow rules and become a good employee. For some people, that's the path that they want to take in life, and they find success and happiness in their lives from doing so. I used to think this was what I wanted for my life, until I began to reach an age and maturity where I was beginning to learn about who I really am and the life that I want to build for myself. Following rules set in place to make me effective at building someone else a fortune, while receiving a minimal slither of the pie– I came to understand that this wasn't the reality I wanted to wake up and live every day.

Therefore, I began to struggle with school, because I had no clear desire or goal I was working towards. It was mostly something that I felt like I should be doing because everybody else was doing it, but I was unhappy, unmotivated, and saw no value in doing the work that was being assigned to me. I realized I was interested in learning *life* skills and growing in my personal development that translate outside of academia, skills that allow me to express myself and be an individual instead of just another number at a massive state institution that makes a fortune off the dreams they sell to young adults and their families that are willing to go into crippling debt to pay for a brighter future for their children. I was there on campus, doing my best to stay engaged with the curriculum and to take what I could away from my instructors– but it had been a while since I had truly been *there*. My physical body was in the classroom trying to make the most of the classes my parents and I had paid for, but my mind and my heart were elsewhere.

Even knowing that I felt this way towards school, I still felt nervous and even slightly guilty to tell my parents that I wasn't interested in finishing my degree on the timetable that I had originally set out to do so. All I ever wanted to do was make my parents proud and the same is still true. They're two of the best human beings I've ever met in my life, and the impact they've had on me as a person cannot be overstated. I eventually reached a maturity to understand that my parents didn't have an emotional, deep connection with college courses and a degree that would be framed and collect dust somewhere in the attic someday.

That emotional connection was with *me*– it was never hot gyms, uncomfortable bleachers, long days at the baseball fields, or anything else that my parents suffered through that got them to make those sacrifices. It was because they loved me and wanted to know that I was happy, doing the things that I loved to do with my life at the time. My mom hated sitting on metal bleachers and driving two hours in rush-hour traffic, but one of her greatest joys was watching her kids do the things we loved to do. My dad hated being gone all weekend and not being able to do his yard work until later in the week, but he put everything on hold to coach and see his kids grow in our abilities at the sports we loved to play. To see the joy it brought my brothers and I, they made those sacrifices. They paid the price of going above and beyond for their kids, and because of their efforts, my brothers and I have stepped into the world prepared to do the same. We witnessed the model examples our entire lives leading up to where we are now, so we have a clear understanding of what making these sacrifices looks like.

It was foolish of me to feel like my parents would think any less of me for postponing my plans of graduating college, but that's the type of pressure that society and its "standards" puts on this generation. Being at the age where you're seemingly being forced to make the decisions that will shape your future, all while trying to find yourself and what it is that you're truly passionate about, it's far from an easy place to be in life. I still plan on finishing my final year of school at some point, for the sole reason that I feel I have been through too much in my experiences to not cross that finish line one day in my life– not because I feel it will complete or validate my skill set and what I bring to the world. Walking away from school and focusing on this book, pursuing what felt right for me in my own personal life– the price was giving up society's definition of success and choosing to discover and pursue my own definition of success. It's a price that I would pay tenfold if given the opportunity to do so.

The most controversial decision I've ever made in my life was moving across the country all alone. The decision to do so had been on my mind for a while but I knew it would be met with opposition and resistance from my family and loved ones. I put it off as long as I could and pushed the thought to the back of my mind, dismissing it as a crazy, impulsive thought that would separate me from my family and friends, with no guarantee of the move being beneficial to me in any shape or form. Coming from the family background that I come from and having the relationships that I have with these people in my life, it was the most difficult decision I've ever had to make in my life to follow my heart and take this chance.

Since moving here, I've become a much more responsible person and have matured exponentially as an adult. Forcing myself to do things that I've never been responsible for, such as keeping my groceries stocked up, paying bills on time, and working full-time to support myself- these responsibilities put my back against the wall each morning that I wake up. I've come to love the version of myself that has his back against the wall because he tends to figure things out and make things happen. The growth I've seen in myself and the confidence that I've found in following my heart and bringing the amazing experiences, people, and life that I'm living into my reality– it's still surreal to me that I followed that crazy nudge in my heart and am slowly figuring it out day-by-day.

The move cost me everything essentially. I can no longer walk downstairs and hug my mom before I leave the house to hang out with my friends. I can no longer go outside and spend time with my dad whenever I want to. I can no longer walk across the hall and play video games or talk about life with my younger brother. I'll only get to see my niece and nephews a few times a year, along with my older brother and his wife. My family and friends from back home, who mean everything to me, are physically out of reach for about 49 out of the 52 weeks in a year– this isn't a matter that weighs in lightly on my mind and my conscience.

Even feeling it in my heart that this chance was the right move for me at this time in my life, I felt incredibly guilty to finally voice this desire that was only growing by the day in my mind. My decision met its fair share of resistance and disapproval, as I expected it would. Honestly, I feel as though I disappointed and confused the people I love most in making the decision– but there comes a point where you have to take into consideration that you only get one life to live, and it is *your* responsibility to do whatever it is that you would like to do with that life. Leaving my family wasn't necessarily ideal for me, but I understood it had to be done if I was going to follow my heart and allow myself to experience the fresh start and amazing experience that moving away has provided me with.

I know this has been an adjustment for my family and it's difficult for them to accept that I'm so far away. I give them credit for making the adjustment and continuing to be as supportive as possible, even though they don't fully understand or agree with my choices. I sincerely hope that they understand that I carry them and the many important values that they instilled in me everywhere I go. Without them, I'm not even a fraction of the person that I am today, and they all mean more to me than they could ever possibly know. Some days are easier than others, but there isn't a day that goes by where I don't think about them and miss them.

I think this irrational fear of losing the respect and support of the people we love in our lives keeps many of us from making the sacrifices that we must make to live the lives that we truly desire to live. The truth is that those who want to be in your life will make the effort and support you, regardless of how they feel about your decisions. I wanted so badly for my entire family to see my life and my decisions from my perspective, for them to accept them, and not feel I was making a mistake. That wasn't the case, but it doesn't change the fact that these people are my family and carrying this last name motivates me every day to make them proud.

As I mentioned earlier, this process of paying the price looks different for all of us because we've all been equipped with different strengths and weaknesses. My struggles may not necessarily be your struggles, but we're all struggling with *something* in our lives. The only way through these struggles is to acknowledge they exist and to give consistent effort to becoming better in these areas of our lives.

Always remember that to whom much is given, much is expected. A good life comes at a higher price than the life of a beggar on the side of the street, but one life is worth the sacrifice, and one isn't. Even once you establish a good life, that price still must be paid daily to maintain the good life that you've built. If you pay the price required, you can have anything that you desire in this life. Nobody can keep you from those things but the person you see when you look in the mirror each morning.

Living your life with faith comes with a price. It's going to cost you your fears and worries that are not serving you well. In a world that is living in fear, it's going to require you to go against the world's trends and operate from a place of peace of mind and security. It's going to cost you leaning on your own emotions and understanding, understanding that being led by the Spirit is always going to help you make those tough decisions to do what is best for yourself and follow the plan that has been made for your life. It's going to cost you your anger and bitterness, learning to see others as brothers and sisters that deserve forgiveness and compassion. All the intricacies of faith-based living present their own different challenges, but it is a price you must be willing to pay if you want to live at peace, with purpose, and with the confidence that this life and all its struggles are worth the struggle and sacrifice. Pay the price.

Living your life with a strong "why" comes with a price. Life can no longer only be lived for your own selfish ambitions and interests. This concept requires you to hold yourself accountable for impacting the lives of others, which is a responsibility that should never be taken lightly. It requires you to choose purpose over pleasure and virtues over

310

vices. Where most of the world is getting their high from distraction and meaningless pursuits, you must find your high in maintaining focus and pursuing something meaningful and purposeful to you and your mission. This strong sense of purpose is going to cost you friends, family, and everything in between at times. It's a price you must be willing to pay if you're going to stay true to your values and give this world everything you've got while you're still here and able to leave the impact that you're meant to leave for the future generations. Pay the price.

Living the life that you desire is going to come with a price. You will have to say no to the thoughts, things, people, and all other aspects of your life that don't align with your desires for your life. You will have to do whatever it is that *you* want to do and allow people to make their judgments. You will lose some things and people along the way, but the life that you live and your experiences will be well worth it in the end. To say yes to yourself, you must say no to everybody else. It's one of the most difficult and uncomfortable situations to put yourself in, but it's a situation you must be willing to put yourself in if you're going to live your life to the fullest and leave nothing to chance. Pay the price.

Connecting with yourself comes with the price of being less connected to the outside world than you currently are. It takes time to get to know yourself and to discover what makes you tick in life. Time alone is necessary to recharge your batteries and reflect on life and its meaning, to keep the main goal the main goal in a world where distraction is the biggest threat to living the life that you're capable of living. You may have to sacrifice some followers and likes to follow your dreams and reach the places you desire to be, along with reducing all other distractions as much as you possibly can. It's a price you must be willing to pay to know yourself and to reach a place of clarity regarding what it is that you desire most in your life and how you want to show up for yourself and others on a daily basis to obtain those desires. Pay the price.

Letting go of comparison comes with a price. You can no longer be consumed by what others are doing with themselves and their time. Instead, you must focus on maximizing your time and energy to build yourself into someone who is capable of building the life you desire to live. You must compete with yourself daily, making that effort to get just a little bit better with each day that passes by. You must learn to be present in the journey, releasing yourself from all of society's standards and timetables. It's a price you must be willing to pay if you're going to avoid the poison that comparison brings into your life and make the choice to live in the truth and fullness of who you are and who you were made to be. Pay the price.

The price of finding the sunshine in life is to endure pain and suffering in the rain. Life is meant to be enjoyed and fulfilling, but it is through challenges, setbacks, and bumps in the road that we find our purpose for being here and meaning in the suffering it requires to see that purpose through. You will be faced with adversity, fear, and many other challenges along the way– these challenges make you a stronger final product that is capable of taking from this life whatever it is that you desire. Learning to face the rain, to learn and grow in the rain, and how to weather the storms in your life is a price you must be willing to pay to get to the better days that your life will bring you in due time. Pay the price.

The price of your new life is going to cost you the poor habits of your old life. You can't build a better life for yourself stuck in the same habits and cycles that have led you to the life that you're living in this very moment. You must become successful in your habits before you become successful in your life, but becoming successful in your habits is the real reward– learning to live your life better, with greater efficiency is what this process is all about. It's important to understand that you can't expect to trade in the life you're living for the life that you desire, without trading in your ways of thinking, acting, and living for better, healthier alternatives. The comfort and instability of your old ways is a price you must be willing to pay to build better habits and a better life for yourself and those you care about most. Pay the price.

The price of looking and feeling your best is going to cost you your undisciplined, comfortable ways of living. You will have to sweat, bleed, and even sometimes shed tears to push yourself and your body to its limits. By breaking the body down and allowing it to heal and recover, you're left with a stronger version of your body than you had before. The physical body must be used to maintain and gain strength, so that's a commitment that must be made to prioritize your physical body and well-being. You must find longevity and feel good doing it to see your grandchildren grow up and to reap all the fruits of your labor. The comfort that keeps you stagnant and complacent, along with your lack of disciplined action, eating, and sleeping is a price you must be willing to pay to keep your body strong and healthy– to do your best work for as long as possible. Pay the price.

The price of building your empire and creating a better future for yourself is going to cost you some hard times that strengthen you to embrace these moments once you finally make it on the other side of the difficulty. There is no such thing as gaining something worth having in life without first sacrificing something. The odds may be against you, the doubts of others may be weighing heavily on you, and this may be causing you to second-guess your every move. You must free yourself from this weight and believe, even when it looks like a lost cause. When you're doubted and counted out, the history books are on your side– there have been great empires built in the face of tragedy, war, and widespread chaos. The path of least resistance and the life that is free of challenge and hardship is a price you must be willing to pay to pursue your empire and better life in the face of all the obstacles standing in your way. Pay the price.

The price of calming yourself and becoming non-reactive to life and its happenings and circumstances is going to cost you battling your pride, flesh, and yesterday's ways to make today's progression. You will be required to get to know yourself better than you know anybody else, to give yourself your own undivided focus and attention. The ways of the world will often go against the flow of your spirit and the direction in which you are meant to be traveling– you must learn to pursue flowing with what's meant for you above anything else or whatever else others may be doing. Pay the price.

While calming yourself and operating from a place of flow, you must not lose your competitive edge and understanding of your power to rise up against great challenges to prevail and serve your ultimate purpose to the world at a high level. Your human nature to live your life reactive, out of control, and untamed is a price you must be willing to pay to live your life in a state of flow, tranquility, and taking daily, purposeful actions to better serve others. Pay the price.

The price of choosing humility and gratitude in your life is going to cost you the urge to be in a rush to the top. It's going to require you to grow where your feet are planted at this very moment, without worrying about what the future may or may not hold. It's going to require you to let go of all trespasses against you, to forgive and find it in yourself to love others despite their flaws and the wrongs they've committed against you. Choosing gratitude is going to require you to make peace with difficult experiences, situations, and truths in life– making the choice to learn from every experience and grow amid the unique difficulty each one presents. Choosing humility is going to require you to believe in yourself to impact others, to lead by example, and to value your life's mission above the price that is demanded of you to complete that mission. Pay the price.

We pay the price in this life because there is no price too high for a life that results in peace, happiness, and fulfillment. That's what this entire journey is all about, finding ways to do what is necessary to reach a state of contentment and peace with where we end up in our lives. Pay the price to be great today and all your tomorrows, and you will eventually become great and live a life that you can only imagine as of right now. Your

315

effort and intentionality will be the true difference in what separates you from everything

and everybody trying to stop you from building the life you desire to live. Leave nothing in

this world to chance. The life of your dreams *is* possible, but it is *not* free. Pay the price.

Sources

Aarnio, Stefan. *Hard Times Create Strong Men: Why the World Craves Leadership and How You Can Step up to Fill the Need*. CLOVERCROFT Publishing, 2019.

Hardy, Allan. "Losing Yourself in the Service of Others." 21 Apr. 2017. Mahatma Gandhi Quote.

Hardy, Darren. *The Compound Effect*. John Murray Publishing, 2022.

Hill, Napoleon. *Outwitting the Devil: The Original Unedited Complete Text, Including Content Never before Published*. Sound Wisdom Publishing, 2020.

Hall, Nancy. "Newton's Laws of Motion - Glenn Research Center." *NASA*, 27 Oct. 2022.

Johnson, Inky. "It's Not Just About You." YouTube. San Bruno, CA, 2017.

Kennedy, John F. "Inaugural Address." Washington D.C.

"A Quote by Bruce Lee." *Goodreads*, June 2020. Bruce Lee Quote.

Manson, Mark. *The Subtle Art of Not Giving a F*ck: A Counterintuitive Approach to Living a Good Life*. HarperLuxe Publishing, 2019.

Fruit of the SPIRIT: Galatians 5:22-23. Written by Apostle Paul. Open Bible Trust, 2012.

The Living Stone and a Chosen People: 1 Peter 2:15. Written by Apostle Peter. Open Bible Trust, 2012.

Bokenkamp, Jon. *The Blacklist*, NBC. Raymond Reddington Quote.

Rohn, Jim. "How to Live a Successful Life and Control Your Future." The Art of Exceptional Living. The Art of Exceptional Living, Anaheim, California.

Wiest, Brianna. *The Mountain Is You Transforming Self-Sabotage into Self-Mastery*. Thought Catalog Books, 2020.

Made in United States
Troutdale, OR
11/02/2023

14254798R00179